Gender and the Court of Justice of the European Union

Offering an alternative exploration of the Court of Justice of the European Union (CJEU) and its work, this book aims to start a conversation between legal, political and gendered examinations of the Court of Justice and some of the substantive areas of law it is concerned with. In doing so, it provides a broader and more holistic view of the Court and its work which can add to our understanding of the institution, its role and its case law as well as the contribution it can and does make to shaping law and policy at EU and national level.

Jessica Guth is Reader in Law at Leeds Beckett University.

Sanna Elfving is Senior Lecturer in Law at the University of Bradford.

To Dr Kathryn Dutton, to sisterhood and friendship

Gender and the Court of Justice of the European Union

Jessica Guth and Sanna Elfving

Routledge
Taylor & Francis Group
LONDON AND NEW YORK

First published 2019
by Routledge
2 Park Square, Milton Park, Abingdon, Oxon OX14 4RN

and by Routledge
52 Vanderbilt Avenue, New York, NY 10017

First issued in paperback 2020

Routledge is an imprint of the Taylor & Francis Group, an informa business

British Library Cataloguing-in-Publication Data
A catalogue record for this book is available from the British Library

Library of Congress Cataloging-in-Publication Data
Names: Guth, Jessica, author. | Elfving, Sanna, author.
Title: Gender and the Court of Justice of the European Union/Jessica Guth and Sanna Elfving.
Description: New York: Routledge, 2018. | Series: Routledge research in eu law | Includes index.
Identifiers: LCCN 2018018600 | ISBN 9780415785792 (hbk)
Subjects: LCSH: Court of Justice of the European Union. | Women judges—European Union countries. | Sex discrimination against women—Law and legislation—European Union countries. | Justice, Administration of—European Union countries. | Judges—Selection and appointment—European Union countries.
Classification: LCC KJE5461. G87 2018 | DDC 341.242/2284082—dc23
LC record available at https://lccn.loc.gov/2018018600

ISBN 13: 978-0-367-58812-0 (pbk)
ISBN 13: 978-0-415-78579-2 (hbk)

Typeset in Galliard
by Apex CoVantage, LLC

Contents

Lists of cases

Court of Justice of the European Union

“CHEZ Razpredelenie Bulgaria” AD v Komisia za zashtita ot diskriminatsia (C-83/14) [2015] EU:C:2015:480
Aissatou Diatta (267/83) [1985] EU:C:1985:67
Anita Cristini v Société nationale des chemins de fer français (32/75) [1975] ECR 1085
Annunziata Matteucci v Communauté française of Belgium and Other (235/87) [1988] ECR 5589
Asma Bougnaoui and other v Micropole SA (C-188/15) [2016] EU:C:2016:553 Opinion of AG Sharpston
Asma Bougnaoui and other v Micropole SA (C-188/15) [2017] EU:C:2017:204
Asociaţia Accept v Consiliul Naţional pentru Combaterea Discriminării (C-81/12) [2013] EU:C:2013:275
Athanasios Vatsouras and Josif Koupatantze v Arbeitsgemeinschaft (ARGE) Nürnberg 900 (C-22/07 and C-23/08) [2009] ECR I-04585
BASF SE v Bundesrepublik Deutschland (C-456/15) [2016] not published, EU:C:2016:567
Baumbast and R v Secretary of State for the Home Department (C-413/99) [2002] ECR I-7091
Bilka-Kaufhaus GmbH v Karin Weber von Hartz (170/84) [1986] ECR 1607
Blaise Baheten Metock and Others v Minister for Justice, Equality and Law Reform (C-127/08) [2008] ECR I-6241
Carole Louise Webb v EMO Air Cargo (UK) Ltd (C-32/93) [1994] ECR I-3567, Opinion of AG Tesauro
Centrum voor gelijkheid van kansen en voor racismebestrijding v Firma Feryn NV (C-54/07) [2008] ECR I-5187
Christos Konstantinidis v Stadt Altensteig-Standesamt and Landratsamt Calw-Ordnungsamt See Case (C-168/91) [1993] ECR I-1191, Opinion of AG Jacobs
Christos Konstantinidis v Stadt Altensteig-Standesamt and Landratsamt Calw–Ordnungsamt (168/91) [1993] ECR I-1191

Christos Konstantinidis v Stadt Altensteig-Standesamt and Landratsamt Calw-Ordnungsamt (C-168/91) [1993] ECR I-1191, Opinion of AG Jacobs
Colin Wolf v Stadt Frankfurt am Main (C-229/08) [2010] ECR I 00001
Commission v Germany (C-329/04) [2005] EU:C:2005:263
Commission v Jégo-Quéré (C-263/02 P) [2004] ECR I-3425
Commission v United Kingdom (C-308/14) [2016] EU:C:2016:436
D and Sweden (C-122/99 P and C-125/99 P) [2001] ECR I-4329, Opinion of AG Mischo
D and Sweden v Council (C-122/99 P and C-125/99 P) [2001] ECR I-4319
D v Council (T-264/97) [1999] ECR-SC I-A-1 and II-1
Defrenne v Belgian State (C-80/70) [1971] ECR 445 (Defrenne I)
Defrenne v Sabena (C-149/77) [1978] ECR 01365 (Defrenne III)
Defrenne v Sabena (C-43/75) [1976] ECR 00455 (Defrenne II)
Deutsche Post AG v Elisabeth Sievers and Brunhilde Schrage (C-270/97 and C-271/97) [2000] ECR I-799
Deutsche Telekom AG, formerly Deutsche Bundespost Telekom v Lilli Schröder (C-50/96) [2000] ECR I-743
DM Levin v Staatssecretaris van Justitie (C-53/81) [1982] ECR 1035
Domnica Petersen v Berufungsausschuss für Zahnärzte für den Bezirk Westfalen-Lippe (C-341/08) [2010] ECR I-47
Doris Povse v Mauro Alpago (C-211/10 PPU) [2010] ECR I-6669
Dorsch Consult Ingenieurgesellschaft mbH v Council and Commission (T-184/95) [1997] ECR II-351
Douglas Harvey Barber v Guardian Royal Exchange Assurance Group (C-262/88) [1990] ECR I-1889
Dr David L Parris v Trinity College Dublin and Others (C-443/15) [2016] EU:C:2016:897
Dr David L Parris v Trinity College Dublin and Others (C-443/15) [2016] EU:C:2016:493, Opinion of AG Kokott
Dr Pamela Mary Enderby v Frenchay Health Authority and Secretary of State for Health (C-127/92) [1993] ECR I-5535
Dynamic Medien Vertriebs GmbH v Avides Media AG (C-244/06) [2008] ECR I-505
Eckhard Kalanke v Freie Hansestadt Bremen (C-450/93) [1995] ECR I-03051
Eileen Garland v British Rail Engineering Limited (12/81) [1982] ECR 359
Elisabeta Dano and Florin Dano v Jobcenter Leipzig (C-333/13) [2014] EU:C:2014:2358
Elisabeth Johanna Pacifica Dekker v Stichting Vormingscentrum voor Jong Volwassenen (VJV-Centrum) Plus (C-177/88) [1991] IRLR 27
ERT (C-260/89) [1991] EU:C:1991:254
Ewaen Fred Ogieriakhi v Minister for Justice and Equality and Others (C-244/13) [2014] EU:C:2014:2068
Félix Palacios de la Villa v Cortefiel Servicios SA (C-411/05) [2007] ECR I-08531

Franca Ninni-Orasche v Bundesminister für Wissenschaft, Verkehr und Kunst (C-413/01) [2003] ECR I-13187
Frédéric Hay v Crédit agricole mutuel de Charente-Maritime et des Deux-Sèvres (C-267/12) [2013] EU:C:2013:823
Geoffrey Léger v Ministre des Affaires sociales and others (C-528/13) [2015] EU:C:2015:288
Geoffrey Léger v Ministre des affaires sociales and others (C-528/13) [2014] EU:C:2014:2112, Opinion of AG Mengozzi
Gerardo Ruiz Zambrano v Office National de l'Emploi (ONEm) (C-34/09) [2011] ECR I-1177
Gisela Rosenbladt v Oellerking Gebäudereinigungsges mbH (C-45/09) [2010] ECR I-9391
Health Service Executive v SC and AC (C-92/12 PPU) [2012] EU:C:2012:255
Hellmut Marschall v Land Nordrhein-Westfalen (C-409/95) [1997] ECR I-6363
Hoekstra (née Unger) v Bestuur der Bedrijfsvereniging voor Detailhandel en Ambachten (75-63) [1964] ECR 177
Inga Rinau (C-195/08 PPU) [2008] ECR I-5271
Internationale Handelsgesellschaft mbH v Einfuhr- und Vorratsstelle für Getreide und Futtermittel (11/70) [1970] ECR 1125
Inuit Tapiriit Kanatami and Others v Parliament and Council (C-583/11 P) [2013] EU:C:2013:21, Opinion of AG Kokott
Inuit Tapiriit Kanatami v Parliament and Council (C-583/11 P) [2013] EU:C:2013:625
J McB v LE (C-400/10 PPU) [2010] ECR I-8965
Jacqueline Förster v Hoofddirectie van de Informatie Beheer Groep (C-158/07) [2008] ECR I-08507
Jasna Detiček v Maurizio Sgueglia (C-403/09 PPU) [2009] ECR I-12193
Jean Noël Royer (C-48/75) [1976] EU:C:1976:57
JEG Achterberg-te Riele and Others v Sociale Verzekeringsbank (48/88, 106/88 and 107/88) [1989] ECR 01963
Jessy Saint Prix v Secretary of State for Work and Pensions (C-507/12) [2014] EU:C:2014:2007
Joan Gillespie and others v Northern Health and Social Services Boards and Others (C-342/93) [1996] ECR I-475
Jobcenter Berlin Neukölln v Nazifa Alimanovic and Others (C-67/14) [2015] EU:C:2015:597
John O'Flynn v Adjudication Officer (C-237/94) [1996] ECR I-2617
Joseba Andoni Aguirre Zarraga v Simone Pelz (C-491/10 PPU) [2010] ECR I-14247
Jürgen Römer v v Freie und Hansestadt Hamburg (C-147/08) [2011] ECR I-03591
Kadi and Al Barakaat International Foundation v Council and Commission (C-402/05 P and C-415/05 P) [2008] EU:C:2008:461

Karim Boudjellal v Rauwers Contrôle SA (C-508/16) [2017] not published, EU:C:2017:6
Katarina Abrahamsson and other v Elisabet Fogelqvist (C-407/98) [2000] ECR I-5539
KB v National Health Service Pensions Agency and Secretary of State for Health (C-117/01) [2004] ECR I-541
Kenneth Scrivner and Carol Cole v Centre public d'aide sociale de Chastre (C-122/84) [1985] ECR 1027
Kuldip Singh and Others v Minister for Justice and Equality (C-218/14) [2015] EU:C:2015:476
Kunqian Catherine Zhu and Man Lavette Chen v Secretary of State for the Home Department (C-200/02) [2004] ECR I-9925
Lisa Jacqueline Grant v South-West Trains Ltd (C-249/96) [1997] EU:C:1997:449, Opinion of AG Elmer
Lisa Jacqueline Grant v South-West Trains Ltd (C-249/96) [1998] ECR I-00621
London Borough of Harrow v Nimco Hassan Ibrahim and other (C-310/08) [2010] ECR I-01065
M Helen Marshall v Southampton and other (C-271/91) [1993] ECR I-4367 (Marshall No 2)
Macarthys Ltd v Wendy Smith (129/79) [1980] ECR-1275
Maria Luisa Jiménez Melgar v Ayuntamiento de Los Barrios (C-438/99) [2001] ECR I-6915
Maria Martínez Sala v Freistaat Bayern (C-85/96) [1998] ECR I-2691
Maria Teixeira v London Borough of Lambeth and other (C-480/08) [2010] ECR I-1107
Mary Brown v Rentokil (394/96) [1998] IRLR 445
Mary Carpenter v Secretary of State for the Home Department (C 60/00) [2002] ECR I-6279
Mary Murphy and others v An Bord Telecom Eireann (C-157/86) [1988] ECR 673
Massam Dzodzi v Belgian State (C-297/88 and C-197/89) [1990] ECR I-3763
Michel Trojani v Centre public d'aide sociale de Bruxelles (CPAS) (C-456/02) [2004] EU:C:2004:488
Murat Dereci and Others v Bundesministerium für Inneres (C-256/11) [2011] ECR I-11315
Naczelnik Urzędu Celnego I w Ł v GM and MS (C-303/15) [2016] EU:C:2016:771
Nadine Paquay v Société d'architectes Hoet + Minne SPRL (C-460/06) [2007] ECR I-08511
Netherlands v Ann Florence Reed (59/85) [1986] ECR 1283
Netherlands v Ann Florence Reed (59/85) [1986] ECR I-1284, Opinion of AG Lenz
Netherlands v Parliament and Council (C-377/98) [2001] ECR I-7079
OL v PQ (C-111/17 PPU) [2017] EU:C:2017:436

Olaitan Ajoke Alarape and Olukayode Azeez Tijani v Secretary of State for the Home Department (C-529/11) [2013] EU:C:2013:290
Omega Spielhallen und Automatenaufstellungs- GmbH v Oberbürgermeisterin der Bundesstadt Bonn (C-36/02) [2004] ECR I-9609
Opinion 2/13 [2014] EU:C:2014:2454
Opinion 2/94 [1996] ECR I-1759
Oumar Dabo Abdoulaye and Others v Régie nationale des usines Renault SA (C-218/98) [1999] ECR I-5723
P v S and Cornwall County Council (C-13/94) [1996] ECR I-2143
Pasquale Foglia v Mariella Novello (C-244/80) [1981] ECR 3045
Pensionsversicherungsanstalt v Christine Kleist (C-356/09) [2010] ECR I-11939
Pensionsversicherungsanstalt v Peter Brey (C-140/12) [2013] EU:C:2013:565
Peter Brey v Pensionsversicherungsanstalt (C-140/12) [2013] EU:C:2013:337, Opinion of AG Wahl
Plaumann and Co v Commission (25/62) [1963] ECR 95
R v Immigration Appeal Tribunal, ex parte Gustaff Desiderius Antonissen (C-292/89) [1991] EU:C:1991:80
R, on the application of Dany Bidar v London Borough of Ealing and other (C-209/03) [2005] ECR I-2119
R, on the application of The Incorporated Trustees of the National Council for Ageing (Age Concern England) v Secretary of State for Business, Enterprise and Regulatory Reform (C-388/07) [2009] I-1569
RH Kempf v Staatssecretaris van Justitie (139/85) [1986] ECR-1741
Rheinmühlen-Düsseldorf v Einfuhr- und Vorratsstelle für Getreide und Futtermittel (166-73) [1974] ECR 33
Rudy Grzelczyk v Centre public d'aide sociale d'Ottignies-Louvain-la-Neuve (C-184/99) [2001] ECR I-6193
S and G v Minister voor Immigratie, Integratie en Asiel (C-457/12) [2014] 3 CMLR 18; [2014] EU:C:2014:136
S Coleman v Attridge Law and Steve Law (C-303/06) [2008] ECR I-5603
S Coleman v Attridge Law and Steve Law (C-303/06) [2008] EU:C:2008:61, Opinion of AG Maduro
Samira Achbita and other v G4S Secure Solutions NV (C-157/15) [2017] EU:C:2017:203
Sarah Margaret Richards v Secretary of State for Work and Pensions (C-423/04) [2006] ECR I-3585
Secretary of State for the Home Department v Hacene Akrich (C-109/01) [2003] ECR I-9607
Secretary of State for the Home Department v NA (C-115/15) [2016] EU:C:2016:259, Opinion of AG Wathelet
Secretary of State for the Home Department v NA (C-115/15) [2016] EU:C:2016:487

Seda Kücükdeveci v Swedex GmbH & Co KG (C-555/07) [2010] ECR I-365
Shirley McCarthy v Secretary of State for the Home Department (C-434/09) [2011] ECR I-3375
SIA „Oniors Bio" v Valsts ieņēmumu dienests (C-233/15) [2016] EU:C:2016:305
Silke-Karin Mahlburg v Land Meckleburg-Vorpommern (C-207/98) [2000] ECR I-549
Srl CILFIT and Lanificio di Gavardo SpA v Ministry of Health (283/81) [1982] ECR I-3415
Steven Malcolm Brown v The Secretary of State for Scotland (197/86) [1988] ECR 3205
Susanna Brunnhofer v Bank der österreichischen Postsparkasse AG (C-381/99) [2001] ECR I-4961
Susanne Lewen v Lothar Denda (C-333/97) [1999] ECR I-7243
Sylvie Lair v Universität Hannover (39/86) [1988] ECR 3161
Tadao Maruko v Versorgungsanstalt der deutschen Bühnen (C-267/06) [2008] I-1757
Tanja Kreil v Bundesrepublik Deutschland (C-285/98) [2000] ECR I-69
Tele Danmark A/S v Handels- og Kontorfunktionærernes Forbund i Danmark (HK) (C-109/00) [2001] ECR I-6993
Telemarsicabruzzo SpA and Others v Circostel, Ministero delle Poste e Telecomunicazioni and other (C-320/90, C-321/90 and C-322/90) [1993] ECR I-393
Toufik Lounes v Secretary of State for the Home Department (C-165/16) [2017] EU:C:2017:407, Opinion of AG Bot
Toufik Lounes v Secretary of State for the Home Department (C-165/16) [2017] EU:C:2017:862
Unión de Pequeños Agricultores v Council (C-50/00 P) [2002] ECR I-6677, Opinion of AG Jacobs
Unión de Pequeños Agricultores v Council (C-50/00 P) [2002] ECR I-6677
Vestische Arbeit Jobcenter Kreis Recklinghausen v Jovanna García-Nieto and Others (C-299/14) [2016] EU:C:2016:114
W v Commission (F-86/09) [2010] EU:F:2010:125
Werner Mangold v Rüdiger Helm (C-144/04) [2005] ECR I-09981
Wienand Meilicke, Heidi Christa Weyde and Marina Stöffler v Finanzamt Bonn-Innenstadt (C-292/04) [2007] ECR I-1835

Other jurisdictions

AT&T Corp v Hulteen and others 556 US 701 (2009)
Attridge Law and Another v Coleman [2007] 2 CMLR 24
Belcacemi and Oussar v Belgium, App No 37798/13 (ECtHR 11 July 2017)
Dakir v Belgium, App No 4619/12 (ECtHR 11 July 2017)
McQuire v Western Morning News [1903] 2 KB 100

Michalak v Mid Yorkshire Hospitals NHS Trust [2011] ET 1810815 (Employment Tribunal)
Sahin v Turkey, App No 44774/98 (ECtHR 29 June 2004)
SAS v France (2015) 60 EHRR 11 Judgment of 1 July 2014
Sen v The Netherlands, App No 31465/96 (ECtHR 21 December 2001)

List of abbreviations

AG	Advocate General
CUP	Cambridge University Press
CoJ	Court of Justice
CJEU	Court of Justice of the European Union
EC	European Community
ECHR	European Convention on Human Rights
ECtHR	European Court of Human Rights
EEC	European Economic Community
EU	European Union
GC	General Court
OUP	Oxford University Press
TEU	Treaty on the European Union
TFEU	Treaty on the Functioning of the European Union
UK	United Kingdom
UP	University Press

Acknowledgements

We would like to thank the team at Routledge for believing in this project and helping us shape our thoughts and ideas into something publishable. Special thanks have to go to Professor Heather MacRae for awaking our interest in the Court of Justice and encouraging us to see it as something other than the simply the author of the judgments we work with every day. Thanks to the participants of various workshops and conferences who introduced us to political science ideas and ways of doing things and who suggested that our ideas were worth pursuing. Receiving the Franscesco Kjellberg Award at the 2014 International Political Science Association Conference for a paper which tentatively proposed the key themes of the book, gave us the confidence to further explore many of the ideas in this book and made us feel like we had something to say. Nonetheless, as is perhaps not unusual for women in academia, we have doubted both ourselves and this project at times (though never each other) so we want to say thank you to our friends and families who have endured endless and sometimes circular conversations about gender, feminism, judges, the EU and law – in isolation and various combinations, sometimes ordered and coherent and sometimes not. We could not have done this without them.

Preface

Writing a book is always a learning curve and throughout this process we have both learned a lot about areas of law with which we thought we were quite familiar, about academic writing, about collaboration, about each other and about ourselves. We have come to this project from different backgrounds and positions with different skills and experiences as well as approaches. Whereas Jess has engaged with feminist ideas since her undergraduate studies and as a significant interdisciplinary background, my academic identity was constructed around being an EU lawyer.

Feminist? Me? I didn't certainly consider myself openly as a feminist before I embarked on writing this book with my colleague, Jess. I had always been the EU lawyer, and that is what I consider myself till today. I used to tell people, part jokingly, part seriously that Jess and I made a great team: she was the gender specialist and EU expert, whereas I didn't know why she needed me on board. I struggled with the concepts of feminist legal theory and the feminist legal research methodology. I spent a lot of time looking for anything I could find about feminist legal method. Then I realised that my fatal mistake was looking for materials from 2013 onwards as I tend to do. It has been hammered to my head that recent legal materials are of most relevance. However, once I managed to locate one recent journal article on the topic, it then lead me to some of the established writings and helped me to gain a basic understand of what I was supposed to be doing. At times understanding feminist legal methodology was like looking at a needle in a haystack, especially since I started with the case law to do with trade and external relations. I remember asking Jess what exactly she thought I was going to bring into the book project since I had no clue what I was doing.

Gradually, we started to write the chapters and exchanged the drafts with one another which further helped me to understand a little bit about Jess was doing and tried to do something similar. However, I also noticed that our ways of working are very dissimilar. Jess likes to write 'on top her head' if you like and doesn't do long-winded explanations, whereas I want to check every fact and detail of a case, paragraph number, and the exact presentation of references. My writing suffers from lack of coherence and my appalling grammar for which

I blame my native tongue which has no indefinite or definite articles. Having a co-author, who ruthlessly cut down my incoherent rambling, and said that we could use it for some other purpose, was extremely comforting and beneficial. Apart from noticing the essential limitations of my ability to write and conduct academic research for our monograph I have certainly become more aware of the pain-staking and largely in-built and irrational discrimination facing women and various minorities, including sexual minorities, disabled persons, and ethnic and racial minorities due to the very characteristics people cannot change about themselves, or at least changing some of these characteristics take a hell of lot of effort. I am talking about characteristics, such as femininity, masculinity, class, age, complexion and other physical features which make people who they are. The discrimination against anyone, who does not fit into the mould of a white, heterosexual, able bodied male, appears to be so ingrained that many of us do not even question it. We just put up with the stereotypes that people have of women, ethnic and sexual minorities, older people, people with regional accents or disabilities.

On the one hand, it has been refreshing to witness the immense influence the members of the American film industry have had on social and conventional media over the course of writing of this book. First, the African American actors criticised the Oscars for complete lack of nominations among non-white screen writers, directors, producers, and actors. The criticism was taken on board as the Oscars in 2017 saw a number of films by African American actors and directors being nominated and winning Oscars. In 2017, we also witnessed the sexual harassment claims by numerous women against prominent film producers and well-known actors. Although it feels that 2017 could have well been a watershed moment for gender equality certainly in the United States and in Europe, it sadly was not so for racial equality because the United States still remains a highly segregated society with deep entrenched racial equality. Therefore, although there is still a lot work to do, I feel that the book is very timely, and the comments I have received from reviewers but also people not necessarily connected with academia, specifically women, on writing this book have been extremely supportive and encouraging. People acknowledge the inherent gender inequality in our societies and I have been positively surprised that there are equally extremely progressive, modern men among my friends and colleagues who do not think that gender equality, or any equality for that matter, does in any deduct from their rights.

Sanna Elfving

For me this book is a culmination of an academic and personal journey which saw me leaving one law school under a cloud of depression and anxiety and join another in a more positive frame of mind. This book is therefore partly about reminding myself, my colleagues and students that there is work to do, that we need feminism, gendered questions and gendered solutions in law, in politics, in academia and in life. I echo all of Sanna's comments above. As we make our way through 2018 I am saddened by the backward steps in law and in politics in my own EU Member State(s) and across the EU but am also hopeful that the wins we have celebrated have built a strong foundation from which we can move forward in the future. Some of those wins and some of those disappointments are laid out in these pages. I hope they start a conversation that will, eventually, one step at a time, change the world.

Jessica Guth

1 Introduction – gendering the Court of Justice of the European Union

There will be enough women on the [US] Supreme Court when there are nine (Ruth Bader Ginsburg).

The Court of Justice of the European Union (CJEU) has been subject to relatively little scrutiny from a gender perspective. Lawyers have tended to focus their examination of the Court and its work on specific decisions or on the workings of the preliminary reference procedure and the relationship between the Court and national courts and legal systems. Political scientists have paid comparatively little attention to the CJEU as an institution of political relevance, initially focusing on it as an agent of the most powerful Member States[1] and later acknowledging though perhaps not unpicking, the Court's independence and possible activism.[2] So while there is a growing body of work considering the European Union (EU) generally as well as EU institutions, actors, policies and processes more specifically from a gendered perspective[3] and there is also a growing body of work which

1 See Geoffrey Garret, 'The European Community's Internal Market' (1992) 46(2) *International Organization* 533; Geoffrey Garret and Barry Weingast, 'Ideas, interests and institutions: Constructing the EC's internal market' in Judith Goldstein and Robert O Keohane (eds), *Ideas and Foreign Policy: Beliefs, Institutions, and Political Change* (Cornell University Press 1993); Anne-Marie Burley and Walter Mattli, 'Europe Before the Court: A Political Theory of Legal Integration' (1993) 47 *International Organization* 41.

2 See eg Joseph Weiler, 'A Quiet Revolution: The European Court of Justice and Its Interlocutors' (1994) 26(4) *Comparative Political Studies* 510; Walter Mattli and Anne-Marie Slaughter, 'Law and Politics in the European Union: A Reply to Garrett' (1995) 49 *International Organization* 183; Walter Mattli and Anne-Marie Slaughter, 'Revisiting the European Court of Justice' (1998) 52(1) *International Organization* 177; Karen Alter, *The European Court's Political Power* (Oxford University Press 2009).

3 See eg Gabriele Abels and Joyce Mushaben (eds), *Gendering the European Union: New Approaches to Old Democratic Deficits* (Palgrave MacMillan 2012); Fiona Beveridge and Samantha Velluti (eds), *Gender and the Open Method of Coordination: Perspectives on Law, Governance and Equality in the EU* (Ashgate 2008); Johanna Kantola, *Gender and the European Union* (Palgrave MacMillan 2010); Emanuela Lombardo and Maxime Forest, *The Europeanization of Gender Equality Policies: A Discursive-sociological Approach* (Palgrave MacMillan 2012); Anna van der Vleuten, *The Price of Gender Equality: Members States and*

examines the CJEU and its work, there is very little which brings those two areas together. As Sally Kenney notes '[p]olitical scientists and feminists alike often fail to recognise courts as political institutions and judgeships as decision-making positions that require a gender balance'.[4] As a result, when considered from a gendered or feminist perspective, we know almost nothing about the CJEU.

The CJEU has often been described as political on the grounds that its judgements favour further integration within the EU, which in essence means the interests of the EU institutions, rather than those of the Member States.[5] The Court has had a prominent role in the development of EU law in that regard because many of its judgements have become a major source of EU law,[6] and gender equality cases have been at the forefront of some of these developments. In the light of this, the Court's argument that it can only act within the limits of powers explicitly provided to it to protect the interests recognised by the Treaties is controversial and not something the Court itself has always strictly adhered to, particularly in the early days.[7] There may be scope for the CJEU to develop strong protection for individuals through its case law in various areas of law. This is primarily because, although the Court attempts to follow its own precedents, it is not bound by its previous decisions.[8] Rather, existing case law is seen as persuasive and is sometimes simply ignored by the Court. Although 'the dynamic approach is reflected in the Court's main methods of interpretation, specifically, the teleological approach, which tries to give the interpretation that best fulfils the purpose of the law in a particular context',[9] the Court is not particularly adventurous or gender aware in its decisions – even though the case law demonstrates some small victories along the history of the Court.

We will argue throughout the book that a gendered look at CJEU jurisprudence will lead to a fuller understanding of that jurisprudence and a more holistic understanding of the Court's decisions and its approach generally. We will also highlight areas where further research, mostly empirical in nature, is required to give us a fuller picture of how the Court works. Key to successfully increasing gender equality within the CJEU and, importantly, also increasing gender awareness ultimately leading to better overall decisions is making the case for a diverse judiciary, not only on the basis of representativeness and legitimacy, but on the basis that a more diverse judiciary is likely to be a better judiciary. In order to do

---

Governance in the European Union (Ashgate 2007); Eugenia Caracciolo di Torella and Annick Masselot, *Reconciling Work and Family Life in EU Law and Policy* (Palgrave Macmillan 2010).

4 Sally J Kenney, *Gender and Justice: Why Women in the Judiciary Really Matter* (Routledge 2013) 108.

5 Sanna Elfving, 'The European Union's animal welfare policy and indigenous peoples' rights: The case of Inuit and seal hunting in Arctic Canada and Greenland' (PhD thesis, University of Surrey 2014) 213.

6 ibid.

7 See Jessica Guth, 'Transforming the European Legal Order: The European Court of Justice at 60+' (2016) 12(1) *Journal of Contemporary European Research* 455.

8 Elfving (n 5) 213.

9 ibid 214.

so, we need to fully understand the CJEU, how it works, how it thinks and what its role is in an increasingly complex EU. This book begins to address that gap in our understanding by highlighting some of the issues relating to gender and setting out a research agenda for the future.

Structure of the book

The book is structured as follows and is broadly split into two parts. The first three chapters following this introduction deal with the theoretical framework of our work and the Court as an institution, whereas the next three chapters after that deal with substantive law topics before our concluding chapters aim at providing some overall insights as well as set out a research agenda for the future.

The theoretical framework (chapter 2)

Chapter 2 explains the theoretical framework we have adopted in this book. An important area of analysis and one where a significant amount of academic material exists is the outcome of the work of the CJEU. The decisions of the Court can be analysed form a gender perspective for a number of reasons: to reveal differing impact of the decisions on men and women; to highlight the way in which the Court deals with gender issues, and to examine the Court's gender awareness in cases which do not deal with gender *per se*. Although individual decisions, or clusters of decisions, have been the subject of this kind of scrutiny in the past, there is no systematic investigation of case law of the CJEU from this perspective. In fact, the Court's case law is not usually subjected to a gendered analysis.[10]

We will argue throughout the book that cases, which do not explicitly raise gender issues, have gendered consequences and also that applying a gender lens to these cases might lead to a different understanding of the issues and the different outcomes. A systematic analysis of the Court's decisions in a variety of policy areas, which considers both the gendered consequences of those decisions in detail as well as what a gendered reading of the cases might add to or change about a decision, is required to better understand the jurisprudence in those areas and the CJEU as a legal and political institution. In order to claim that the CJEU consistently makes gender-aware decisions, we need to not only examine those decisions, which have an obvious and direct impact on gender, but also those cases where gender implications are not obvious, and gain an understanding how the Court deals with them. While considering all policy areas where gender may have a role is obviously beyond the scope of a single book, it is worth looking

10 There are, of course, some exceptions; for example Caracciolo di Torella and Masselot (n 3); Jessica Guth, 'When Is a Partner Not a Partner? Conceptualisations of "Family" in EU Free Movement Law' (2011) 33(2) *Journal of Social Welfare and Family Law* 193 and works cited throughout this book.

at a number of areas to illustrate the argument as well as the point that CJEU jurisprudence would benefit from a detailed gender analysis.

We also acknowledge that, although taking a gendered approach to the Court's decisions may not necessarily result in a different outcome in the cases, there is a potential that it may do. What we can say with certainty is that it is likely to result in better reasoning which shows more clearly whether and why each case is different, and hence warrants an assessment of individual circumstances of the applicants. We argue that gender and questions of traditional family models cannot be de-coupled from situations where women and families are involved.

Who the judges are matters: the composition of the court (chapter 3)

One obvious place to begin an examination of the CJEU from a gendered perspective is to look at the Court itself and simply count the number of female judges employed by the Court. Understanding the gender balance within an institution is an important starting point and yet the composition of the CJEU has received only limited academic attention.[11] The Treaties now dictate that there must be one judge from each of the Member States to ensure representativeness and fairness. Why this argument holds true for nationality but not for other characteristics such as race or ethnic background, sexual orientation or, of course, gender is however not clear and has not been fully explored. There is a linked issue here which is the more general theoretical question as to why a diverse judiciary might be important. Paul Collins and his colleagues note that 'although some studies have identified gender differences in judicial decision making, others have failed to uncover systematic differences between male and female judges'.[12] This seems obvious given that it is the diversity in experience that might make for an overall better judiciary rather than the fact that men and women will always and inherently make different decisions. However, they also raise an interesting question about female judges which might be important in the CJEU context, namely whether critical mass makes a difference? If the number of women on a judiciary exceeds a certain number or proportion, do women then decide cases differently or reason differently? Collins and his colleagues found that when women serve with other women they decide cases differently. They note that '[w]hile it is clear that the influence of gender varies across policy areas, it is also evident that the impact of gender may be in part, contingent upon the presence of other women in the decision-making environment'.[13]

The question therefore arises that if there were more women on the CJEU, would they bring a more gender-aware voice to the Court and would that be

11 See eg Kenney, *Gender and Justice* (n 4); Sally J Kenney, 'Breaking the Silence: Gender Mainstreaming and the Composition of the European Court of Justice' (2002) 10 *Feminist Legal Studies* 257.

12 Paul M Collins, Jr, Kenneth L Manning, and Robert A Carp, 'Gender, Critical Mass, and Judicial Decision Making' (2010) 32(2) *Law and Policy* 260, 275. See also Rosemary Hunter, 'More Than Just a Different Face? Judicial Diversity and Decision-making' (2015) *Current Legal Problems* 1 doi:10.1093/clp/cuv001.

13 Collins and others (n 12) 275.

reflected in the final decisions of the Court. Until there are more women on the CJEU it is impossible to assess this. However, empirical work in other courts can further develop the work started by Collins and his colleagues, and detailed qualitative work with judges can shed further light on the factors that influence the Court's decision making.

How the court works and why it matters (chapter 4)

The focus of Chapter 4 is how the Court carries out its work. This necessitates asking questions such as how cases are brought to the CJEU, how it hears them, and how its decisions are arrived at. There is scope for significant gendered approaches in investigating the workings of the Court, and it is in this area where the case of a diverse judiciary can be made. However, assessing the impact of diversity generally, and gender specifically, in the case of the CJEU is difficult. This is because judgements are given by chambers of various compositions, rather than by individual judges. Therefore, individual voices are difficult to isolate and examine. Even more difficult is an assessment of the implications of the processes and procedures which lead to cases being heard at the Court. There are questions here generally about whether access to justice is gendered, which in itself has implications for the type of cases and claimants who come to the CJEU, and particularly the cases referred from Member States' courts to the Court of Justice through the preliminary reference procedure. However, there are also other gender issues inherent in the way cases are brought, processed, presented and eventually decided upon.

We also look at the relative lack of gender implications in the area of direct actions brought against the acts of the institutions. Although the Treaty of Lisbon[14] was thought to relax the rules on standing and access to the Court for direct actions, the Court continues to apply the strict approach in most proceedings involving private individuals.[15] Hence, the gendered implications of this area are very limited since natural persons are commonly unsuccessful in achieving standing. This in itself may have gendered implications though. The CJEU has rejected a broad interpretation of standing rules in conformity with the right to a fair trial and the right to an effective remedy in line with the Charter of Fundamental Rights[16] and the European Convention of Human Rights.[17] Instead, it has indicated that it is up to the Member States to provide individuals with direct legal remedies under national law.

After having looked at the composition and the working of the Court, the next obvious issue to consider is the outcome of the Court's work and the next three chapters turn to this.

14 Treaty of Lisbon Amending the Treaty on European Union and the Treaty Establishing the European Community [2007] OJ C306/01.
15 Elfving (n 5) 189.
16 Charter of Fundamental Rights of the European Union [2010] OJ C 83/389.
17 Convention for the Protection of Human Rights and Fundamental Freedoms (European Convention on Human Rights, as amended).

Gendering EU gender equality case law (chapter 5)

Chapter 5 is the first chapter in a series of chapters covering substantive law areas. We examine in detail the gender equality case law and apply a gendered reading to those cases. We also seek to understand why and how the Court championed gender equality and note that gender equality was not necessarily the primary factor in the decision making of the Court. Although it is often assumed that the CJEU has done a lot for gender equality, such an assumption is based on a handful of key judgements which can be argued to have advanced women's rights. However, making decisions which benefit women is not the same as being gender aware and genuinely promoting equality. The claims about the gender awareness of the CJEU's decisions requires a far more detailed examination, which is based on careful case law analysis.

EU rhetoric suggests that gender equality is one of the founding principles of the EU and that the CJEU has driven gender equality forward through its decisions. While most academics writing in this area are a little more sceptical, there is wide recognition that the EU has helped to drive progress in Member States. The key case in gender equality law is *Defrenne*[18] which concluded that the provisions relating to gender equality were directly effective and therefore citizens could rely on those provisions in their national courts. Other important decisions relate to equal pay cases,[19] decisions about part-time workers,[20] and cases about access to certain jobs in the military.[21] However, there are also decisions which question the gender awareness of the Court. Disappointingly, the Court has also proved regressive by deciding that positive action is unlawful because it goes beyond the promotion for equal treatment.[22] Although the Court has also recognised that where women are under-represented an equally qualified woman can be hired over a man,[23] it seems clear that this does not acknowledge the historic disadvantage women still face. Agata Brzezińska has noted the importance of gender quotas in employment in her 2009 work:

> So if only the ECJ relaxed its case law, the Member States could start introducing measures such as quotas in employment. It is for the ECJ to adapt its reasoning to social needs and to fully follow the substantive model of equality.[24]

18 Case 43/75 *Defrenne v Sabena (No 2)* [1976] ECR 455; Case 149/77 *Defrenne v Sabena (No 3)* [1978] ECR 1365.

19 eg Case C-262/85 *Douglas Harvey Barber v Guardian Royal Exchange Assurance Group* (1990) IRLR 240; Case C-381/99 *Susanna Brunnhofer v Bank der österreichischen Postsparkasse AG* [2001] ECR I-04961.

20 eg Case 170/84 *Bilka-Kaufhaus GmbH v Karin Weber von Harz* [1986] ECR 1607.

21 eg Case C-285/98 *Tanja Kreil v Bundesrepublik Deutschland* [2000] ECR I-69.

22 eg Case C-450/93 *Eckhard Kalanke v Freie Hansestadt Bremen* [1995] ECR I-3051; Case C-407/98 *Katarina Abrahamsson and Leif Anderson v Elisabet Fogelqvist* [2000] ECR I-5539.

23 Case C-409/95 *Hellmut Marschall v Land Nordrhein- Westfalen* [1997] ECR I-6363.

24 Agata Brzezińska, 'Gender Equality in the Case Law of the European Court of Justice' (2009) *Institute for European Studies Working Paper* 2/2009 doi:10.2139/ssrn.157775117.

Rather convincingly she also notes that without the quotas 'equality between men and women in the procedure of selecting employees remains a fiction'.[25] Quotas may not be popular, but the reality is that comparing women with men without taking cultural and societal context into account is not a fair comparison. Decisions comparing women and men on a like-for-like basis miss the point because men and women are not in the same position. This like-for-like comparison may be at least in part based on the underlying economic rationale of all EU provisions which also presume equal labour market participation. Although the Court has rather progressively stated in its case law that Treaty provision on equal pay[26] 'constitutes the expression of a fundamental human right',[27] we argue that there is still a long way to go to reach equality in terms of equal pay and more generally.

It's not just gender that's gendered: equality case law more broadly (chapter 6)

Chapter 6 discusses a much more inclusive approach to discrimination cases which could be applied to all cases involving individual citizens in one which puts human dignity at the heart of the consideration. The wider equality case law deals with alleged discrimination on grounds of a number of other protected characteristics, including race, religion and disability. The former Portuguese Advocate General (AG) of the Court, Poiares Maduro, in his opinion in *Coleman*[28] attempted to establish a foundation to equality jurisprudence which governs the interpretation of the Framework Directive[29] and which sees 'human dignity' as fundamental to equality. His approach has been welcomed by some and criticised by others.[30] Although the AG's approach was ultimately not taken up by the Court, it would facilitate the consideration of gender alongside other factors, may be more sensitive to gender implications, and could be employed in a variety of policy areas. Additionally, the consideration of other protected grounds allows us to evaluate the Court's engagement with fundamental rights and consider the impact its sometimes strained relationship with the European Court of Human Rights might have on equality overall. We also look at the issues to do with intersectionality in this chapter which helps us explore how ignoring gendered questions leads to decisions which simply do not consider the reality of claimants' lives. Here we argue that it makes no logical sense to create a legal framework which protects people on paper only but which cannot take lived experience into account in any meaningful way.

25 ibid.
26 Treaty on the Functioning of the European Union [2012] OJ C 326/47, art 157.
27 Cases C-270/97 and C-271/97 *Deutsche Post AG v Elisabeth Sievers and Brunhilde Schrage* [2000] ECR I-929 para 57.
28 Case C-303/06 *S Coleman v Attridge Law and Other* [2008] EU:C:2008:61, Opinion of AG Maduro.
29 Council Directive 2000/78/EC of 27 November 2000 Establishing a General Framework for Equal Treatment in Employment and Occupation [2000] OJ L303/16.
30 See eg Errol P Mendes, 'Taking Equality into the 21st Century: Establishing the Concept of Equal Human Dignity' (2000) 12(1) *National Journal of Constitutional Law* 3, 10–12.

European Union citizenship – free movement for all? (chapter 7)

Another chapter where case law is worthy of a closer examination through a gender lens relates to the decisions concerning free movement of persons and EU citizenship. This chapter takes an area of law which is less explicitly about women's rights or equality, and applies a gendered reading to the case law. It demonstrates how applying a gender lens to key cases concerning EU citizenship can highlight the way in which economic, rather than social drivers still shape the concept of EU citizenship and the way in which an alternative reading of the cases allows us to take into account a different set of factors which may lead to more considered decision making.

In 2011, the Court of Justice handed down a controversial judgement in *Zambrano*[31] which was quickly followed by the decision in *McCarthy*.[32] While we deal with these cases in more detail in Chapter 7, these two cases read together suggest that there has to be a relationship of care for the derived residence rights to apply. Although this is not something the Court made explicit in its judgements, previous decisions concerning a parent of a minor EU citizen suggest that the right of residence is usually granted.[33] The CJEU seems rather more sceptical of partners and spouses in general and even more so where the EU citizen claiming the right is economically inactive.[34] While the acknowledgement of the importance of carers' rights enhances women's rights, these rights have not been acknowledged with the primary aim of enhancing gender equality because the Court does not consider citizenship decisions from a gendered or even gender-aware perspective. In fact, the citizenship case law suggests that women have to do it all: they need to be able to work and ideally work in a Member State other than their own in order to benefit from the right to have their third-country national family member join them. If there is a relationship of caring present, chances of rights being granted seem to increase dramatically. These cases taken together are just one example of how market-driven citizenship has gendered implications that the Court has shown little awareness of.

Concluding thoughts

Our concluding thoughts take us back to our starting point and questions concerning whether more women in the EU judiciary would make a tangible

31 Case C-34/09 *Gerardo Ruiz Zambrano v Office National de l'Emploi ONEm* [2011] ECR I-1177.

32 Case C-434/09 *Shirley McCarthy v Secretary of State for the Home Department* [2011] ECR I-3375.

33 Case C-200/02 *Kunqian Catherine Zhu and Man Lavette Chen v Secretary of State for the Home Department* [2004] ECR I-9925; Case C-310/08 *London Borough of Harrow v Nimco Hassan Ibrahim and Other* [2010] ECR I-1065; Case C-480/08 *Maria Teixeira v London Borough of Lambeth and Other* [2010] ECR I-1107.

34 See also Case C-109/01 *Secretary of State for the Home Department v Hacene Akrich* [2003] ECR I-9607; Case C-127/08 *Blaise Baheten Metock and Others v Minister for Justice, Equality and Law Reform* [2008] ECR I-6241.

difference to the decisions of the Court and the outcomes of cases. We argue that it probably would because, in the areas examined in this book, being more gender aware and being more explicit about the gendered impacts of these decisions could have led to better, more holistic, more transparent and possibly more coherent decision making by the Court. We conclude that the Court has obviously advanced (gender) equality, and although we would rather be with its protection than without, it can, and must, do better. In particular, we argue that it needs to move away from a focus on market citizenship and free movement rationales to embrace fundamental rights more explicitly and that a more gender-aware approach is one step in that direction.

Conclusions

We argue throughout the book that the CJEU needs to be subjected to a full analysis which not only considers gender implications, but also what a more gender-aware consideration of the Court as a political institution could add to our understanding of how the EU works. The composition of the CJEU matters not only because the composition impacts on its representativeness and legitimacy, but because a more diverse judiciary will ultimately be a better judiciary. Further, the way in which cases are brought to the Court, particularly through the preliminary reference procedure, has gendered consequences. Much is dependent on the judiciary in the home State as to the extent to which preliminary references are made and, indeed, the extent to which gender questions are seen as important and worthy of referral. It seems clear that this procedure might have different implications and impacts on men and women. Although there have been a number of decisions which advance the rights of women and have done much for gender equality in the EU, the gender-awareness and pro-equality stance of the CJEU, and perhaps the EU generally, has often been overstated. Many of these decisions were economically motivated, and the same way as gender considerations often lose out when competing with other factors in general policy making,[35] so will gender considerations lose out when competing with other considerations in judicial decision making. That is to say, when presented with a gender questions, the CJEU has a relatively good record of making gender-aware decisions which try and promote equality in most cases. However, where gender is not an obvious factor or not directly at issue, the Court does not appear to be any better at demonstrating gender awareness or at mainstreaming gender than any of the other EU institutions.

Bibliography

Abels G and Mushaben J (eds), *Gendering the European Union: New Approaches to Old Democratic Deficits* (Palgrave MacMillan 2012)

35 Heather MacRae, 'The EU as a Gender Equal Polity: Myths and Realities' (2010) 48(1) *Journal of Common Market Studies* 155.

Alter KJ, *The European Court's Political Power* (Oxford University Press 2009)
Beveridge F and Velutti S (eds), *Gender and the Open Method of Coordination: Perspectives on Law, Governance and Equality in the EU* (Ashgate 2008)
Brzezińska A, 'Gender Equality in the Case Law of the European Court of Justice' (2009) *Institute for European Studies Working Paper* 2/2009 doi:10.2139/ssrn.157775117
Burley AM and Mattli W, 'Europe Before the Court: A Political Theory of Legal Integration' (1993) 47 *International Organization* 41
Caracciolo di Torella E and Masselot A, *Reconciling Work and Family Life in EU Law and Policy* (Palgrave Macmillan 2010)
Collins PM Jr, Manning KL and Carp RA, 'Gender, Critical Mass, and Judicial Decision Making' (2010) 32(2) *Law and Policy*
Elfving S, 'The European Union's Animal Welfare Policy and Indigenous Peoples' Rights: The Case of Inuit and Seal Hunting in Arctic Canada and Greenland' (PhD thesis, University of Surrey 2014)
Garret G, 'The European Community's Internal Market' (1992) 46(2) *International Organization* 533
Garret G and Weingast B, 'Ideas, Interests, and Institutions: Constructing the European Community's Internal Market' in Goldstein J and Keohane RO (eds), *Ideas and Foreign Policy* (Cornell University Press 1993)
Guth J, 'Transforming the European Legal Order: The European Court of Justice at 60+' (2016) 12(1) *Journal of Contemporary European Research* 455
———, 'When Is a Partner Not a Partner? Conceptualisations of "Family" in EU Free Movement Law' (2011) 33(2) *Journal of Social Welfare and Family Law* 193
Hunter R, 'More Than Just a Different Face? Judicial Diversity and Decision-making' (2015) *Current Legal Problems* 1–23
Kantola J, *Gender and the European Union* (Palgrave MacMillan 2010)
Kenney SJ, 'Breaking the Silence: Gender Mainstreaming and the Composition of the European Court of Justice' (2002) 10 *Feminist Legal Studies* 257
———, *Gender and Justice: Why Women in the Judiciary Really Matter* (Routledge 2013)
Lombardo E and Forest M, *The Europeanization of Gender Equality Policies: A Discursive-Sociological Approach* (Palgrave MacMillan 2012)
MacRae H, 'The EU as a Gender Equal Polity: Myths and Realities' (2010) 48(1) *Journal of Common Market Studies* 155
Mattli W and Slaughter AM, 'Law and Politics in the European Union: A Reply to Garrett' (1995) 49 *International Organization* 183
———, 'Revisiting the European Court of Justice' (1998) 52(1) *International Organization* 177
Mendes EP, 'Taking Equality into the 21st Century: Establishing the Concept of Equal Human Dignity' (2000) 12(1) *National Journal of Constitutional Law* 3
van der Vleuten A, *The Price of Gender Equality: Members States and Governance in the European Union* (Ashgate 2007)
Weiler J, 'A Quiet Revolution: The European Court of Justice and Its Interlocutors' (1994) 26(4) *Comparative Political Studies* 510

2 The theoretical framework

> Through a political science lens, legal scholarship seems anecdotal, lost in details, fatally flawed because the influences of extra-legal factors are not seriously explored, or unpersuasive because of a tendency to say that everything matters. Through a legal lens, political science work seems woefully misinformed about law and the legal process, simplistic if not crude, stating the obvious as if it were newly discovered, and ignorant or in denial of important cases that seem to disprove the argument made.[1]

The idea for this book came from conversations with European Union (EU) lawyers, political scientists, students and other colleagues, friends and family. Those conversations highlighted that taking a slightly different perspective, freeing ourselves from the traditional approach to legal reasoning and case analysis and asking slightly different questions of institutions and their outputs could reveal otherwise hidden biases and assumptions which can tell us something important about law, gender, the institutions, case law and the world we live in. The conversations also highlighted that seeing the Court of Justice of the European Union[2] (CJEU or the Court) as a political as well as a legal institution and acknowledging its role as both a legal and political actor can help uncover those biases

1 Karen J Alter, Renaud Dehousse and Georg Vanberg, 'Law, Political Science and EU Legal Studies: An Interdisciplinary Project' (2002) 3(1) *European Union Politics* 113-114.

2 There have been changes in the structure of the Court in the course of its existence. The titles of the two remaining courts have changed and the third court forming part of this institution, the Civil Service Tribunal, is no longer in existence since it ceased operations on 1 September 2016. Hence, currently, the CJEU consists of the General Court and the Court of Justice. It is important to note that prior to the amendment of the Treaties in 2009, the Court of Justice was known as the European Court of Justice (ECJ). Hence, many of the materials, including academic writings and judgements of the Court predating 2009 frequently refer to the ECJ. Additionally, the General Court was known as the 'Court of First Instance' until 2009. For ease we refer to the Court of Justice of the European Union or CJEU when we mean the entire institution. We refer to the General Court (GC) or the Court of Justice (CoJ) when we mean that specific court. Where we have quoted materials referring to the ECJ we have kept the original reference.

and assumptions. Subsequently, our approach in this book has involved taking a conscious departure from the traditional approach to legal analysis by asking different questions, or the same questions, but differently. We have tried to identify the assumptions made, question them, and see what happens when, or if, we make different assumptions. Our approach is interdisciplinary, and in many ways personal. This chapter attempts to share that approach with our readers.

Interdisciplinary research always necessitates a clear exploration of theoretical and methodological issues. Even in closely related disciplines, such as political science and law, meaning and methodological approaches may be subtly different and theoretical concepts may be interpreted differently. There is a real risk that we talk past each other rather than to one other. In this chapter we have therefore attempted to articulate our approach to this project, our ways of thinking and our ways of working, so that readers can set this work in a context, understand it in the way we intended it to be understood, and take it further through debate and critique. In addition, we have tried to offer definitions, or at least possible explanation, of the key ideas and concepts used throughout this book. Although they are not the only possible definitions and explanations, they are the ones which have proven useful in our analysis. This chapter begins with setting out our approach to research generally, and this project specifically, before explaining what we did throughout the research and writing process, and examining and challenging our own assumptions and biases. We explore some of the key theoretical issues raised by studying the CJEU and its case law and have tried to explain how we have engaged with ideas drawn from political science and law and how we have treated the Court as an institution which is both political and legal.

Our approach

We acknowledge that there is no single feminist method or methodology, one way to analyse and think about law and legal and political institutions, or one feminist way to do so.[3] Through this book we have tried to set out our thinking, our way of doing this, without saying that our approach is the only or the best way of analysing the Court and its case law. What we are saying is that our way of thinking and doing things should be part of the conversation. We realise that as lawyers by training we have much to learn from other disciplines and that it is likely that we have, mostly, based what we do on an understanding that is grounded in our disciplinary background.

We are often led to believe that legal method is something objective and something that can be learned. Law students and (academic) lawyers are trained to

3 Gabriele Abels and Heather MacRae (eds), *Gendering European Integration Theory: Engaging New Dialogues* (Barbara Budrich 2016) 11; Rosemary Hunter, 'The Power of Feminist Judgments?' (2012) 20(2) *Feminist Legal Studies* 13 doi:0.1007/s10691-012-9202-0; Yavuz Selim Alkan, 'Feminist Legal Methods: Theoretical Assumptions, Advantages, and Potential Problems' (2012) 9(2) *Ankara Law Review* 157, 158.

'think like lawyers'.[4] Lawyers are trained to read cases; they are taught how to interpret statutory material using different methods and are well acquainted with legal research methods. They can decode citations, find law reports, track down statutory instruments or white papers and know where to search for the latest judgements or government proposals, treaties and other legal materials. Lawyers can explain what the law says and what it means in a given practical scenario; what lawyers are less good at is acknowledging that legal method is no different, no more objective, than any other approach to research. Lawyers are taught to think of legal reasoning, statutory interpretation and legal research in general as an objective exercise; one which is divorced from the researcher's, in fact, from anyone's, personal view or perspective. Law then is rational, objective and dispassionate, and those who practise it, whether as practitioners or academics, are, like the oft-cited man on the Clapham omnibus,[5] objective, dispassionate, rational and reasonable. In discussing socio-legal work in the context of the EU, Jo Shaw captures this way of thinking about what lawyers do: 'This [work on the Court of Justice as a political institution] has involved some collaboration with lawyers, principally seen as "technicians" feeding in a data set of what the Court (objectively) "does" . . .'.[6]

However, the law and legal processes studied in this book are more than objectively measurable rules and procedures or an objective data set. Like any other analysis, legal analysis is inextricably linked with the researcher's own position, experience and biography and, perhaps even more importantly, an individual's experience of the law will be shaped by their background and context. Although understanding this is the key to our approach in this book, unravelling all these elements is not always straightforward. However, as Shaw notes: 'without a developed sense that law in the EU context is a problematic enterprise, socio-legal studies on the EU will provide little more than a contextualised explanation of existing legal models rather than a critical exploration'.[7] In order to provide that critical exploration, this book engages with the law, with interdisciplinary, theoretical debates and with our own assumptions and biases. As Michael Adler puts it:

> Because the facts do not speak for themselves, because concepts need to be constructed and because the process of concept construction needs to

4 Fiona Cownie, Anthony Bradney, and Mandy Burton, *English Legal System in Context* (4th edn, Oxford University Press 2007). For an explanation as to what doctrinal or classic legal method involves, see Terry Hutchinson and Nigel Duncan, 'Defining and Describing What We Do: Doctrinal Legal Research' (2012) 17 *Deakin Law Review* 83; Elies van Sliedregt, 'International Criminal Law: Over-studied and Underachieving?' (2016) 29 *Leiden Journal of International Law* 1.

5 The man on the Clapham omnibus is the hypothetical 'reasonable man' and possibly makes his first appearance in *McQuire v Western Morning News* [1903] 2 KB 100 at 109 where Collins MR refers to Lord Bowen having used the phrase several years earlier as a junior counsel in a criminal case in 1871.

6 Jo Shaw, 'Socio-legal studies and the European Union' in Philip A Thomas (ed), *Socio-Legal Studies* (Ashgate Dartmouth 1997) 313.

7 ibid 317.

> be theoretically informed, empirical socio-legal researchers need to have a good grasp of legal, political and social theory. This is clearly the case if the research is intended to advance theory but it is, arguably, also the case if the research is intended to deepen understanding, challenge complacency, or inform and evaluate policy.[8]

The approach we take is therefore unapologetically qualitative in nature and it treats law and policy documents as any other documents to be interrogated without assigning them any special status. Documents about the Court, case law and commentary form our data and we are as interested in what is left out as we are in what is included. Norman Denzin and Yvonna Lincoln note that:

> Three interconnected, generic activities define the qualitative process. They go by a variety of different labels, including theory, analysis, ontology, epistemology and methodology. Behind these terms stands the personal biography of the researcher, who speaks from a particular class, gender, racial cultural and ethnic community perspective. . . . Every researcher speaks from within a distinct interpretive community that configures in its special way the multicultural, gendered components of the research act.[9]

Our interpretive community can perhaps be said to be disciplinary-aware legal feminists, or feminist EU lawyers, or feminists with an interest in EU law and EU studies more generally – depending on the work we are currently immersed in and colleagues were are currently closely connected to. Our underpinning and guiding theoretical framework is drawn from feminist legal theory, which generally challenges traditional and dominant legal doctrine as feminist legal scholars analyse and seek reform of existing legal approaches.[10] In general it can be argued that feminist legal scholars criticise dominant legal methods for 'representing male power structures, considering only a male view of the world, and ignoring the female view'.[11] Rita Dhamoon calls the feminist critique of law 'a form of social critique' to address existing gender relations.[12] To counter the one-sided presentation of words, feminist legal scholars have attempted to incorporate the

8 Michael Adler, *Recognising the Problem: Socio-Legal Research Training in the UK* (University of Edinburgh 2007) 1.

9 Norman K Denzin and Yvonna S Lincoln, 'Introduction: The discipline and practice of qualitative research' in Norman K Denzin and Yvonna S Lincoln (eds), *Handbook of Qualitative Research* (3rd edn, Sage 2005) 21.

10 Alkan (n 3).

11 Lydia Cloughtery, 'Feminist Legal Methods and the First Amendment Defense to Sexual Harassment' (1996) 75 *Nebraska Law Review* 1, 2. See also eg Katharine T Bartlett, 'Feminist Legal Methods' (1990) 103 *Harvard Law Review* 829.

12 Rita Kaur Dhamoon, 'Feminisms' in Georgina Waylen, Karen Celis, Johanna Kantola and S Laurel Weldon (eds), *Oxford Handbook on Gender and Politics* (Oxford University Press 2013) 89.

experience of women and women's voices into jurisprudence.[13] In this sense, feminist legal theory challenges traditional legal assumptions and methods with a view to exploring alternative approaches using specialist discourse and methodology to expose those features of law that disadvantage women.[14] Although traditional legal method may be argued to 'male-identified in its current incarnation', feminist legal method can be seen to contribute to the constant reformulation of methodological conventions, with the aspirations to 'transform not only lawyers' views of gender justice, but their views of how to use law to persuade and produce social change'.[15] Dealing with method is important because, as Catharine MacKinnon noted, it 'organises the apprehension of truth; It determines what counts as evidence and it defines what is taken as verification.'[16]

Rosemary Auchmuty has noted that feminism is a late entrant to law, and while feminist jurisprudence may have become an accepted and growing field, it remains separate and marginal.[17] This marginality is not helped by the fact that feminism or a feminist approach does not signify one specific way of doing law or even one particular theory of law; a lack of unity of definition means that feminist approaches can appear disjointed, 'bitty' or even contradictory. It is therefore useful to outline and understand some of the differing strands and how they have informed our work. Katherine Bartlett's 1990 work on feminist legal methods provides a useful basis for further discussion.[18] While her analysis and arguments have been subject to critical questioning due the reflexivity of the approach, her work is one of the most frequently cited in the existing literature focusing on feminist legal methods.[19] Moreover, even though existing literature focuses on the 'feminist legal theories', very little literature focusing exclusively upon 'feminist legal methods' has been written since 2000. Instead, existing literature commonly refers to Bartlett to provide general information about the theoretical background of the feminist legal methods, which is subsequently applied to case law.[20] Bartlett's work outlines three main feminist legal methods, which she names as 'asking the woman question', 'feminist practical reasoning' and 'consciousness raising'. She further analyses three theories of knowledge that emerged from within feminist theory; 'rational empiricism', 'standpoint epistemology' and 'postmodernism'.[21] Bartlett subsequently proposes a fourth stance entitled 'posi-

13 Alkan (n 3) 159.
14 ibid.
15 Kathryn Abrams, 'Feminist Lawyering and Legal Method' (1991) 16 *Law and Social Inquiry* 373, 375.
16 Catharine Mackinnon, 'Feminism, Marxism, Method and the State: An Agenda for Theory' (1982) 7(3) *SIGNS: Journal of Women in Culture and Society* 515, 527.
17 Rosemary Auchmuty, 'Feminist Approaches to Sexuality and Law Scholarship' (2015) 15(1) *Legal Information Management* 4.
18 Bartlett (n 11).
19 Alkan (n 3) 160.
20 ibid.
21 Bartlett (n 11) 837–867.

tionality', which, according to her, provided 'for feminists the best explanation of what it means to be 'right' in law'.[22]

In our approach we have borrowed from Bartlett's feminist practical reasoning as it seems to us to be a useful way of ensuring that the voices of the excluded can be taken into account more easily. It allows for the importance of context to be recognised as it suggests that the nature of the (legal) issue or problem as well as the possible solutions all arise from the intricacies and specific factual situations and context.[23] This approach coupled with what Bartlett has termed positionality has proved useful in our analysis of the Court and its work. Bartlett argues that positionality helps us make sense of the differing and competing feminist claims. It 'acknowledges the existence of empirical "truths", values and knowledge and also their contingencies'.[24] It recognises that there is no one truth that can be deemed final because truth and knowledge arise out of the social context and is shaped by us and knowledge can be expanded by moving beyond our own truth and seeking out additional perspectives. This made inherent sense to us as we sought to first apply traditional legal reasoning and then seek out alternative interpretations of the legal issues and questions raised and their possible solutions within a fixed but ultimately flexible legal framework.

The discussions above however do not really take us any further in defining what the key factors are on which we as feminist scholars want to focus. It could be argued that despite different theoretical perspectives among, for instance, liberal and radical feminists,[25] three central tenets amongst feminist critical theories exist.[26] First, on a political level, different feminist approaches aim to endorse equality between women and men.[27] Second, on a substantive level, the aim of feminist critical frameworks focusing on gender analysis is to 'reconstitute legal practices that have excluded, devalued, or undermined women's concerns'.[28] Third, on a methodological level, the critical frameworks seek to define 'the world in ways that correspond to women's experience and. . . [to] identify the fundamental social transformations necessary for full equality between the sexes'.[29]

Feminist legal scholars disagree among themselves as to whether they should adopt some aspects of traditional legal methods or whether they should completely

22 ibid 829.

23 ibid 851. See also Amelie Rorty, *Mind in Action: Essays on the Philosophy of Mind* (Beacon Press 1988).

24 Bartlett (n 11) 880.

25 Alkan (n 3) 158. Although we recognise that even the notion of equality is in itself problematic and has divided feminists.

26 See eg Nancy Levit and Robert Verchick, *Feminist Legal Theory: A Primer* (New York University Press 2006) 15–88. For historical evolution of feminist legal scholarship, see Martha Fineman, 'Feminist Theory and Law' (1995) 18 *Harvard Journal of Law and Public Policy* 349; Katherine Bartlett, 'Feminist Legal Scholarship: A History Through the Lens of the California Law Review' (2012) 100 *California Law Review* 381.

27 Deborah Rhode, 'Feminist Critical Theories' (1990) 42 *Stanford Law Review* 617, 619.

28 ibid.

29 ibid.

reject, for instance, the deductive model of legal reasoning.[30] According to Bartlett, feminist practical reasoning is not the polar opposite of the model of legal reasoning which has been considered being inherently 'male' in its form.[31] Carol Smart has argued that the structure, language and power of law exclude and damage women and that 'in accepting law's terms in order to challenge law, feminism always concedes too much'.[32] We struggled with how to reconcile the power of law to define issues in a particular way that often excludes women and therefore how we could work within the legal framework to show the difference a gendered approach can make.

However, Bartlett's work highlights that feminist practical reasoning, for example, is not the opposite of 'rationality', but a feminist rationality which 'acknowledges greater diversity in human experiences', 'openly reveals its positional partiality', and instead of limiting new situations within prescribed categories of analysis, opens up the possibilities for such situations.[33] Although some feminist scholars consider it impossible to attain their goals 'under existing ideological and institutional structures',[34] Alkan has argued that no compelling arguments have been provided as to when legal feminist scholars should discard traditional approaches and when they would be better advised to work within those boundaries.[35] Therefore, whether or not challenging traditional legal doctrine means adaptation or mere careful examination of case law, institutional actors and socio-economic and cultural actors engaging in the field of law and policy, feminist legal theory has brought new insights into traditional legal approaches,[36] and can allow us to do the same.

A perhaps more recent and powerful method of legal critique and a form of feminist legal strategy, namely feminist judgement writing, engages with law in terms not envisaged by early feminist legal scholars.[37] The methodology involves an attempt to contradict some of the arguments of early feminist legal scholars that law as a powerful discourse has exclusionary and damaging impacts for women.[38] Rosemary Hunter has criticised early scholars, such as Smart, for asserting that the representation of women and gender in law not only ignores or leaves women out of the legal accounts, but it also actively disqualifies women's

30 Alkan (n 3) 162.
31 Bartlett (n 11) 855.
32 Carol Smart, *Feminism and the Power of Law* (Routledge 1989) 5. In her later work Smart is less critical of law as an institution and acknowledges the positive impact law can have on resolving the issues facing women although she always remains an advocate of non-legal solutions. These issues are further explored in Rosemary Auchmuty and Karin van Marle (eds), 'Special Issue: Carol Smart's Feminism and the Power of Law' (2012) 20(2) *Feminist Legal Studies*.
33 Bartlett (n 11) 857–858.
34 Rhode (n 27) 619.
35 Alkan (n 3) 162.
36 ibid 161.
37 Hunter (n 3).
38 ibid referring to Smart (n 32).

experience and knowledge.[39] Therefore, law's understanding of women ousts and delegitimises alternative interpretations proposed by women themselves.[40] This occurs as a result of the ability of law to persuasively claim that it 'speaks the truth about social experience'.[41] Because of the power of such claims to speak the truth, law's knowledge about women is taken to be accurate. As a result, law disqualifies competing knowledges, which are unable to invoke such powerful support for their claims to speak the truth.[42] Accordingly, Smart identified as a major obstacle to feminist interventions in law the most commonly used legal method[43] which the courts employ when resolving disputes before them. This is despite the assumption that this method is not only presumed to be neutral, objective and impartial, but also to result in 'correct' decisions.[44] Similarly, according to Mary Jane Mossman, the legal method used by the courts is structured in such a way that it is impermeable to a feminist perspective.[45] However, rather than accepting this argument, feminist judgement writing attempts to introduce a feminist perspective into law by means of legal method.[46] This notion is an attractive one to us as it allows us to think about how a feminist approach might make law better rather than having to accept the suggestion that law is inherently anti-feminist.

The feminist judgement writing methodology involves re-writing judgements in selected cases based on the assumption that the law is full of 'decisions which feminists might perceive to be unjust'.[47] This provides feminist legal theory practical effect in judgement form, which subsequently creates a mixture of critique and suggestions for law reform.[48] The principal idea of this method is that an alternative feminist analysis of the issues and legal principles involved in a particular case chosen for analysis is not conducted merely as an academic exercise or for an academic audience, but the aim of the scholars is to influence a wider audience beyond academia, including activists, lawyers and judges.[49] Consequently, the reasoning in feminist judgement writing aims at persuading their audience to either contribute to the development of laws indirectly or to generate change in the

39 ibid referring to Smart (n 32) 2, 11, 21.
40 Hunter (n 3).
41 ibid.
42 ibid.
43 Songer and his colleagues note that the legal model is based on the view that judges are 'neutral arbiters of the law'. Rather than making the law, judges decide the case before them by analogy. In essence, judges start off by examining the law and its application in precedents after which they assess the similarity of the case before them with existing case law and finally apply legal doctrine to it. Donald R Songer, Cynthia Lynne Ostberg, and Matthew Wetstein, *Law, Ideology, and Collegiality: Judicial Behaviour in the Supreme Court of Canada* (McGill-Queen University Press 2012) 46.
44 Hunter (n 3); Smart (n 32) 2, 11, 21.
45 Mary Jane Mossman, 'Feminism and Legal Method: The Difference It Makes' (1987) 3 *Wisconsin Women's Law Journal* 147, 165.
46 Hunter (n 3).
47 ibid.
48 ibid.
49 ibid.

law.[50] Additionally, by assuming legal personas and forms, the feminist judgement writing visibly demonstrates that these cases could have been reasoned or decided differently with the legal and other materials available to the court at the time of the decision.[51] In doing so, this method exposes the eventuality and biases of existing decisions and questions the unique authority of the courts and legal decision making.[52] On the other hand, the legal forms which this method takes remain largely unchallenged. Judgement writing is accepted as a particular genre, which is subject to particular constraints. Therefore, it strives to operate within that genre and it is subject to the same constraints as those binding appellate judges. Hence, the method does not attempt to open up legal forms or legal method.[53]

For our own work this approach has been helpful and insightful. While we have kept in mind the more traditional legal feminist approaches such as the one outlined by Smart, we have also learned a great deal from the feminist judgements projects. Our approach to the decisions of the CJEU that we have considered throughout this book was not to re-write the judgements themselves but to ask different questions about them and consider the choices that could have been made, *inter alia*, in terms of questions referred, arguments made, precedents selected and conclusions drawn. We have then sought to set that in the context of a body of case law in each of our chosen areas, which has enabled us to learn not only about individual cases, but about substantive law dealing with a particular topic and the influence the Court has had, and could have had, in that area.

A diversity of possible feminist judgements could be written in any given case. As outlined further below we have, in our approach to the case law, taken some of the methodology of feminist judgement writing on board in order to enable us to reimagine the cases, ask questions that were left unasked and offer different explanations and views. Other questions could be asked and other explanations could be offered and the more open we are to all of them the richer our understanding of the Court and its case law will become.

Understanding gender and applying a gender lens

Our understanding of a feminist approach is not only shaped by feminist legal theory but also draws on feminist approaches more generally and in particular looks to social sciences for an interpretation of gender. This is not an easy task since there is no single theory of gender in social sciences,[54] nor is there a single gendered approach to analysing the European legal system, the decisions of the CJEU or a theory that would explain judicial decision making. An obvious place to look may be the broadly defined discipline of gender studies. Just as there

50 ibid.
51 ibid.
52 Hunter (n 3).
53 ibid.
54 Abels and MacRae (n 3) 12.

is no one feminism, the concept of 'gender' also has different definitions and using gender as a lens to analyse questions of EU law and policy means that how we understand gender is also shaped by our general theoretical framework. The collection considering a gendered analysis of EU integration theories edited by Gabriele Abels and Heather MacRae highlights this effectively.[55] Abels and MacRae have argued that:

> gender is a socially constructed [meta-theoretical] category that profoundly shapes people's lives; it is not a naturally given fact. Men and women, masculinity and femininity, sexual identities are not biologically given essentials, but are constructed and given meaning through human interaction.[56]

At the same time, they note that 'gender is not stable category, but its meaning is contested'.[57] According Toni Haastrup and Meryl Kenny, gender can be understood as 'a constitutive element of social relations based upon perceived (socially constructed and culturally variable) differences between women and men, and as a primary way of signifying (and naturalising) relationships of power and hierarchy'.[58] Therefore, gender does not operate only at interpersonal level, but is also a feature of institutions and social structures, and 'part of the symbolic realm where gender meanings are construed'.[59] Similarly, Hans-Jürgen Bieling and Thomas Diez highlight the 'unequal power relations between men and women' and 'the related life plans of different kinds of men and women' inherent in the concept of gender.[60] Hence, they consider it as 'a theoretical concept sensitive to social power relations, social hierarchies and established modes of domination, and also the manifold forms of discrimination inscribed in them'.[61]

MacRae has argued that rather than being a variable, gender is a viewpoint as gendered perspective seeks to look at the world through a particular 'gender lens'.[62] However, the conceptual potential of a gender-sensitive perspective, or the use of a gender lens to examine the workings of the CJEU, does not mean that we have attempted to generate a single theory with which it is possible to explain the workings of the Court. This is because gender-sensitive perspective is not a substantive theoretical approach, and an attempt to develop a gender theory of the working of the Court runs the danger of providing a one-sided

55 ibid.
56 Abels and MacRae (n 3) 11.
57 ibid.
58 Toni Haastrup and Meryl Kenny, 'Gendering institutionalism: Feminist institutionalist approach to EU integration theory' in Abels and MacRae (n 3) 201.
59 ibid.
60 Hans-Jürgen Bieling and Thomas Diez, 'Linking gender perspectives to integration theory: The need for dialogue' in Abels and MacRae (n 3) 280.
61 ibid.
62 Heather MacRae, 'Neo-functionalism: Spilling over to gender studies' in Abels and MacRae (n 3) 71.

gender reductionist view. Indeed, the function which the term 'gender' has as an analytical category is immensely useful since it helps us as legal scholars to 'reveal hidden biases and assumptions upon which many traditional categories of analysis are built'.[63] Using gender analysis, or a gender lens, we are able to frame a set of research questions, such as how power operates in the production of sex, gender and sexuality within the context of the CJEU.[64] This necessitates asking questions which define the parameters of gender analysis as they reveal both obvious and embedded masculinities underlying power and hierarchies as well as highlights the way in which practices, which are considered 'standard' or normal, serve to reproduce existing hierarchies and gendered regimes.[65] MacRae argues that, for instance, the structure on which the EU is built is inherently gendered, which can be inferred from the emphasis placed on economic and labour market integration.[66] Naturally, the critique of the unequal integration between Member States' economic and social policies extends to the CJEU and the legitimacy of the Court.[67] Dagmar Schiek notes that:

> the disproportionate power of judges in adjudicating the Internal Market has led some authors to suggest that direct effects and supremacy of EU law should no longer be recognised or that there should be an EU level mechanism for Member States to challenge contentious rulings by the Court of Justice. While some of these authors demand protection of Member States' authority (including for social policy) from the European Court of Justice's adjudication, the prioritisation of legislation over adjudication is not necessarily linked to a preference for national social policymaking.[68]

We would not go as far as advocating abandoning the longstanding principles of EU law as established in the Court's jurisdiction, considering that it would involve nullifying decades of a body of Court's case law giving effective meaning, for instance, the 'fundamental status' of EU citizenship.[69] Eradicating case law that 'has been, and continues to be, carried out progressively and in close cooperation with national courts in the context of references for a preliminary

63 Abels and MacRae (n 3) 11.

64 For similar arguments in the context of the theories gendering European integration theories, see Abels and MacRae (n 3) 11.

65 MacRae (n 62) 71.

66 ibid.

67 Dagmar Schiek, 'Towards More Resilience for a Social EU: The Constitutionally Conditioned Internal Market' (2017) 13(4) *European Constitutional Law Review* 611, 618 doi:10.1017/S1574019617000311.

68 ibid 618 (footnotes omitted).

69 Case C-165/14 *Alfredo Rendón Marín v Administración del Estado* [2016] EU:C:2016:75, Opinion of AG Szpunar, para 110. See also Charlotte O'Brien, 'The ECJ Sacrifices EU Citizenship in vain: Commission v. United Kingdom' (2017) 54 *Common Market Law Review* 209.

ruling'[70] would simply not serve any meaningful purpose. Instead, we propose to examine the judgements, some of them arguably 'controversial, complex, and subtle',[71] from a gendered perspective, which in this context would ask why social policy is less important in comparison with the economic policy and how is it possible that, whereas economic integration and market liberalisation appear to be beneficial to everyone, they may, in fact, be detrimental to specific groups of women.[72] In line with the feminist constructivist theory it would be possible to argue that, although some institutions within the EU, such as the Commission, have made a resolute effort to construct, maintain or change gender roles within the EU, identities and practices, gender rules look remarkably persistent throughout the history and across the cultures.[73]

Abels and MacRae have argued that feminist scholarship forms part of 'polyphonic chorus of dissident voices' in theories debating European integration in a sense that gender issues remain 'side-lined and marginalised' in the academic journals and debates on 'mainstream' theories of European integration.[74] They are of the opinion that this is partly due to the conscious choice by the gender scholars to engage in policy issues, rather than theoretical debates and, hence, gender scholars should make a conscious effort to engage with political scientists due to continuing events threatening the significant achievements of the European integration project since its inception. Abels and MacRae cite as examples capable of exerting pressure on further European integration, *inter alia*, the 2008 financial crisis; the rise of populism; political unrest in the European neighbourhood; and the sudden influx of irregular migrants to Europe as a result of civil wars in the Middle East and North African region.[75] More recently Guerrina and Masselot make similar points in relation to the United Kingdom's (UK) decision to withdraw from the EU (Brexit).[76] We would like to complement Abels and MacRae's list by adding events that are likely to have highly gendered impacts, for instance the aftermath of the adoption of the Treaty of Lisbon[77] in 2009 when several Member States adopted restrictive policies towards EU migrants from Bulgaria and Romania.[78] Indeed, as we argue in Chapter 7, the right to free movement under EU citizenship law has been interpreted increasingly

70 *Rendón Marín* (n 69) para 110.

71 O'Brien, 'The ECJ Sacrifices EU Citizenship in vain' (n 69) 209.

72 MacRae (n 62) 71.

73 Ulrike Liebert, 'Gendering Europeanisation: Making equality work in theory and practice' in Abels and MacRae (n 3) 155.

74 Abels and MacRae (n 3) 10.

75 Abels and MacRae (n 3) 11.

76 Roberta Guerrina and Annick Masselot 'Walking into the Footprint of EU Law: Unpacking the Gendered Consequences of Brexit' (2018) *Social Policy and Society* 1 doi:10.1017/S1474746417000501.

77 Treaty of Lisbon amending the Treaty on European Union and the Treaty establishing the European Community [2007] OJ C306/1.

78 See eg James Hampshire and Tim Bale, 'New Administration, New Immigration Regime: Do Parties Matter After All? A UK Case Study' (2015) 38(1) *West European Politics* 145, 153 doi:10.1080/01402382.2014.925735.

restrictively both by Member States' governments and the Court. This has resulted in gendered impacts due to the marginalisation of women working in part-time positions, and particularly lone parents, who are likely to be women more often than men.[79]

Further, the economic austerity measures introduced by a number of Member States governments following the 2008 financial crises have had a more profound impact on women.[80] There is evidence that women working in the UK are more frequently employed on contracts which confine them to low-paid jobs, with limited working hours and constrained working and employment opportunities.[81] The Office for National Statistics has noted that workers on contracts where they are not guaranteed any specific number of hours and, hence, may not work at all one week, 'are more likely to be young, part-time, women, or in full-time education when compared with other people in employment'.[82] Abels and MacRae's list can also be complemented with the infringement of rule of law in some of the Central and Eastern European Member States in the course of 2017 as this can be argued to have gendered impacts.

Abels and MacRae's edited collection shows how a gendered lens can be applied to different theoretical approaches to EU integration, including that affecting Member States' legal systems.[83] Auchmuty provides a further example in her work as to how a gender lens is applied in practice. According to her, this

79 See eg Charlotte O'Brien, 'The Pillory, the Precipice and the Slippery Slope: The Profound Effects of the UK's Legal Reform Programme Targeting EU Migrants' (2015) 37(1) *Journal of Social Welfare and Family Law* 111-112 and 124 doi:10.1080/09649069.2015.1005997. O'Brien has argued that the 'xenosceptic' law making and administrative culture of the UK government have imported neoliberal ideals into the welfare system by challenging the basic principles of equality and human rights and by attacking the right to free movement and equal treatment for all citizens.

80 Roberta Guerrina, 'Gendering European economic narratives: Assessing the costs of the crisis to gender equality' in Johanna Kantola and Emanuela Lombardo (eds), *Gender and the Economic Crisis in Europe: Politics, Institutions and Intersectionality* (Palgrave MacMillan 2017); Akwugo Emejulu and Leah Bassel, 'Whose crisis counts? Minority women, austerity and activism in France and Britain' in Johanna Kantola and Emanuela Lombardo (eds), *Gender and the Economic Crisis in Europe: Politics, Institutions and Intersectionality* (Palgrave MacMillan 2017).

81 See eg Charlotte O'Brien, 'Civis Capitalist Sum: Class as the New Guiding Principle of EU Free Movement Rights' (2016) 53(4) *Common Market Law Review* 937-938; Colette Fagan and Jill Rubery, 'Advancing Gender Equality Through European Employment Policy: The Impact of the UK's EU Membership and the Risks of Brexit' (2017) *Social Policy and Society* 1 doi:10.1017/S1474746417000458; Jo McBride, Andrew Smith, and Marcell Mbala, '"You end up with Nothing": The Experience of Being a Statistic of "in-work Poverty" in the UK' (2017) 1 *Work, Employment and Society* 1, 2 doi:10.1177/0950017017728614; Office for National Statistics, 'People in Employment on a Zero-hours Contract: Mar 2017' 2 <www.ons.gov.uk/employmentandlabourmarket/peopleinwork/earningsandworkinghours/articles/contractsthatdonotguaranteeaminimumnumberofhours/mar2017> accessed 26 November 2017.

82 Office for National Statistics (n 81) 2.

83 See Jessica Guth, 'Law as the object and agent of integration: Gendering the Court of Justice of the European Union, its decisions and their impact' in Abels and MacRae (n 3).

involves asking gender questions and questions about gender, highlighting issues such as that the world is not composed solely of men; women's experiences are different from men; and the relationship between sexes is not necessarily one of equality, but sometimes it is that of overt discrimination and oppression.[84] Auchmuty has argued that the fact that the UK legal professions consisted of virtually no women before 1920 was not because women had no interest in practising law until then, but it was because 'men used every possible legal and extra-legal means to keep women out of the [legal] profession'.[85] According to her, the classic problem that pervades most knowledge and scholarship is the virtual absence of women in mainstream work and the use of universal words to describe the experience of men only.[86] The continuing acceptability of accounts that focus solely on male concerns is problematic because women are often situated in a very different place from men.[87] Since a central feature of feminism is that gender is socially constructed, the goal of many feminist scholars is the creation of a world in which the biological sex of a person makes no social difference.[88] However, as long as gender makes a difference, a feminist legal scholar must ask of her sources whether the situation is different for men and for women; does the law in question apply equally and in the same way to men and women; who campaigned for it, and why; and who benefits.[89]

The Court as a political and legal institution

The CJEU has attracted some considerable examination as a legal and as a political institution. Early analysis focused on the Court as a key player shaping the legal developments. It was seen as the key legal institution in the (then) Community structure. The European Court of Justice, as it was, has been subject to analysis from a political science perspective since at least the 1990s.[90] While

84 Auchmuty (n 17) 4.
85 ibid.
86 ibid.
87 ibid 5.
88 ibid.
89 ibid.
90 See eg Geoffrey Garrett, 'International Cooperation and Institutional Choice: The European Community's Internal Market' (1992) 46 *International Organization* 533; Geoffrey Garrett, 'The Politics of Legal Integration in the European Union' (1995) 49 *International Organization* 173; Walter Mattli and Anne-Marie Slaughter, 'Law and Politics in the European Union: A Reply to Garrett' (1995) 49 *International Organization* 183; Walter Mattli and Anne-Marie Slaughter, 'Revisiting the European Court of Justice' (1998) 52 *International Organization* 177; Alec Stone Sweet, 'Path dependence, precedent, and judicial power' in Martin Shapiro and Alec Stone Sweet (eds), *On Law, Politics, and Judicialization* (Oxford University Press 2002); Alec Stone Sweet and James A Caporaso, 'From free trade to supranational polity: The European Court and integration' in Wayne Sandholtz and Alec Stone Sweet (eds), *European Integration and Supranational Governance* (Oxford University Press 1998); Lisa Conant, 'The Politics of Legal Integration' (2007) 45 *Journal of Common Market Studies* 45; Karen J Alter, 'Who Are the "Masters of the Treaty"? European

some scholars have drawn on principal–agent theory to highlight the Court's position as an agent of the Member States, thinking about the Court in these terms means that the Court is seen as doing the bidding of the most powerful States and thus inherently governed by politics rather than the rule of law.[91] This however underestimates the level of independence the Court has exhibited and overestimates the control even the most powerful Member States exert over it.[92] Geoffrey Garrett and Walter Mattli and Anne-Marie Slaughter in their exchange set out the arguments clearly and we do not intend to rehash them here. Karen Alter suggests that the truth lies somewhere between those two positions; with the Court having significant autonomy without being immune to political processes and Member State or EU institutional interests.[93] It nevertheless appears that such debates are not unique to the CJEU since increased political role of courts and the growing activities of justices have been argued to be part of a global 'phenomenon in which courts have become increasingly active in the politics of both well-established and emerging democracies'.[94] In essence, what we are doing is analysing the doctrinal development of the CJEU and provide normative commentary on the appropriate exercise of power by the Court.

Although judicial politics scholarship is not only valuable for situating the decisions of the CJEU in their political environments, but also for its careful analyses of the independence and accountability of the European judiciary *vis-à-vis* European legislature, literature on judicial politics focuses primarily on American federal courts.[95] Hence, it has paid far less attention to other important questions such as the impacts of limited and renewable terms of office of the Court's judges and the significance of open voting and separate opinions, which are an important variable in supranational courts, as well as the complex interactions

---

Governments and the Court of Justice' (1998) 52 *International Organization* 121; Karen Alter, *Establishing the Supremacy of European Law* (Oxford University Press 2001); Ulrich Haltern, *Europarecht und das Politische* (Mohr Siebeck 2005); Ulrich Haltern, *Was bedeutet Souveränität?* (Mohr Siebeck 2007).

91 See Garret (n 90); Geoffrey Garret and Barry Weingast, 'Ideas, interests and institutions: Constructing the EC's internal market' in Judith Goldstein and Robert O Keohane (eds), *Ideas and Foreign Policy: Beliefs, Institutions, and Political Change* (Cornell University Press 1993); Anne-Marie Burley and Walter Mattli, 'Europe Before the Court: A Political Theory of Legal Integration' (1993) 47 *International Organization* 41. See further Jessica Guth, 'Transforming the European Legal Order: The European Court of Justice at 60+' (2016) 12(1) *Journal of Contemporary European Research* 455; Guth, 'Law as the object' (n 83).

92 See eg Joseph HH Weiler, 'A Quiet Revolution: The European Court of Justice and Its Interlocutors' (1994) 26 *Comparative Political Studies* 510; Mattli and Slaughter, 'Law and Politics in the European Union' (n 90); Mattli and Slaughter, 'Revisiting the European Court of Justice' (n 90); Alter, *Establishing the Supremacy of European Law* (n 90).

93 Karen Alter, *The European Court's Political Power* (Oxford University Press 2009).

94 Songer, Ostberg and Wetstein (n 43) 42 and 165.

95 Jeffrey L Dunoff and Mark A Pollack, 'The Judicial Trilemma' (2017) 111(2) *American Journal of International Law* 225, 233 doi:10.1017/ajil.2017.23. The judicial politics literature theorises and empirically studies the relationships between judges and their political environments and interlocutors.

among judicial independence, judicial accountability, and judicial transparency.[96] Although this is a gross oversimplification, judicial politics scholarship typically focus on explaining measurable judicial behaviour by theorising judges as 'utility-maximising rational actors' who seek to realise their goals within the variable constraints imposed by institutions and constitutional structures.[97] There is a growing consensus among judicial politics scholars that judges are 'policy-seekers' who interpret the law in light of their ideology and policy preferences.[98] Scholars disagree, however, on the question whether judges are free to follow their sincere preferences or whether they are constrained by other institutional actors, which in the context of the EU include the Council and the Commission.[99]

As lawyers we look at the extent of legal and political influence of the Court slightly differently compared to political scientists. A political scientist may argue that the mechanisms in which the Court shapes EU legislation in the areas, which are exclusive competence of the Member States and where they are unable to agree on a common position in the Council, is ultimately determined by whether the 'Council takes up judicial considerations in policy-making'.[100] Hence, such a position may imply questions such as whether the court has superseded legislature in making policy; whether it is merely engaging in a running dialogue with the latter; and what role the court should play in policy making.[101] While it may seem obvious that the areas falling within the exclusive competence of the Member States will not be covered by EU legislation unless the Member States agree on a common approach, a lawyer immediately rules out the possibility that the implementation of case law would be uncertain in a case where the Council failed to pay attention to the Court's case law. This is because, due to the supremacy of EU law, the Member States have to take the Court's decision into account – even if the Court's decisions were no codified in any primary or secondary EU law instrument. Hence, the Court's case law has as much influence in the EU as the legislation drawn up by the EU institutions.

There are a number of policy areas where the Court's decisions have seemingly forced Member States to coordinate their laws in areas, such as social policy, energy, common European asylum policy and recognition of professional qualifications. On the other hand, the Member States reluctance to take a consistent approach towards coordination of national asylum policies, alongside the creation of internal energy market,[102] has been remarkably strong. Although we return

96 Dunoff and Pollack (n 95) 233.

97 ibid.

98 ibid.

99 ibid.

100 Fabio Wasserfallen, 'The Judiciary as Legislator? How the European Court of Justice Shapes Policy-making in the European Union' (2010) 17(8) *Journal of European Public Policy* 1128, 1129 and 1135.

101 Songer, Ostberg and Westein (n 43) 166.

102 The creation of a fully integrated single energy market within the EU has posed challenges, primarily due to the reluctance of the EU Member States to implement common

to some of these issues in Chapter 4 in the context of the preliminary reference procedure, it is worth noting that there is some evidence of the Court's use of its political power, especially in relation to EU citizenship (Chapter 7) and fundamental rights (Chapter 6). While commentators may argue that 'legalisation of politics' may benefit primarily social elites because the legal process is inherently favourable to the wealthier echelons of the society and hence is likely to undermine democracy and harm the underprivileged, there are also concerns that the courts 'may become the "pawn" of social activist'.[103] Whereas it may be possible to argue against the further expansion of the concept of EU citizenship case law, from a feminist point of view the Court's increasing role in protecting fundamental rights can be viewed as a manifestation of its independence and courage of supporting rights claims which are unpopular or advanced by disadvantaged groups.[104] It is possible to argue that the comprehensive reading of many decisions[105] involving economically inactive EU citizens adopted after 2009 have been specifically adopted to prevent further expansion of the scope of the EU citizenship law due to increasing discontent among the Member States.[106] While we return to these issues in Chapter 7, it is worth noting that O'Brien has argued that the Court uses political power in its decisions concerning the EU citizenship. In her opinion, the Court was mindful of the impact of its 2016 decision in *Commission v UK*,[107] delivered only a week before the UK's referendum on its EU membership in June 2016:

> It is impossible to know the intersection of legal and political in the minds of judges, but those minds do not operate in a vacuum. If we were to disregard the desire to maintain the Union, then we would be hard-pressed to explain

standards. See eg Sanna Elfving, 'The potential of United Kingdom shale gas regulation to inform the EU level harmonising measures' in Ioanna Mersinia and Sirja-Leena Penttinen (eds), *Energy Transitions: Regulatory and Policy Trends* (Intersentia 2017); Sanna Elfving, 'Prospective Governance and Legal Framework Between the EU and MENA in Renewable Energy Cooperation' (2016) 7(2) *Renewable Energy Law and Policy Review* 157.

103 Songer, Ostberg and Westein (n 43) 42–43.

104 For similar comments in relation to the Supreme Court of Canada, see Songer, Ostberg and Westein (n 43) 166. The Supreme Court of Canada has also been very accommodating towards the rights of the country's indigenous populations. See eg Sanna Elfving, 'The European Union's animal welfare policy and indigenous peoples' rights: The case of Inuit and seal hunting in Arctic Canada and Greenland' (PhD thesis, University of Surrey 2014).

105 See eg Case C-333/13 *Elisabeta Dano and Florin Dano v Jobcenter Leipzig* [2014] EU:C:2014:2358; Case C-67/14 *Jobcenter Berlin Neukölln v Nazifa Alimanovic and Others* [2015] EU:C:2015:597.

106 eg in the UK, the decision in *Dano* was hailed as a victory to curb unwanted EU immigration and the Government saw it as an authorisation to restrict access to non-contributory social benefits such as housing benefits and tax credits for EU citizens who were not workers, jobseekers or former workers. See eg Rebecca Zahn, '"Common Sense" or a Threat to EU Integration? The Court, Economically Inactive EU Citizens and Social Benefits' (2015) 44(4) *Industrial Law Journal* 573 doi:10.1093/indlaw/dwv031.

107 Case C-308/14 *Commission v United Kingdom* [2016] EU:C:2016:436.

> the Court's choices to avoid engaging with key legal provisions, to embroider conditions into others, and to sacrifice the last vestiges of EU citizenship upon the altar of the UK's nativist tendencies.[108]

Despite the differences in approach, the way in which political scientist approach the Court makes intuitive sense to us and has shaped how we have approached our work, and we have tried to step away from traditional judicial doctrines and way of thinking. Instead, we have attempted to see the cases we analyse in their political context rather than simply as examples of legal reasoning, or even feminist legal reasoning. Throughout the chapters dealing with substantive areas of law we have tried to draw attention to potential political influence which may explain or contribute to an explanation of how the case arrived at the Court or how the Court reached its decision. We hope that by doing so we are able to convey both the detail with which legal scholarship often concerns itself as well as the broader context, and extra-legal factors which political science scholarship considers important.

What we actually did

In a desk-based piece of research such as this, it seems a little odd to explain our methods in addition to explaining our overall approach above. However, we felt that it was important to lay out clearly what this project did and did not involve, how we came to write about the things we have written about and how we drew our conclusions. For us this is part of our feminist project.

The first part of this book deals with the CJEU, its composition and its ways of working. Although empirical work with the Court was outside the scope of this project we realise that empirical work would offer unique insights and a detailed exploration of the private life of the Court, as it were. Our analysis is limited to what we might call the public life of the Court. We have drawn on information which is publicly available about the Court, its composition and how it works. In addition, we have engaged with the now quite substantial literature on the Court by both lawyers and political scientists, some of which we have alluded to above. Our analysis therefore paints a picture about what we know about the Court without having spoken to or heard directly from the people who make up the Court itself. This, of course, has implications on our analysis because our information is limited. We make assumptions about who the individuals working in Court are and how they operate. Although those assumptions are based on the information we have obtained and the research we have conducted, they remain assumptions. We also only know how the documents available suggest the Court functions. We do not know how the individuals working within the institution think it works, to what extent the actual working of the Court differs from the processes set out on paper, and we have no sense of how informal structures

108 O'Brien, 'The ECJ Sacrifices EU Citizenship in vain' (n 69) 209.

and dynamics play out. As a feminist piece of work, in particular, this is perhaps a major flaw in our project. We are relying on public (legal) documents rather than on the stories and lived experience of those from within the institution. This is not the usual feminist approach. The lack of empirical work and desk-based approach is certainly something which occupied much of our thinking time earlier on as we wondered whether we could build additional work into the project.

However, not doing the empirical work required to fully understand the ins and outs of the Court and how it works has also offered opportunities. It allowed us to focus solely on what for most people is knowable about the Court. It allowed us to explore the legitimacy and representativeness of the Court based on the documents and information that is publicly available and consider the extent to which the Court can be seen to be gender aware. It allowed us to keep our focus firmly on the institution as a whole rather than on individual judges, Advocates-General or other staff working at the Court. Not doing empirical work shifts the focus onto the public life of the Court and therefore forces a more detailed engagement with the questions of legitimacy and representativeness as set out in Chapter 3. Although empirical work would add a further and extremely valuable dimension to this perspective, we believe that our analysis starts a conversation which can be built on in the future. Understanding the public life of the Court sets a solid foundation for exploring the private life of the same institution.

Our first steps for the second area of work presented in this book were to identify the areas of law we wanted to consider. The choices here were mostly pragmatic drawing on our respective areas of expertise in EU law and, therefore, we chose to start our analysis with equality law, citizenship and human rights. As we point out in our concluding chapter when we set out the future research agenda, we now need to turn our attention to areas of law where gender is not an obvious issue to be considered.

Once we had decided our focus in terms of areas of law, we needed to choose the focus of our case law analysis. In areas routinely taught in EU law courses in universities, the first phase of doing this was relatively simple. We started our analysis by consulting some EU law textbooks written by distinguished EU law scholars such as Paul Craig and Gráinne de Búrca for the landmark case law included on any given topic.[109] We did so because the Court has drawn all the major legal principles from its landmark jurisdiction, which, at least arguably, consist of the most important cases in EU law. However, we have noted above the fact that feminist legal scholarship remains marginal in the mainstream legal scholarship in general as well as the textbooks on the law curriculum. Therefore, it is possible for both undergraduate and postgraduate students undertaking a law degree at a university in the UK to meet no feminist input throughout their entire degree programme.[110] Although women constitute more than half the law students on

109 Paul Craig and Gráinne de Búrca, *EU Law: Texts, Cases and Materials* (6th edn, Oxford University Press 2015).

110 Auchmuty (n 17) 4.

many degree programmes in the UK and elsewhere – and thus, the market for law books – neither academics nor publishers have traditionally questioned the fact that most books contain very little material that would be applied specifically to women.[111] As such, simply taking the case law identified as continuing the main body of Court's jurisdiction in the leading textbooks used on the law curriculum in the UK universities, without asking any further questions, or further exploration of possible additional cases, would have perpetuated the potentially flawed notion that what is included in the textbooks represents an objective selection of important cases and legal principles in EU law – when, in fact, it might simply replicate traditional legal reasoning and method without question. So, while we took those cases as our starting point, we subsequently asked ourselves questions about why they had been selected, what they told us, whether there were other cases which had not been included, what they told us and whether we would have chosen a different set of cases. We searched the database of EU cases[112] as well as well-known legal databases to ensure we covered cases we might not otherwise be familiar with. Through this process we arrived at our initial lists of cases for consideration, but we added to them as we worked through them and as we read additional literature in each of our substantive law areas.

For each of the substantive law areas we first took a fairly traditional approach to legal analysis in the sense that we started our research with an analysis of the Treaty provisions and secondary legislation to make sure we could situate the case law in the legal framework as it prevailed at the time of the decisions in question. This legal analysis often highlighted questions and issues important to a feminist analysis and gendered reading of the law and, where this was the case, we noted them to see to what extent they might be picked up in the case law. Our case law analysis then focused on understanding the reasoning of the Court in as much detail as possible, drawing on the judgement, the opinions of the Advocates-General and any other official documentation relating to the case law at EU level. Where possible we also drew on discussions of cases at national level although language barriers made this problematic in many cases, leaving us simply with the academic literature available. Once clear about the context of the Court's decision we asked a series of questions along the lines of the following:

1. What were the questions referred in this case and why were those particular questions referred?
2. What other questions could have been referred or how could the question have been phrased differently?
3. What facts were deemed relevant and what facts were deemed irrelevant? Would a gendered lens change this?

111 ibid.

112 The EUR-Lex and Curia databases provide free access to judgements and orders of the Court of Justice of the European Union in the 24 official EU languages. See Curia, <https://curia.europa.eu/> accessed 25 January 2018; EUR-Lex, <http://eur-lex.europa.eu/homepage.html?ptab=caselaw> accessed 25 January 2018.

4. If different facts were seen as important or relevant, would the legal arguments have been different? How so?
5. Could the principles have been interpreted differently?
6. What would a gendered reading of the facts, the question(s) referred, the arguments and the decision add to our understanding of the law?
7. Would a gendered reading make a difference?

In our analysis we have then looked at both individual cases as well as series of cases taken together. While the individual analysis tells us something about the Court's approach and gender awareness, looking at a series of cases together highlights hidden biases and assumptions and tells us something about the state of the law overall. Both components are useful because the individual analysis can raise consciousness about particular issues and specific decisions, which can either advance or hinder gender equality. A number of cases together can potentially reveal a pattern, which can highlight progress on the one hand, or systemic failures on the other hand, to recognise gendered issues. We argue that these two components are interdependent because gendered issues cannot be identified and addressed without individual analysis. Similarly, gendered issues are easily dismissed as one offs, trivial and unimportant without understanding the pattern or collective impact of a series of cases. We hope therefore that our analysis of the cases chosen and areas dealt with contextualise the case law and offer insights into individual judgements and bodies of case law overall.

Working in partnership with a co-author is always a stimulating, rewarding and sometimes challenging undertaking. We were keenly aware that our expertise and interests differed slightly and that we had vastly different writing styles. We did not want this book to read like an edited collection and the point of working on this project together was to challenge each other in our assumptions and biases and explore the topics together. Nonetheless, due to pressures of time and the practicalities of writing, we did often take responsibility for developing areas and arguments individually before coming back together to discuss and explore them. This does have implications. When writing in areas of familiarity about case law with which we engage regularly through teaching or our other writing, it can be easy to slip into the orthodox and traditional way of thinking about the issues without sufficiently questioning the assumptions we make. It is worth noting that our own (legal) education was almost completely devoid of feminist legal analysis or method and that our work contexts are not necessarily encouraging or supportive of such an approach making it all the easier to slip back into traditional (but flawed) legal analysis, outdated thinking about power dynamics and seeing law as something more objective than it really is. Questioning assumptions, biases, approaches and the status quo is far easier, we found, in areas of law with which we are a little less familiar, areas of law we do not routinely teach and have not previously spent much time researching. Therefore, our different backgrounds and areas of expertise allowed us to keep asking questions of each other when selecting material for analysis, when discussing our work and key themes and arguments and when reviewing drafts. Our chapters have passed between us countless times for drafting, redrafting and editing with responsibility always lying with both of us irrespective who started the chapter. The result is one of genuine co-working and co-authorship which, we believe, has led to a more rounded and insightful analysis. Being able to challenge each other about why we argue what we argue and think what we think has made us look at familiar case law in a new light and at new case law we might otherwise have (dis)missed.

Before beginning our project though, it was necessary to consider some key definitions, or interpretations to ensure that we were directing our thinking in the same way. We have outlined above that we do not believe that there is one feminism and we agreed to work with different strands and approaches in order to come to a more holistic understanding. As such, we have found Bartlett's notion of 'positionality' helpful because it allows us to articulate and argue why our approach helps us to a better version of law.[113] We have gone no further in defining our feminism in this project precisely because we have not set out to argue from a particular feminist standpoint. We have, maybe in line with the feminist judgement writing projects, simply acknowledged that there are many different perspectives of feminism, which have competing and sometimes contradictory aims, approaches and priorities. What we have taken them to all have in common is that they seek to engage with law in a different way and/or ask different questions of the law and its institutions.

We also outline above the problematics of the term 'gender' with its multiple layers endorsing existing social hierarchies, power relations and modes of domination,[114] and what it might mean to apply a gendered lens. It has been argued that the terms 'gender', 'men', 'women', 'femininity', 'masculinity' and our sexual identities are socially construed analytical categories that constantly shape individual's lives through human interaction.[115] We believe this to be true. In this book, the term 'gender' is used in this context and thus recognises the distinction between the term 'sex', which has a biological base, and the term 'gender' which is 'an ascription of roles to women'.[116]

In this book we therefore use feminist legal methodologies to help us apply a gendered lens to our analysis of the CJEU. We do so to better understand and challenge the perceived prevailing structures of power within the Court in a number of ways: (1) by highlighting weaknesses in composition of the Court and its potential implications, (2) by exploring how the ways of working of the Court often renders it 'gender blind' at best, (3) by exposing bias against women (and other minorities) in traditional legal methods, (4) by showing how rebuilding the Court's decision making to take into account women's points of view, or voice, can lead to fairer judicial decisions, and (5) to argue for the employment of feminist legal methods as a means to identifying inherent gender bias in the Court's decision making.

113 Bartlett (n 11).
114 Bieling and Diez (n 60) 280.
115 Abels and MacRae (n 3) 11.
116 See Dagmar Schiek, 'Intersectionality and the Notion of Disability in EU Discrimination Law' (2016) 53(1) *Common Market Law Review* 35, 45.

Conclusion

Writing an interdisciplinary book brings with it the danger that we talk past all of the disciplines we are trying to engage. By spending time setting out our approach we hope we have minimised that risk. We hope that we have managed to apply a gendered lens to the anecdotal, the detail, the legal and the extra-legal. We hope we have provided a legal analysis which takes account of at least some of the thinking drawn from political science and that we have in the process asked some searching and important questions. We have not always been able to give answers but where we have we hope that our readers will question them as we have questioned those of others and move the discussion on. Where we have not been able to answer our own questions, we hope that our readers will think about them and that collectively we will keep working towards a more holistic understanding of the CJEU and its work.

Bibliography

Abels G and MacRae H (eds), *Gendering European Integration Theory: Engaging New Dialogues* (Barbara Budrich 2016)

Abrams K, 'Feminist Lawyering and Legal Method' (1991) 16 *Law and Social Inquiry* 373

Adler M, *Recognising the Problem: Socio-Legal Research Training in the UK* (University of Edinburgh 2007)

Alkan YS, 'Feminist Legal Methods: Theoretical Assumptions, Advantages, and Potential Problems' (2012) 9(2) *Ankara Law Review* 157

Alter K, *Establishing the Supremacy of European Law* (Oxford University Press 2001)

———, *The European Court's Political Power* (Oxford University Press 2009)

———, 'Who Are the "Masters of the Treaty"? European Governments and the Court of Justice' (1998) 52 *International Organization* 121

Alter KJ, Dehousse R and Vanberg G, 'Law, Political Science and EU Legal Studies: An Interdisciplinary Project' (2002) 3(1) *European Union Politics* 113-114

Auchmuty R, 'Feminist Approaches to Sexuality and Law Scholarship' (2015) 15(1) *Legal Information Management* 4

Auchmuty R and van Marle K (eds), 'Special Issue: Carol Smart's Feminism and the Power of Law' (2012) 20(2) *Feminist Legal Studies*

Bartlett K, 'Feminist Legal Methods' (1989) 103 *Harvard Law Review* 829

———, 'Feminist Legal Scholarship: A History Through the Lens of the California Law Review' (2012) 100 *California Law Review* 381

Bieling HJ and Diez T, 'Linking Gender Perspectives to Integration Theory: The Need for Dialogue' in Abels G and MacRae H (eds), *Gendering European Integration Theory: Engaging New Dialogues* (Barbara Budrich 2016)

Burley A-M and Mattli W, 'Europe Before the Court: A Political Theory of Legal Integration' (1993) 47 *International Organization* 41

Cloughtery L, 'Feminist Legal Methods and the First Amendment Defense to Sexual Harassment' (1996) 75 *Nebraska Law Review* 1

Conant L, 'The Politics of Legal Integration' (2007) 45 *Journal of Common Market Studies* 45

Cownie F, Bradney A and Burton M, *English Legal System in Context* (4th edn, Oxford University Press 2007)

Curia, <https://curia.europa.eu/> accessed 25 January 2018

Denzin NK and Lincoln YS, 'Introduction: The Discipline and Practice of Qualitative Research' in Denzin NK and Lincoln YS (eds), *Handbook of Qualitative Research* (3rd edn, Sage 2005)

Dhamoon RK, 'Feminisms' in Waylen G, Celis K, Kantola J and Weldon SL (eds), *Oxford Handbook on Gender and Politics* (Oxford University Press 2013)

Dunoff JL and Pollack MA, 'The Judicial Trilemma' (2017) 111(2) *American Journal of International Law* 225 doi:10.1017/ajil.2017.23

Elfving S, 'Prospective Governance and Legal Framework Between the EU and MENA in Renewable Energy Cooperation' (2016) 7(2) *Renewable Energy Law and Policy Review* 157

———, 'The European Union's Animal Welfare Policy and Indigenous Peoples' Rights: The Case of Inuit and Seal Hunting in Arctic Canada and Greenland' (PhD thesis, University of Surrey 2014)

———, 'The Potential of United Kingdom Shale Gas Regulation to Inform the EU Level Harmonising Measures' in Mersinia I and Penttinen S-L (eds), *Energy Transitions: Regulatory and Policy Trends* (Intersentia 2017)

Emejulu A and Bassel L, 'Whose Crisis Counts? Minority Women, Austerity and Activism in France and Britain' in Kantola J and Lombardo E (eds), *Gender and the Economic Crisis in Europe: Politics, Institutions and Intersectionality* (Palgrave MacMillan 2017)

EUR-Lex, <http://eur-lex.europa.eu/homepage.html?ptab=caselaw> accessed 25 January 2018

Fagan C and Rubery J, 'Advancing Gender Equality Through European Employment Policy: The Impact of the UK's EU Membership and the Risks of Brexit' (2017) *Social Policy and Society* doi:10.1017/S1474746417000458

Fineman M, 'Feminist Theory and Law' (1995) 18 *Harvard Journal of Law and Public Policy* 349

Garret G and Weingast B, 'Ideas, Interests and Institutions: Constructing the EC's Internal Market' in Goldstein, J and Keohane RO (eds), *Ideas and Foreign Policy: Beliefs, Institutions, and Political Change* (Cornell University Press 1993)

———, 'International Cooperation and Institutional Choice: The European Community's Internal Market' (1992) 46 *International Organization* 533

———, 'The Politics of Legal Integration in the European Union' (1995) 49 *International Organization* 173

Guerrina R, 'Gendering European Economic Narratives: Assessing the Costs of the Crisis to Gender Equality' in Kantola J and Lombardo E (eds), *Gender and the Economic Crisis in Europe: Politics, Institutions and Intersectionality* (Palgrave MacMillan 2017)

Guerrina R and Masselot A, 'Walking into the Footprint of EU Law: Unpacking the Gendered Consequences of Brexit' (2018) *Social Policy and Society* 1 doi:10.1017/S1474746417000501

Guth J, 'Law as the Object and Agent of Integration: Gendering the Court of Justice of the European Union, Its Decisions and Their Impact' in Abels G and MacRae H (eds), *Gendering European Integration Theory: Engaging New Dialogues* (Barbara Budrich 2016)

———, 'Transforming the European Legal Order: The European Court of Justice at 60+' (2016) 12(1) *Journal of Contemporary European Research* 455

Haastrup T and Kenny M, 'Gendering Institutionalism: Feminist Institutionalist Approach to EU Integration Theory' in Abels G and MacRae H (eds), *Gendering European Integration Theory: Engaging New Dialogues* (Barbara Budrich 2016)
Haltern U, *Europarecht und das Politische* (Mohr Siebeck 2005)
Hampshire J and Bale T, 'New Administration, New Immigration Regime: Do Parties Matter After All? A UK Case Study' (2015) 38(1) *West European Politics* 145 doi: 10.1080/01402382.2014.925735
Hunter R, 'The Power of Feminist Judgments?' (2012) 20(2) *Feminist Legal Studies* doi:10.1007/s10691-012-9202-0
Hutchinson T and Duncan N, 'Defining and Describing What We Do: Doctrinal Legal Research' (2012) 17 *Deakin Law Review* 83
Levit N and Verchick R, *Feminist Legal Theory: A Primer* (New York University Press 2006)
Liebert U, 'Gendering Europeanisation: Making Equality Work in Theory and Practice' in Abels G and MacRae H (eds), *Gendering European Integration Theory: Engaging New Dialogues* (Barbara Budrich 2016)
McBride J, Smith A and Mbala M, 'You end up with Nothing': The Experience of Being a Statistic of "in-work Poverty" in the UK' (2017) *Work, Employment and Society* 1 doi:10.1177/0950017017728614
Mackinnon C, 'Feminism, Marxism, Method and the State: An Agenda for Theory' (1982) 7(3) *SIGNS: Journal of Women in Culture and Society* 515
MacRae H, 'Neo-Functionalism: Spilling over to Gender Studies' in Abels G and MacRae H (eds), *Gendering European Integration Theory: Engaging New Dialogues* (Barbara Budrich 2016)
Mattli W and Slaughter A-M, 'Law and Politics in the European Union: A Reply to Garrett' (1995) 49 *International Organization* 183
———, 'Revisiting the European Court of Justice' (1998) 52 *International Organization* 177
O'Brien C, 'Civis Capitalist Sum: Class as the New Guiding Principle of EU Free Movement Rights' (2016) 53(4) *Common Market Law Review* 937
———, 'The ECJ Sacrifices EU Citizenship in-vain: Commission v. United Kingdom' (2017) 54 *Common Market Law Review* 209
———, 'The Pillory, the Precipice and the Slippery Slope: The Profound Effects of the UK's Legal Reform Programme Targeting EU Migrants' (2015) 37(1) *Journal of Social Welfare and Family Law* 111 doi:10.1080/09649069.2015.1005997
Office for National Statistics, 'People in Employment on a Zero-Hours Contract: Mar 2017' 2 <www.ons.gov.uk/employmentandlabourmarket/peopleinwork/earningsandworkinghours/articles/contractsthatdonotguaranteeaminimumnumberofhours/mar2017> accessed 26 November 2017
Rhode D, 'Feminist Critical Theories' (1990) 42 *Stanford Law Review* 617
Rorty A, *Mind in Action: Essays on the Philosophy of Mind* (Beacon Press 1988)
Schiek D, 'Intersectionality and the Notion of Disability in EU Discrimination Law' (2016) 53(1) *Common Market Law Review* 35
———, 'Towards More Resilience for a Social EU: The Constitutionally Conditioned Internal Market' (2017) 13(4) *European Constitutional Law Review* 611 doi:10.1017/S1574019617000311
Shaw J, 'Socio-Legal Studies and the European Union' in Thomas PA (ed), *Socio-Legal Studies* (Ashgate Dartmouth 1997)

Songer DR, Ostberg CL and Wetstein M (eds), *Law, Ideology, and Collegiality: Judicial Behaviour in the Supreme Court of Canada* (McGill-Queen's University Press 2012)

Stone Sweet A, 'Path Dependence, Precedent, and Judicial Power' in Shapiro M and Stone Sweet A (eds), *On Law, Politics, and Judicialization* (Oxford University Press 2002)

Stone Sweet A and Caporaso JA, 'From Free Trade to Supranational Polity: The European Court and Integration' in Sandholtz W and Stone Sweet A (eds), *European Integration and Supranational Governance* (Oxford University Press 1998)

Treaty of Lisbon Amending the Treaty on European Union and the Treaty Establishing the European Community [2007] OJ C306/1

van Sliedregt E, 'International Criminal Law: Over-studied and Underachieving?' (2016) 29 *Leiden Journal of International Law* 1

Wasserfallen F, 'The Judiciary as Legislator? How the European Court of Justice Shapes Policy-making in the European Union' (2010) 17(8) *Journal of European Public Policy* 1128

Weiler JHH, 'A Quiet Revolution: The European Court of Justice and Its Interlocutors' (1994) 26 *Comparative Political Studies* 510

Zahn R, ' "Common Sense" or a Threat to EU Integration? The Court, Economically Inactive EU Citizens and Social Benefits' (2015) 44(4) *Industrial Law Journal* 573 doi:10.1093/indlaw/dwv031

3 Who the judges are matters

The composition of the court

> This is the idea that the judge has no will, makes no value choices, but is just a calculating machine.[1]

This chapter sets out the composition of the Court of Justice of the European Union (CJEU) and considers the extent to which this composition has gender implications. It engages in arguments relating to the representativeness and legitimacy of the Court as an institution and considers the importance of how we perceive and think about the judges of the Court, including the way they are presented to the public through the Court's website. The chapter then focuses on the benefits of a more diverse judiciary and seeks to argue that the gender balance within a court can make a significant difference to judicial decision making. It draws on literature concerning judicial diversity from across the globe and considers the way judges are appointed to the courts forming part of the CJEU, namely the Court of Justice and the General Court,[2] and what that means for a gendered consideration of these issues.

Part of our task in this chapter is to outline what an ideal judiciary is, or rather should be, and what it should look like. Once we have established that, we can begin to think about whether or not the Court lives up to those ideals and, if not, why this may be. We can then also assess the implications of any shortcomings in terms of gendered implications. A useful starting point for our analysis is provided by a 2017 speech by the current President of the Supreme Court of the United Kingdom (UK), Lady Brenda Hale. In her speech Lady Hale outlined her thoughts on what should be the characteristics of a judiciary in a democratic State. She suggested that the characteristics of a judiciary that 'we want to achieve by our selection processes . . . would be independent; it would be incorruptible; it would be of high quality; and it would be diverse'.[3] Although our focus throughout

1 Richard A Posner, 'Judicial Self-Restraint' (1983) 59 *Indiana Law Journal* 1, 3.

2 Consolidated version of the Treaty on European Union [2012] OJ C326/13 (TEU), art 19(1): 'The Court of Justice of the European Union shall include the Court of Justice, the General Court and specialised courts.'

3 Lady Hale, 'Judges, Power and Accountability: Constitutional Implications of Judicial Selection' (Constitutional Law Summer School, Belfast, 11 August 2017) <www.supremecourt.uk/docs/speech-170811.pdf> accessed 17 November 2017.

this chapter will be chiefly on Lady Hale's final point, namely the diversity within the judiciary, it is worth also considering the other points in relation to the CJEU briefly. Although we do not think that it is controversial to assume that any judiciary should be independent,[4] incorruptible and of high quality, it is worth exploring what exactly does this mean in the context of the CJEU.

Sophie Turenne has questioned the independence of the Court, citing as reasons for this, *inter alia*, the short tenure of judges,[5] the reliance on their Member State for reappointment and, in some cases, careers post their work at the Court.[6] Although there is high variability among the actual length of service within the CJEU, on average judges and Advocates-Generals (AGs) of the Court of Justice and the judges of the General Court serve from seven to nine years.[7] Additionally, many of the judges appointed to the Court may only serve one term if their tenure is not renewed after six years.[8] The fairly short tenures of the judges arguably hamper the Court's work and productivity because the new judges require a couple of years to familiarise themselves with the Court's high degree of procedural formalism, originating from the French legal tradition which is aimed at minimising the discretion of judges.[9] Additionally, every three years, half of the judges at the Court are subject to renewal as part of the Court's standard triennial renewal procedure under Article 253 of the Treaty on the Functioning of the European Union (TFEU).[10] The arguments concerning the short duration of the tenures could well be supported by findings of so-called 'attitudinalist' judicial political scholars who have argued that the 'US federal judges, who are granted lifetime tenure, are free to vote and rule in line with their individual ideological or policy views, and that these attitudes are in fact the best predictors of judicial votes'.[11] However, seven to nine years served by European judges is not substantially different from other international courts since judges at virtually every international court serve for

4 According to Dunoff and Pollack, judicial independence is 'central to virtually all plausible theories of well-functioning courts' and in the context of supranational courts it can be understood to mean 'the freedom of judges to decide disputes upon the facts and the law, free of outside influences such as the preferences of powerful states'. See Jeffrey L Dunoff and Mark A Pollack, 'The Judicial Trilemma' (2017) 111(2) *American Journal of International Law* 225-226 and 233 doi:10.1017/ajil.2017.23.

5 Treaty on the Functioning of the European Union [2012] OJ C 326/47, art 253 stipulates the term for a judge is to be six years renewable and that 'Every three years there shall be a partial replacement of the Judges and Advocates-General, in accordance with the conditions laid down in the Statute of the Court of Justice of the European Union.'

6 Sophie Turenne, 'Institutional Constraints and Collegiality at the Court of Justice of the European Union: A Sense of Belonging?' (2017) 24(4) *Maastricht Journal of European and Comparative Law* 565.

7 Angela Huyue Zhang, 'The Faceless Court' (2016) 38 *University of Pennsylvania Journal of International Law* 71, 92.

8 ibid.

9 ibid 103.

10 See n 5. See also Zhang (n 7) 92.

11 Dunoff and Pollack (n 4) 233.

nine-year terms, some without the possibility of renewal.[12] There are nevertheless opinions that extending a six-year renewable terms to longer, non-renewable terms of nine or even 12 years would reduce the accountability of the judges of international courts to their home States.[13]

While Turenne notes that the lack of individual judgements, or dissents, offer some protection to the sitting judges in that the individual justices and their views on the issues under scrutiny cannot be identified in the judgements, she argues that:

> there is a lack of a transparent process and criteria for renewal [of judicial appointments] at the CJEU in many Member States; non-renewal may also take place for reasons which have little to do with the judge's professional merit, and more to do with some internal 'political haggling' . . . . [14]

While judges' compensation packages are generous, their pensions are guaranteed and their dismissal is all but impossible other than in cases of very serious misconduct[15] – which has never happened in the history of the Court – the judges' dependence on Member States for their initial appointment and subsequent reappointment coupled with the lack of judicial transparency[16] arguably puts the independence of the judiciary at risk and may also indicate that the judiciary is not therefore incorruptible. According to Erik Voeten, there is evidence that, like any other profession, the judiciary are 'at least partially motivated by material or career incentives'.[17] Angela Zhang has similarly argued that the high judicial salaries and lack of procedural safeguards for the judicial appointments in the CJEU may in fact attract political appointees who are more interested in the pay package of the job than carrying out justice.[18] Even if the judicial appointments were not driven by any particular policy agenda or goals, 'personal connections to the appointing executive and party credentials' may be considered vital in

12 ibid 234. For instance, judges of the International Court of Justice serve for nine-year terms, and may be reappointed, while judges of the European Court of Human Rights and the International Criminal Court judges also serve for nine-year terms, but are not eligible for reappointment.
13 ibid 247.
14 Turenne (n 6) 574.
15 A judge may be removed during their term of office 'only if, in the unanimous opinion of the Judges and Advocates-General of the Court of Justice, he no longer fulfills the requisite conditions or meets the obligations arising from his office'. Protocol No 3, On the Statute of the Court of Justice of the European Union [2010] OJ C83/210, art 6.
16 Judicial transparency can be understood as 'mechanisms that permit the identification of individual judicial positions, primarily through the publication of separate votes or opinions'. Dunoff and Pollack (n 4) 226.
17 Erik Voeten, 'The Politics of International Judicial Appointments' (2008) 9(2) *Chicago Journal of International Law* 387-388.
18 Zhang (n 7) 71.

some Member States.[19] In some cases, the nominating Member State has used judicial appointment as a form of patronage to reward loyal representatives or as an opportunity to remove an undesirable political opponent.[20] Indeed, Sally Kenney argued in 2002 that:

> Appointments to the Court sometimes display many of the same features of diplomatic appointments: exile for a party luminary who is in trouble, a retirement prize for exemplary public service, the removal of a competitor within a party, a consolation prize for a failed judicial appointment at home.[21]

This argument has been echoed by former judges of the Court of Justice. Sir Konrad Schiemann made a similar point in 2012, outlining concerns which particularly smaller Member States might have about appointing judges on merit only, without regard for nationality:

> [V]arious governments . . . use European Union posts to reward those whom they wish to reward or to park those whom they prefer to see away from home. In some Member States the allocation of such posts is traditionally a matter of considerable political haggling – your party can nominate a judge in Luxembourg if my party can appoint its nominee to the presidency of our top Administrative Court.[22]

However, it can also be argued that, in this regard, the Court is not so different from other international tribunals in that, theoretically, governments can been seen to use the appointment process to exert influence over the decisions of international judges.[23] We will return to these questions of independence, accountability and integrity when discussing the representativeness and legitimacy of the Court below.

Lady Hale's point about a judiciary being 'high quality' is one about merit. The concept of merit has received a great deal of attention in relation to appointments to senior positions across business, politics and law, and the concept itself has proven to be a notoriously difficult one to pin down and define. We grapple with the notion of merit below. For now, though, it is worth noting that even without interrogating the concept itself, it is clear that 28 Member States are likely to have different ideas about what makes a good judge and that, even if

19 Sally J Kenney, 'Breaking the Silence: Gender Mainstreaming and the Composition of the European Court of Justice' (2002) 10 *Feminist Legal Studies* 257, 260; Zhang (n 7) 82.

20 Zhang (n 7) 82.

21 Kenney (n 19) 260.

22 European Union Committee, Follow-up Inquiry into the Workload of the Court of Justice of the European Union: Oral and written evidence (HL 2012–13) 65 <www.parliament.uk/documents/lords-committees/eu-sub-com-e/FollowupworkloadCJEU/CJEU-Follow-upWrittenOralevidence290413.pdf> accessed 13 December 2017.

23 Zhang (n 7) 82.

they could agree on what makes a good domestic judge, they are unlikely to do so in relation to a judge of the CJEU. Turenne notes that: 'Processes and criteria [used by Member States] will reflect the boundaries between law and politics specific to each country, with distinct roles allocated to parliament, judges or the legal doctrine in driving legal developments.'[24] The appointment of the Court's judges is therefore to be understood in the context of each Member State as well as the European Union (EU) as a whole. Hence, the questions of legitimacy, representativeness and effectiveness must be understood in that context. This chapter proceeds to outline the composition of the Court and who the judges and AGs are. Following this presentation of the Court, the chapter explores the notions of diversity, legitimacy and representativeness in more detail and asks why and how a diverse judiciary might be better and what exactly this means for the Court. Finally, the chapter concludes with an assessment of the implications of the Court's composition and asks whether the ways of working of the Court can mitigate against or, in fact, add to the gender-blindness of the Court. We focus on this theme again in Chapter 4 where we consider how the Court occupies itself with its normal activities.

The composition of the Court

The CJEU as an institution employs approximately 2,000 permanent and temporary staff out of whom approximately 60% are female.[25] However, when we take a look at the composition of the judiciary, the picture looks rather different. The Court, which, until 2016, was made up of three distinct courts with separate jurisdictions, namely the Court of Justice, the General Court, and the Civil Service Tribunal, had a total of 229 Members. The Court of Justice is currently made up of 28 judges, one from each Member State, five of whom are women.[26] Out of the 11 AGs of the Court, two are women. Under Article 252 TFEU the Council may unanimously increase the number of AGs upon the request of the Court of Justice. Whereas six of the Court's AGs are appointed from the largest Member States, namely Germany, France, Spain, Poland, the UK and Italy,

24 Turenne (n 6) 574 and 570. See also Sophie Turenne, *Fair Reflection of Society in Judicial Systems: A Comparative Study* (Springer 2015) 1.

25 Court of Justice of the European Union, *Annual Report 2016: Management Report* (European Union 2017) <https://curia.europa.eu/jcms/upload/docs/application/pdf/2017-06/rapport_gestion_2016_en_.pdf> accessed 14 December 2017.

26 On 28 February 2018, the Member States appointed new female judge, Ms Lucia Serena Rossi (Italy), and reappointed one of the five current female judges, Ms Alexandra (Sacha) Prechal (Netherlands) to the Court of Justice of the European Union. Both judges will start their six-year term of office on 7 October 2018. However, since the term of office of another 14 judges and five AGs expires on 6 October 2018, five judges more and two AGs still have to be either reappointed or appointed in 2018. Council, 'Court of Justice of the European Union: Appointment of Nine Judges' (28 February 2018) <www.consilium.europa.eu/en/press/press-releases/2018/02/28/court-of-justice-of-the-european-union-appointment-of-nine-judges/> accessed 7 March 2018.

the final five positions rotate among the remaining Member States.[27] Although there may not be an obvious direct linkage, Rachel Cichowski has argued that 'Germany, the Netherlands, and the UK possess a comparatively high degree of legal expertise in the area of gender equality law' and, hence, these legal systems may afford greater legal protection from sex discrimination.[28] As a consequence, the Court always has a German or British (for now) Advocate General, who should in principle have experience of gender equality law. Although Cichowski could not have foreseen this in 1995, the current two female AGs of the Court are, indeed, from Germany and the UK. Cichowski has also observed that, compared to other Member States more German and Dutch advocates bring cases before national courts to 'systematically test the scope of both EU law and their own national laws by providing real situations for previously vague EU equality laws'.[29] This may influence the stance taken by AGs from those countries, but, of course, does not guarantee it. It is also worth noting that gender-aware decisions are relatively easy to make in cases directly concerning gender but demonstrating gender awareness in seemingly unrelated decisions is much more difficult and may not automatically follow experience with equality law.

In the General Court, ten out of the 46 judges in post at the time of writing are women, and in the former Civil Service Tribunal, which ceased operations in September 2016, two out of the seven and one of the three temporary judges were female. Women are therefore noticeably in the minority among the members of the judiciary at the EU level. Looking at the composition of the Court historically the picture looks even bleaker since there were very few women listed amongst the previous members of the European Court of Justice and the Court of First Instance.[30] The homogeneity of the judiciary extends further and is starkly visible when examining the portraits of the judges available on the Court's website. The complete absence of ethnic and racial diversity is striking among the members of the Court, as is the absence of visible disability. There are so few women among the portraits that they are easy to miss when scrolling through the pictures. In fact, one could be almost forgiven for concluding that European judges constitute 'a uniform bloc of white men'.[31] All members of the Court present a unified ethic group and the average age of the EU judiciary is above 60, whilst a significant number of justices are over the age of 70. In terms of their qualifications, the backgrounds of the judges look fairly varied on paper, but this is to be expected as they come from different jurisdictions with different legal systems. On closer

27 Zhang (n 7) 76–77.

28 Rachel A Cichowski, 'Women's Rights, the European Court, and Supranational Constitutionalism' (1995) 38 *Law and Society Review* 489, 497–498 doi:10.1111/j.0023-9216.2004.00055.

29 ibid 498.

30 Court of Justice of the European Union, 'The Court in Figures' <https://curia.europa.eu/jcms/jcms/P_80908/en/> accessed 12 October 2017. The Court of First Instance is now the General Court.

31 Maya Sen, 'Diversity, Qualifications, and Ideology: How Female And Minority Judges Have Changed, or Not Changed, over Time' (2017) 2 *Wisconsin Law Review* 367, 369.

examination their education, training and experience is quite homogenous. All members of the Court are highly educated and trained to the highest levels in their home countries and internationally. All judges hold at least an undergraduate law qualification but, because there is a variation in the names of academic qualifications, it is difficult to see whether some of the qualifications are similar in content and structure. Several of the Court's members hold doctoral qualifications. Many of the judges of the Court have held or currently hold academic positions at European universities, have published in international legal journals, and sit on the editorial board of such journals.[32] Some have previously worked as a judge in their national courts, at the Civil Service Tribunal or the General Court, or as an AG before becoming a judge at the Court of Justice, whereas others may have held positions at national ministries or even the European Parliament.

The membership of the Court seems to consistently follow very similar pattern from year to year. In the course of the history of the Court approximately a third of the Court members have been civil servants (27%), academics (19%), or national court judges (28%) immediately before joining the Court.[33] A small minority of the justices were engaged in private practice, with most such judges originating from the common law jurisdictions of the UK and Ireland.[34]

In conclusion, we can see that the judges and AGs of the Court are most likely to be white, able-bodied males over the age of 60. We can also learn that all the judges are, unsurprisingly, highly educated, relatively privileged individuals who have received the benefit of extensive legal education and training. This may make them more similar to, rather than different from, one another, even if that education and training has taken place in different jurisdictions at different times. The official portraits, which accompany the brief biography listed on the website, render the members of the Court almost genderless. The individual biographies are concerned only with the qualifications and narrowly defined legal or political work experience of the judges and AGs, providing qualifications and universities where these were obtained as well as dates for significant judicial work. This then is what is presented as important and all other information we might like to know is judged irrelevant or insignificant. Other than education and previous positions, the members' background and experience and who they are is deemed irrelevant. Yet, as we argue below, who the judges are matters and, if it does indeed matter, then we should be able to know.

Composition of the chambers

Given the low number of female members of the judiciary in the Court, it is inevitable that some chambers remain 'all-male chambers'.[35] There is no single

32 eg Rosario Silva de Lapuerta is a co-director of the journal Noticias de la Unión Europea.
33 Zhang (n 7) 87.
34 ibid.
35 This is similar to the concept of 'all-male panel' used to critique the lack of gender diversity in situations where 'the best experts' on the topic invited to speak publicly in events such as seminars, lecture series and the media consist exclusively of men. See eg Saara Särmä, 'Congrats, You Have an All-Male Panel!' (2016) 18(3) *International Feminist Journal of*

chamber that would consist of members who are all women. In fact, because of the limited number of female judges at the Court, the maximum number of women in any of the five-member chambers is two. Significantly, this means that women never form the majority in any of the Court's chambers. Even if an AG appointed to provide their opinion in a given case was female, at least half of the members of the chamber considering the case are men. In effect, the composition of the Court means that as a rule all chambers are dominated by men. Therefore, it is difficult to see what role women's voices can play in these circumstances. This elicits questions such as: how can the voices of female judges be heard; how can these voices be acknowledged and taken into account; what happens to the dynamics in the Court; how credible are the conclusions reached by the chambers, particularly where they concern issues which have an explicitly gendered dimension; and how does the male dominance in the Court shape the arguments brought to the Court and the deliberations within it? Although only empirical work can answer many of these questions, we can draw on work done with other courts as well as theoretical arguments to make some suggestions and we do so throughout the rest of this chapter.

How are the judges appointed to the court?

Without questioning Lady Hale's suggestions outlined above, we have accepted high quality of a judiciary as one of its desirable characteristics. It therefore follows logically that judges should be appointed on merit. However, as Lady Hale noted '[t]he difficulty, as always, lies in defining and assessing merit'.[36] The definition of the term 'merit' has played a key role in the discussion about gender equality across the board. Essentially, appointments made 'on merit' often risk merely perpetuating gendered divisions in the labour market and the hierarchies within it. In her speech Lady Hale isolated the problem: '[i]t is always so much easier to recognise merit in people who are like the people who have always done the job, especially if they are people like oneself'.[37] Hence, definitions of merit are often simply based on the characteristics of the people currently doing the job and little thought is given to whether or not the definitions of merit may in themselves be based on stereotypes and gendered assumptions.[38] Lady Hale further noted that there was 'a niggling nervousness in some quarters that diversity and merit are indeed competing rather than complementary values. We must prove

---

Politics 470 doi:10.1080/14616742.2016.1189671; Maryanne Dever and Lisa Adkins, 'All Male Panel: Interview with Saara Särmä' (2015) 30(85) *Australian Feminist Studies* 283.

36 Lady Hale (n 3).

37 ibid.

38 See eg Lord Sumption, 'Home Truths About Judicial Diversity' (Bar Council Law Reform Lecture, London, 15 November 2012) 11 <www.supremecourt.uk/docs/speech-121115-lord-sumption.pdf> accessed 12 December 2017.

them wrong.'[39] Her suggestion is that we 'abandon our traditional assumptions about who gets which sort of judicial job and look for the best wherever it may be found'.[40] Therefore, it appears that despite having accepted that judges should be appointed on merit, the concept 'merit' is ridden with bias. It follows that, unless the Court is required to seriously rethink what merit means and what we mean by 'the best', the number of female judges is likely to remain pitifully low.

Of course, abandoning entirely the way in which appointments have been made may be problematic in an EU context. Looking for 'the best wherever it may be found' would run counter to the principle of having one judge in the Court of Justice per Member State as the best candidates for judicial office at European level are not likely to neatly split into one person per Member State. The political wrangling associated with the expansion of the General Court is testament to the difficulties in this area. Member States were, for several years, unable to agree to an expansion because they could not agree on how to set up a system of rotation of judges. Expansion was only finally achieved when the proposal to do so was accepted on the basis of appointing two judges per Member State by 2019.[41] The notion of merit is therefore already skewed in the international context where rules exist to ensure national representation or, indeed, any sort of quotas.

The requirements for judicial appointments to the Court are set out in the Treaties. Article 19(2) of the Treaty on European Union (TEU) stipulates that '[t]he Court of Justice shall consist of one judge per Member State' and is assisted by AGs. Article 19 TEU further stipulates that the General Court shall consist of at least one judge per Member State and that:

> The Judges and the Advocates-General of the Court of Justice and the Judges of the General Court shall be chosen from persons whose independence is beyond doubt and who satisfy the conditions set out in Articles 253 and 254 of the Treaty on the Functioning of the European Union.

Under Article 253 TFEU those conditions are that the justices and AGs of the Court must:

> possess the qualifications required for appointment to the highest judicial offices in their respective countries or who are jurisconsults of recognised competence; they shall be appointed by common accord of the governments of the Member States for a term of six years, after consultation of the panel provided for in Article 255.

The conditions for the General Court are almost identical, but here the requirement is only to 'possess the ability required for appointment to high judicial

39 Lady Hale (n 3).
40 ibid.
41 See eg Turenne (n 6).

office'.[42] There has, perhaps surprisingly, been very little research into the appointment of judges to the Court.[43] Much of what is available criticises the process of appointment for its lack of accountability and transparency in the context of varied and often arbitrary procedures found in the Member States prior to the coming into force of the Treaty of Lisbon[44] on 1 December 2009.[45]

The Treaty amendment introduced an expert panel which has as its task to provide an opinion on the suitability of the candidates nominated by Member States' governments to perform the duties of Judge and AGs of the Court of Justice and the General Court prior to those appointments are made under Articles 253 and 254.[46] The panel's membership is set out in Article 255:

> The panel shall comprise seven persons chosen from among former members of the Court of Justice and the General Court, members of national supreme courts and lawyers of recognised competence, one of whom shall be proposed by the European Parliament. The Council shall adopt a decision establishing the panel's operating rules and a decision appointing its members. It shall act on the initiative of the President of the Court of Justice.

However, it is disheartening to note that although the panel was established to scrutinise the credentials of Member State nominees as well as current members of the Court, who were up for reappointment, it merely gives its opinion. It does not select the candidates itself, and, in theory, its opinion could be wholly ignored by the Member State. The process simply allows the panel to give an opinion on the candidates put forward by the national government after which the Member States either appoint that candidate or they do not. One might therefore argue that the panel lacks any meaningful power in practice or that its value is purely symbolic. However, the evidence from its operations suggests otherwise. The panel's opinion, regardless whether favourable or not, has always been followed by the Member States.[47] Additionally, as Tomáš Dumbrovský and his col-

42 TFEU, art 254.

43 Some notable exceptions include Antonin Cohen, 'Ten Majestic Figures in Long Amaranth Robes: The Formation of the Court of Justice of the European Communities' (2010) 60(2) *Revue française de science politique* 227; Derk Siebert, *Die Auswahl der Richter am Gerichtshof der Europäischen Gemeinschaften: zu der erforderlichen Reform des Art 167 EGV* (Peter Lang 1997); Sally J Kenney, 'The Members of the Court of Justice of the European Communities' (1998) 5 *Columbia Journal of European Law* 101; Tomáš Dumbrovský, Bilyana Petkova, and Marijn van der Sluis, 'Judicial Appointments: The Article 255 TFEU Advisory Panel and Selection Procedures in the Member States' (2014) 51(2) *Common Market Law Review* 455.

44 Treaty of Lisbon amending the Treaty on European Union and the Treaty Establishing the European Community [2007] OJ C306/1.

45 Iyiola Solanke, 'Diversity and Independence in the European Court of Justice' (2009) 15 *Columbia Journal of European Law* 91.

46 TFEU, art 255.

47 Council, 'Fourth Activity Report of the Panel Provided for by Article 255 of the Treaty on the Functioning of the European Union' (28 March 2017) <https://curia.europa.eu/jcms/upload/docs/application/pdf/2017-03/rapport_activite__c255_-_en.pdf> accessed 4 December 2017.

leagues argue, the panel and its way of working have had a significant impact on the way Member States select their preferred candidate.[48] The existence of the panel has encouraged a more transparent process in a number of Member States, particularly as the panel can, and does, request information about how the preferred candidate has been selected.[49]

The 2017 report on the activities of the panel reveals that the assessment criteria of the panel are more comprehensive than the standards stipulated in the Treaty. It, for instance, considered that judges or AGs for the Court of Justice should possess a minimum of 20 years of experience with high-level duties and that judges at the General Court should have a minimum of 12 or 15 years' experience with similar duties.[50] Shorter experience is unlikely to be deemed sufficient, unless a candidate can demonstrate exceptional legal expertise.[51] Although the panel stated that it assesses 'the soundness of the candidate's grasp of key legal issues, of issues connected with the principle of the rule of law, and of the main aspects of EU law', it does not 'seek to assess the scope and comprehensiveness of candidates' legal expertise, particularly with regard to European Union law'.[52] It appears that the requirement to speak the working language of the Court, French, remains a soft constraint as the panel expects the candidates to at least 'acquire proficiency, within a reasonable time'.[53] Additionally, according to Zhang, one of the criteria for appointment to the Court of Justice is that the candidate should possess 'the qualifications required for appointments to the national Supreme Court'.[54]

Despite the panel's best efforts to guarantee that appointees to the Court are experienced legal professionals, in practice the Member States retain a high level of discretion as to how they select 'their' judges. Kenney has argued that the judicial appointments to the Court of Justice 'are not made strictly on merit' and are in fact political.[55] Hence, the criteria for functioning as an effective and efficient judge as established in Articles 253 and 254 TFEU leave considerable room for Member State discretion as regards nominations and appointments to the CJEU. Although 'EU judges need to possess three important skills: first, knowledge of EU Law; second, superb legal and research skills and an astute legal mind; and third, fluency in the French language',[56] there are problems in the appointments. As surprising as it sounds, the Member States often nominate candidates who are unsuitable for judicial appointments.[57] Between 2010 and 2013 the panel delivered seven unfavourable opinions out of 67 nominees for the General

48 Dumbrovský, Petkova and van der Sluis (n 43).
49 ibid.
50 Council (n 47) 23.
51 ibid.
52 ibid 24.
53 ibid.
54 Zhang (n 7) 87.
55 Kenney (n 19) 260.
56 Solanke (n 45) 105; Kenney (n 19) 267; Zhang (n 7) 83.
57 Zhang (n 7) 85.

Court.[58] Similarly, between 2014 and 2016, the panel delivered five unfavourable opinions out of 64 nominees to the General Court and one unfavourable opinion concerning a nomination to the Court of Justice.[59] A few of these candidates were rejected on the basis that their 'length of high-level professional experience' was 'manifestly too short'.[60] Even more disturbingly, some candidates were rejected due to their 'insufficient familiarity with EU law'.[61]

The reason that Member States continue to nominate political appointees appears to be at least partly historical. According to Zhang, a little over half of historical appointees to the CJEU have had prior judicial experience in the national courts.[62] Less than a fifth of the past appointees' primary work experience was in the judiciary and approximately a third of the appointees' immediate positions prior to joining the Court were in the judiciary. In fact, more than half of the past judges appointed to the CJEU have worked in Member State governments prior to joining the Court.[63] Many of the former and current judges working for the Court of Justice have a background as ministers, legal advisors at the Ministry of Justice, members of the diplomatic missions and some have even served in the national parliaments.[64] The preference for government officials is unsurprising because the 'secret deliberation rule' prevents Member States from monitoring the voting preference of their nominating appointees.[65] Hence, Member States tend to choose candidates who they believe will act in the national interests. Jeffrey Dunoff and Mark Pollack note that this has implications of the accountability of judges because the candidates and the potential reappointees nominated by Member States are *de facto* accountable to only one State, which is effectively responsible for deciding whether the individual is nominated or renominated.[66] Therefore, they posit that the nominees have strong and direct accountability to their home State and only very limited accountability to other States. In the context of the appointments to the international courts, Voeten has argued that, although governments cannot predict how judges are likely to behave while on the bench, they may attempt to 'select judges whom they expect to make decisions that match their perceived interests' based on the appointees' past behaviour, interviews, or the political and professional backgrounds.[67] Addi-

58 Council, 'Third Activity Report of the Panel Provided for in Article 255 of the Treaty on the Functioning of the European Union' SN11118/2014 (13 December 2013) 9 <http://curia.europa.eu/jcms/upload/docs/application/pdf/2014-02/rapport-c-255-en.pdf> accessed 11 December 2017. See also Dumbrovský, Petkova and van der Sluis (n 43) 459; Zhang (n 7) 85.

59 Council (n 47) 11.

60 ibid 25.

61 ibid.

62 Zhang (n 7) 81.

63 ibid.

64 Kenney (n 19) 260; Zhang (n 7) 82.

65 Zhang (n 7) 82.

66 Dunoff and Pollack (n 4) 235.

67 Voeten (n 17) 388.

tionally, governments may also 'use (threats of) ex post sanctions and rewards to provide incentives to judges'.[68]

However, the Member States' preference to appoint political candidates is likely to result in problems in the independence of the judiciary since, the less capable the Court's judges are, the more they need to rely on the Court's law clerks, dubbed as the 'hidden workforce within the Court',[69] to carry out their judicial functions.[70] Zhang has raised concerns that some of the inexperienced judges may be dominated by their law clerks, which may result in the voices of the latter being amplified due to their essential role in the Court's decision-making process.[71] The vast majority of the Court's law clerks are experienced lawyers who have worked, *inter alia*, as linguists and researchers in the Court, in private practice, academia, at the Commission, or served in their respective national governments.[72]

Hence, even with the panel in place and seemingly working relatively well, some of its key stipulations of the qualities that the candidates should possess seem rather superficial because ultimately the Member States remain in control over appointments. Therefore, national motivations and processes remain opaque, even if some progress has been made. Additionally, although under Article 253 TFEU Member States' governments are supposed to appoint each judge 'by common accord' after consultation of the panel, critics have argued that, in practice, Member States hardly ever disagree with one another's nomination. Consequently, each Member State appoints its own judges following its own judicial appointment process, which is often opaque and political.[73] Kenney has noted that the Member States simply need to inform the Council of their decision and that the judicial appointments do not attract any wider attention in the media or among the public.[74] This in turn means that '[t]he influence of the Member States on issues such as the possible specialisation of judges or gender diversity is immense'.[75] There is no incentive or reason for the Member States to consider the overall composition of the Court and, as such, no incentive to consider gender balance in that institution. As Turenne puts it: '[a]t the level of the CJEU, diversity is the responsibility of every Member State, and consequently, individually that of no one'.[76] This also effectively means that the other key EU

68 ibid.
69 Zhang (n 7) 94.
70 ibid 85.
71 Zhang (n 7) 71, 85 and 94.
72 Most of the clerks come from a fairly small pool of suitable candidates, drawn primarily from Belgium, France, Luxembourg and Germany due to the requirement to be fluent in French. Zhang (n 7) 100.
73 ibid 81; Kenney (n 19); Henri de Waele, 'Not quite the bed Procrustes built' in Michal Bobek (ed), *Selecting Europe's Judges: A Critical Review of the Appointments to the European Court* (Oxford University Press 2015) 24.
74 Kenney (n 19) 260.
75 Turenne (n 6).
76 ibid 572.

institutions, such as the Commission, have very little input in the process, despite having dried to drive gender mainstreaming of the institutions. Further, this is in spite of the importance of gender balance at the Courts, specifically in the future appointments to the General Court, has been recognised in EU law in the form of Regulation 2015/2422/EU[77] which amended the Statute of the Court. Recital 11 of the Preamble to the Regulation states that:

> It is of high importance to ensure gender balance within the General Court. In order to achieve that objective, partial replacements in that Court should be organised in such a way that the governments of Member States gradually begin to nominate two Judges for the same partial replacement with the aim therefore of choosing one woman and one man, provided that the conditions and procedures laid down by the Treaties are respected.

Although it is too early to assess whether this notion is going to have the desired impact, Turenne is not optimistic noting:

> It is doubtful whether this provides the panel with any constraining power in relation to gender diversity – especially as the panel has previously stated that it does not have the competence to determine the composition of the Court of Justice or of the General Court.[78]

What is interesting about Recital 11 is that is asserts the high importance of gender balance without giving any reasons as to why. It is stated as though the significance of appointing both women and men should be obvious. Although we would argue that it should, of course, be blindingly obvious, the need for gender diversity is not often treated as such. Hence, it is possible to ask why it would not be appropriate for women to challenge a system of appointments and, with it, the culture of the Court, which hitherto has been based on and marked by patronage, male privilege, elitism and unaccountability.[79] Surely more egalitarian processes in relation to the appointment of judges and AGs to the Court would be better for the representativeness and the legitimacy of the Court. The next section is therefore concerned with making the argument for gender balance and diversity more generally.

77 Regulation (EU, Euratom) 2015/2422 of the European Parliament and of the Council of 16 December 2015 amending Protocol No 3 on the Statute of the Court of Justice of the European Union [2015] OJ L341/14.

78 Turenne (n 6) 572.

79 Judicial accountability can be understood to focus on an individual judge, rather than the court as an institution and include 'structural checks on the exercise of individual judicial authority manifested most prominently in international courts via reappointment processes'. Dunoff and Pollack (n 4) 226 and 233.

Why does the composition of the court matter?

Saying that gender balance is important, counting the women and bemoaning the fact that there are so few, and highlighting the general lack of diversity amongst the judges does not help us to establish why having more women in the Court is important. We must look beyond merely looking at the numbers because this can lead to tokenism and evening up the scales for the sake of it. The important point is not that there should be a more equal gender balance, but that a more equal gender balance can bring a number of associated benefits.

Maya Sen has argued that there are strong reasons to think that diverse representation makes important contributions to both the 'descriptive' and 'substantive representation' of the Court.[80] The concept of 'descriptive representation':

> builds on the idea that the importance of having a diverse judiciary does not necessarily come from the fact that women and minorities behave differently once appointed, . . . [but] their importance attaches with the mere fact that they are *present*, as this lends the courts a stronger sense of legitimacy and authority.[81]

According to Sen, descriptive representation is by itself normatively desirable as it means that the courts are more reflective of the greater population they serve.[82] Thus, the very presence of women and minorities in the judiciary may serve to remind their white male colleagues about the history of discrimination and bias that could present gendered and race-based[83] issues which are legally significant.[84] Although the normative implications of the 'substantive representation' of female and minority judges remain to be explored, the concept infers that women and minorities have experiences which are different from those of white men and which are rooted in their identity.[85] Hence, female and minority judges will have different viewpoints and they 'can share and represent the political, legal, moral, and popular interests of. . . [individuals and groups who] might not otherwise be heard'.[86]

Increasing importance has been given to the concept of 'the compositional similarity' between representatives and those represented.[87] The first and perhaps

80 Sen (n 31) 373.
81 ibid.
82 ibid.
83 Although this chapter is aimed at identifying the extent of gender disparities at the Court, we note that addressing racial or ethnic disparities requires addressing social constructs of concepts 'race' and 'racial groups' which are not based on substantive biological or genetic differences. See eg Richard Delgado and Jean Stefancic, *Critical Race Theory: An Introduction* (3rd edn, New York University Press 2017) 9.
84 Sen (n 31) 377.
85 ibid 379.
86 ibid 375.
87 Ana Espírito-Santo, 'Citizens' Attitudes Towards Descriptive Representation: The Case of Women in Portugal' (2016) 23(1) *European Journal of Women's Studies* 43-44.

most obvious reason for descriptive and substantive representation is that a more equal gender balance simply looks fairer. It gives women who bring cases before the Court confidence that the judges hearing their case have an understanding of the issues they may be bringing; that the judges are not 'other' to them, and that they can relate to them. There are, of course, all sorts of other reasons why litigants may still feel that the judges cannot relate, or fully appreciate, the context in which they are bringing the case. While we acknowledge that although a more gender-balanced judiciary does not tackle problems of race, sexual orientation, class or age imbalances, it is a start. The EU institutions have noted the importance of gender balance across the institutions over two decades ago when the Council recognised that 'balanced participation of women and men in the decision-making process is a requirement for democracy'.[88] Further, the 1999 report commissioned on the EU judiciary noted that 'the judiciary influences society at all levels and it is therefore crucial that women form a significant presence within it'.[89]

What has not been explored in detail in existing literature on the Court is why a more gender-balanced, or a more diverse, judiciary at the EU level might add to the legitimacy of the Court or, indeed, why representativeness and legitimacy go hand in hand. In the context of national representativeness this seems uncontroversial in the literature. The EU has recognised the need for the Court to be representative, albeit only in terms of the nationality of the judges and the AGs since the composition of the Court in terms of nationality requirements is set out in Article 19 TEU.[90] If the EU recognises that representativeness is important in terms of the need for the judges to represent each of the 28 Member States, then it has already recognised that representativeness enhances the legitimacy. This further enhances the acceptance of the Court's decisions because Member States are more likely to agree with and enforce decisions which they have – at least at institutional level, even if not directly, been involved in. Kenney highlights this by questioning 'whether Ireland would accept a decision by the court that it had to allow the advertisement of abortion services available in London if no Irish judge had sat on that case?'[91]

This argument is somewhat diluted when judges sit in chambers where, of course, judges from other Member States may decide a case relating to a particular Member State. However, while these chambers might make decisions relating to Member States other than their own, the legitimacy of the overall institution remains intact. The importance of retaining one judge per Member State,

88 Recommendation 96/694/EC of 2 December 1996 on the balanced participation of women and men in the decision-making process [1996] OJ L319/11.

89 Miriam Anasagasti and Nathalie Wuiame, *Women and Decision-making in the Judiciary in the European Union* (European Communities 1999) 21.

90 TEU, art 19 notes that the Court of Justice consists of one judge from each Member State and that is assisted by AGs. Similarly, the General Court includes at least one judge per Member State.

91 Kenney (n 19) 266.

even in the enlarged EU of 28 Member States is clear: politically nothing else would be acceptable and the legitimacy of the Court in the eyes of those Member States without judicial representation is likely to be reduced significantly. We have already briefly mentioned the issues which arose out of the expansion of the General Court. As far back as 1999 the General Court requested additional judges but, in spite of further proposals to expand the General Court, Member States could not agree on a process for rotation. Hence, a revised proposal which doubled the number of judges to two per Member State by 2019 was finally adopted in 2015.[92] These political difficulties serve as a useful reminder that appointments to the Court are sensitive and political and that the representativeness in terms of nationality is crucial to legitimacy at least at Member State government level. Having said that, there is little systematic research which explores these questions of representativeness and legitimacy empirically within the Member States, rather than simply with the Member States themselves, so we do not know the extent to which EU citizens feel that the nationality of the members of the Court is important.

However, if there is an acceptance that representativeness enhances legitimacy, then we must acknowledge by analogy that diversity enhances legitimacy because the 500 million population of the EU is far more diverse than its judiciary would suggest. This makes it even more worrying that there is little diversity among the justices of the Court in terms of gender as well as other characteristics, such as race. If decisions are predominantly made by white, able-bodied men over the age of 60, it is perhaps more difficult for the women and minorities to fully embrace those decisions, particularly where those decisions are about issues where gender or membership to a minority plays an obvious role. However, the argument is more complex than that; there are a number of decisions made by all-male chambers which can be seen to significantly advance women's rights. Significantly, Sen has noted the existence of 'panel effect', or the influence that one judge could have over her peers.[93] This is however not fatal to the argument that the visibility of women, or rather a visibly diverse judicial body, is important for legitimacy. In fact, if the 'panel effect' works as described by Sen, it provides a tangible substantive benefit stemming from diverse judiciary because it may enable female and minority judges to influence their colleagues directly.[94] However, the reach of the panel effect needs more investigation at the level of the CJEU as it is impossible to see individual judges' opinions in the judgements handed out by the Court.

Exactly how important diversity of the judiciary is in the context of the CJEU is something we do not really know and cannot find out without detailed empirical work with citizens across the EU. Qualitative work which explores what the

92 Franklin Dehousse and Benedetta Marsicola, 'The Reform of the EU Courts (II): Abandoning the Management Approach by Doubling the General Court' (2016) *Egmont Paper* 83 <www.tepsa.eu/wp-content/uploads/2016/03/paper.pdf> accessed 13 July 2017.

93 Sen (n 31) 377.

94 ibid.

EU citizens want from the personnel of the Court and how and why that might differ from what they want from their national judiciary would help us to a fuller understanding of how and why (gender) diversity at the Court is important. However, an argument often brought against measures that increase the number of female judges is the fact that this would interfere with the idea of merit and appointing the best person for the job. However, as Kenney demonstrates, the question of merit in the case of the CJEU is already highly skewed:

> Choosing the best woman judge is no more antithetical to applying merit standards than choosing the best Cypriot judge. The difference is that requiring diversity of nationality or geography has been accepted as a representative restriction, whereas gender diversity has not.[95]

In addition, factors and characteristics taken into account for objectively assessing merit are often highly gendered. It seems that when we consider what it is we want from our judiciaries we often think about what we already know, rather than what it should be. Additionally, we associate characteristics, which are seen as 'male' – *inter alia*, logic, rationality, ability to apply legal rules to facts without distraction, and detachment – as characteristics we should value in judges. This often results in sidelining of more female traits such as empathy and emotional intelligence. Thus, 'one of the greatest obstacles to a diverse judiciary has been and remains the image of the default judge and our unwillingness to embrace fully the reality that who the judge is matters'.[96] The pursuit of an 'ideal' judge with the arguments that judges need to be appointed on ever elusive 'merit' may nevertheless be flawed because it is likely to be biased towards women in favour of men.

In order to overcome some of the barriers to bringing more women and others from non-traditional backgrounds into the Court, a fuller understanding of the way lawyers reach the required level for appointment in the judiciary at the national level is necessary. If the path to the level required for appointment to the Court in a Member State is highly gendered, the chances of a woman being in a position where she might be considered for the Court are limited. Even where women reach those positions, careful consideration needs to be given to how they are then appointed to the Court.[97] As outlined above, the composition of

95 Sally J Kenney, *Gender and Justice: Why Women in the Judiciary Really Matter* (Routledge 2013) 128. Greaves has criticised the requirement to appoint one judge per each Member State contrary to the appointment of judges to other international courts. See Rosa Greaves, 'The effectiveness of EU law in proceedings before national courts' in Eugène Buttigieg (ed), *Enforcing One's Rights Under EU Law* (Gutenberg Press 2011); Rosa Greaves, 'Reforming some aspects of the role of Advocates General' in Anthony Arnull, Catherine Barnard, Michael Dougan and Eleanor Spaventa (eds), *A Constitutional Order of States: Essays in EU Law in Honour of Alan Dashwood* (Hart 2011).

96 Erika Rackley, *Women, Judging and the Judiciary: From Difference to Diversity* (Routledge 2013) 196.

97 Kenney (n 95).

the Court is important for a variety of reasons. A more diverse judiciary not only looks better but it also appears more legitimate because it is more representative. More importantly though, a more diverse judiciary is – at least theoretically – a better judiciary because it benefits from a wider variety of experiences and views.[98]

Better judging

In addition, and perhaps more importantly, the question of why a more diverse judiciary might make a better judiciary needs exploring. Lady Hale hints at this when she notes '[w]e need judges who can recognise and counter their own biases, whether conscious or unconscious'.[99] Erika Rackley has explored this question in some detail and she argues convincingly that 'who the judge is matters, since it will determine both the way the judge sets about deciding cases and the substantive conclusions they reach'.[100] The US Supreme Court Justice Sonia Sotomayor has further argued that one of the reasons that who the judge is matters is because 'personal experiences affect what facts judges choose to see'.[101] Lady Hale puts this even more clearly:

> We like to think that the outcome of any particular case is determined by the law and the evidence and not by the predilections of the individual judge. We like to think that we are not predictable in the way in which we will decide the hard cases where the outcome is not clear. But we cannot have it both ways – we have already accepted that it matters who the judge is.[102]

This is the crux of our argument. If it matters who the judges are, then the law loses its objective status and can be seen as something that is much more personal and individual with different impacts and implication, depending on who we are. If it matters who the judges are, then it is important that the judges in our courts are the right ones because it is more than merely their legal competence that will determine the outcome of the cases before them and future development of the law. As the comments above suggest, a judge's background and experience will shape their approach to cases; determine what they see as relevant and important; how they interpret the legal provisions in questions put forward to them by the national court, and what they think the outcome should be. In addition to that, it has been argued above that the mere presence of a female judge, or indeed a judge representing a minority, can influence the arguments put forward and submissions made. Advocates may feel confident to address issues to a female judge

98 See also Rosemary Hunter, 'More Than Just a Different Face? Judicial Diversity and Decision-making' (2015) 68 *Current Legal Problems* 119 doi:10.1093/clp/cuv001.
99 Lady Hale (n 3).
100 Rackley (n 96) 165.
101 Sonia Sotomayor, 'A Latina Judge's Voice' (2002) 13 *Berkeley La Raza Law Journal* 87, 92.
102 Lady Hale (n 3).

that they may have couched in different terms or sidelined altogether with a male judge or a panel of all-male judges.

Rackley notes, in the context of discussion of Justice Ginsburg's role and influence in the judgement delivered by the US Supreme Court in *AT&T Corp v Hulteen*[103] about the impact of maternity leave on pension rights, that 'her presence ensured that arguments about workplace equality were aired and addressed'.[104] A more diverse judiciary is therefore important because it allows claimants to feel like they have had their day in court, that they were listened to and that the issues which are important to them got a fair hearing even if they are not ultimately successful in their claims. Where, staying with the example of workplace equality, arguments are not made, or clearly not accepted, as important or relevant by an all-male judiciary, female claimants are likely to feel silenced and that their concerns have not been fully addressed because they have not been understood. Representativeness and legitimacy therefore do often go hand in hand. It also seems obvious that 'a judiciary with a diversity of experience . . . is more likely to achieve the most just decision and the best outcome for society'.[105] In fact, gender and other forms of diversity are not mutually exclusive, since female judges have a wide range of different experiences, including working class background and memberships of ethnic and sexual minorities.[106]

However, maybe this is not that obvious though and it is certainly worthy of further exploration. A key general legal principle is that similar cases must be treated in a similar way and legal certainty can only be upheld if this is the case. However, if we accept that who the judge is matters because it influences not only what arguments, and therefore whose voices, are heard, but also which facts are considered relevant, how the decision making is approached, and ultimately what the final decision might be, then must we also accept that a diverse judiciary is likely to lead to diversity in outcomes? While this is a concern, Rackley convincingly argues that:

> the promise of a diverse judiciary is not the promise of a multiplicity of approaches and values fighting for recognition. But of a judiciary enriched by its openness to viewpoints previously marginalised and of decision-making which is better for being better informed.[107]

Sen has noted that, for instance, African-American judges in the US are more likely to rule in a liberal direction in cases involving discrimination on the basis of gender and to side with plaintiffs belonging to sexual minorities.[108] Similarly,

103 *AT&T Corp v Hulteen and others* 556 US 701 (2009).
104 Rackley (n 96) 170.
105 Terence Etherton, 'Liberty, the Archetype and Diversity: A Philosophy of Judging' (2010) *Public Law* 728.
106 Hunter (n 98) 122.
107 Rackley (n 96) 177.
108 Sen (n 31) 376. Cf Leslie J Moran, 'Judicial Diversity and the Challenge of Sexuality: Some Preliminary Findings' (2006) 28 *Sydney Law Review* 565, 568 who notes the existence of sexual orientation bias among the judiciary.

scholars have noted that 'female and black appellate court judges decide diversity-specific cases differently from their white, male colleagues and affect their colleagues' decision making'.[109] However, the same scholars also note that, while such insights are significant, 'much remains unknown about the presence and degree of diversity representation within . . . political [and legal] institutions'.[110] A diverse judiciary therefore brings a multitude of experiences, backgrounds, viewpoints and opinions and adds them to one big melting pot, which is stirred through discussion and debates both formally and informally, both in relation to specific cases and more generally. As Rackley notes, '[j]udging is a collective enterprise'.[111] However, this collective enterprise is difficult to unpick at EU level. Hence, it is almost impossible to study the impact of diversity, including gender, because judgements are given by the Court as a whole without the reasoned views of the minority judges (dissenting opinions), or of those judges who disagree with the Court's reasoning while agreeing with the final decision. We deal with this issue further in Chapter 4.

Paul Collins and his colleagues rightly note that 'although some studies have identified gender differences in judicial decision making, others have failed to uncover systematic differences between male and female jurists'.[112] This seems obvious, given the discussion earlier in this chapter which argued that it is the diversity in experience that might make for an overall better judiciary rather than the fact that men and women will always and inherently make different decisions. However, Collins and his colleagues raise an interesting question about female judges which might be important in the context of the CJEU on issues such as whether critical mass makes a difference; whether women decide cases differently or reason differently in cases where the number of women on a judiciary exceeds a certain number or proportion. They further found that when women serve with other women they decide cases differently. They note that '[w]hile it is clear that the influence of gender varies across policy areas, it is also evident that the impact of gender may be in part, contingent upon the presence of other women in the decision-making environment'.[113]

To make matters more impenetrable in research terms, we must also acknowledge that judges at the Court swear an oath which includes the obligation to uphold the secrecy of the Court's deliberations.[114] There appears to be different interpretations of this rule since some judges of the Court themselves have

109 Sen (n 31) 376. See also Christina L Boyd, 'Representation on the Courts? The Effects of Trial Judges' Sex and Race' (2016) 69(4) *Political Research Quarterly* 788 doi:10.1177/1065912916663653.
110 Boyd (n 109) 789.
111 Rackley (n 96) 169.
112 Paul M Collins, Jr, Kenneth L Manning, and Robert A Carp, 'Gender, Critical Mass, and Judicial Decision Making' (2010) 32(2) *Law and Policy* 260-261 doi:10.1111/j.1467–9930.2010.00317.x.
113 ibid 275.
114 Protocol (No 3) on the Statute of the Court of Justice of the European Union, annexed to the Treaties [2010] OJ C83/210, as amended, art 35: 'The deliberations of the Court of Justice shall be and shall remain secret'.

interpreted to the Statute of the Court as meaning that the Statute precludes the writing of separate opinions because their publication 'would necessarily reveal, at least to some extent, elements of the court's deliberations, in particular the identity and arguments of those who depart from the majority of the court on specific issues'.[115] According to Azizi, 'the full secrecy of deliberations also excludes to reveal the mere number of judges who have adhered to the final judgement and to specify the reasons why they partly or entirely disagree with that judgement'.[116] While this may be a conceivable reading of the Court's Statute, judges on other international courts routinely issue separate opinions without triggering claims that doing so violates similar rules on the secrecy of deliberations contained in the statutes of these courts.[117]

What we do have is the possibility of looking at the opinions of AGs. However, since there is only one opinion per case, we cannot compare different approaches and the influence gender may have here. We could compare the AG's opinion with the final judgement of the Court of Justice in specific cases, which may give us some, albeit limited, insights. Alternatively, we could compare the approaches of male and female AGs across a series of cases and consider any differences in approach. However, all these approaches are potentially more limited and more problematic in the case of the CJEU as opposed to a national court because there are several more factors which may account for difference. The judges and AGs all come from different national contexts with different legal traditions, processes and norms. Their cultural backgrounds are different, their training to become a lawyer and judge has been different, their approach to law may be very different, and, indeed, the role and visibility of women in law, or more generally, may also vary dramatically between Member States. All of this means that, without carefully constructed and detailed empirical work with the judges of the Court and those who work with them, isolating gender as a factor and exploring its importance and impact is almost impossible.[118]

Conclusion

This chapter has set out the composition of the Court of Justice of the European Union and highlighted some of the issues arising from that composition and the manner in which members of the Court are appointed. We have argued that representativeness and legitimacy are important and that a more diverse judiciary is likely to lead to better decision making because a variety of experience and background are brought to the table. The number of female judges and AGs at the Court of Justice and the General Court is still very low, with many cases being

115 Dunoff and Pollack (n 4) 245.
116 Josef Azizi, 'Unveiling the EU Courts' Internal Decision-Making Process: A Case for Dissenting Opinions?' (2011) 12 *ERA Forum* 49, 52.
117 Dunoff and Pollack (n 4) 245.
118 Silje Hermansen, Malcolm Langford, Daniel Naurin, and Vegard Vibe, 'A Different Voice in International Courts? Gender and Judicial Behavior in Sexual and Reproductive Rights' (Law and Society Association's Annual Meeting, Mexico City, June 2017).

heard by all-male chambers. This is problematic because it means that women's voices are not heard in the decision-making process and fundamentally they may also not be heard during the case itself. The composition of the judiciary at EU level does not therefore hold out much promise for a gender-aware reading of EU law, policy and case facts coming before it. Yet there have been cases in the Courts' history that show a degree of gender awareness. We therefore now turn to considering the way the Courts operate and work in order to examine the gendered implications of those processes and ways of working. We also ask whether or not these factors might mitigate against the lack of diversity of the membership of the Courts.

Bibliography

Anasagasti M and Wuiame N, *Women and Decision-making in the Judiciary in the European Union* (European Communities 1999)
AT&T Corp v Hulteen and Others 556 US 701 (2009)
Boyd CL, 'Representation on the Courts? The Effects of Trial Judges' Sex and Race' (2016) 69(4) *Political Research Quarterly* 788 doi:10.1177/1065912916663653
Cichowski RA, 'Women's Rights, the European Court, and Supranational Constitutionalism' (1995) 38 *Law and Society Review* 489 doi:10.1111/j.0023-9216.2004.00055
Cohen A, 'Ten Majestic Figures in Long Amaranth Robes: The Formation of the Court of Justice of the European Communities' (2010) 60(2) *Revue française de science politique* 227
Collins PM Jr, Manning KL and Carp RA, 'Gender, Critical Mass, and Judicial Decision Making' (2010) 32(2) *Law and Policy* 260–261 doi:10.1111/j.1467–9930.2010.00317.x
Consolidated Version of the Treaty on European Union [2012] OJ C326/13 (TEU)
Council, 'Court of Justice of the European Union: Appointment of Nine Judges' (28 February 2018) <www.consilium.europa.eu/en/press/press-releases/2018/02/28/court-of-justice-of-the-european-union-appointment-of-nine-judges/> accessed 7 March 2018
Council, 'Fourth Activity Report of the Panel Provided for by Article 255 of the Treaty on the Functioning of the European Union' (28 March 2017) <https://curia.europa.eu/jcms/upload/docs/application/pdf/2017-03/rapport_activite__c255_-_en.pdf > accessed 4 December 2017
Council, 'Third Activity Report of the Panel Provided for in Article 255 of the Treaty on the Functioning of the European Union' *SN11118/2014* (13 December 2013) <http://curia.europa.eu/jcms/upload/docs/application/pdf/2014-02/rapport-c-255-en.pdf> accessed 11 December 2017
Court of Justice of the European Union, *Annual Report 2016: Management Report* (European Union 2017) <https://curia.europa.eu/jcms/upload/docs/application/pdf/2017-06/rapport_gestion_2016_en_.pdf> accessed 14 December 2017
———, 'The Court in Figures' <https://curia.europa.eu/jcms/jcms/P_80908/en/> accessed 12 October 2017
Dehousse F and Marsicola B, 'The Reform of the EU Courts (II): Abandoning the Management Approach by Doubling the General Court' (2016) *Egmont Paper* 83 <www.tepsa.eu/wp-content/uploads/2016/03/paper.pdf> accessed 13 July 2017

Delgado R and Stefancic J, *Critical Race Theory: An Introduction* (3rd edn, New York University Press 2017)

Dever M and Adkins L, 'All Male Panel: Interview with Saara Särmä' (2015) 30(85) *Australian Feminist Studies* 283

Dumbrovský T, Petkova B and van der Sluis M, 'Judicial Appointments: The Article 255 TFEU Advisory Panel and Selection Procedures in the Member States' (2014) 51(2) *Common Market Law Review* 455

Dunoff JL and Pollack MA, 'The Judicial Trilemma' (2017) 111(2) *American Journal of International Law* 225 doi:10.1017/ajil.2017.23

Espírito-Santo A, 'Citizens' Attitudes Towards Descriptive Representation: The Case of Women in Portugal' (2016) 23(1) *European Journal of Women's Studies* 43

Etherton T, 'Liberty, the Archetype and Diversity: A Philosophy of Judging' (2010) *Public Law* 728

European Union Committee, *Follow-up Inquiry into the Workload of the Court of Justice of the European Union: Oral and Written Evidence* (HL 2012–13) 65 <www.parliament.uk/documents/lords-committees/eu-sub-com-e/Followup-workloadCJEU/CJEU-Follow-upWrittenOralevidence290413.pdf> accessed 13 December 2017

Greaves R, 'Reforming Some Aspects of the Role of Advocates General' in Arnull A, Barnard C, Dougan M and Spaventa E (eds), *A Constitutional Order of States: Essays in EU Law in Honour of Alan Dashwood* (Hart 2011)

———, 'The Effectiveness of EU Law in Proceedings Before National Courts' in Buttigieg E, (ed), *Enforcing One's Rights Under EU Law* (Gutenberg Press 2011)

Hale (Lady), 'Judges, Power and Accountability: Constitutional Implications of Judicial Selection' (Constitutional Law Summer School, Belfast, 11 August 2017) <www.supremecourt.uk/docs/speech-170811.pdf > accessed 17 November 2017

Hermansen S, Langford M, Naurin D and Vibe V, 'A Different Voice in International Courts? Gender and Judicial Behavior in Sexual and Reproductive Rights' (Law and Society Association's Annual Meeting, Mexico City, June 2017)

Hunter R, 'More Than Just a Different Face? Judicial Diversity and Decision-making' (2015) 68 *Current Legal Problems* 119 doi:10.1093/clp/cuv001

Kenney SJ, 'Breaking the Silence: Gender Mainstreaming and the Composition of the European Court of Justice' (2002) 10 *Feminist Legal Studies* 257

———, *Gender and Justice: Why Women in the Judiciary Really Matter* (Routledge 2013)

———, 'The Members of the Court of Justice of the European Communities' (1998) 5 *Columbia Journal of European Law* 101

Moran LJ, 'Judicial Diversity and the Challenge of Sexuality: Some Preliminary Findings' (2006) 28 *Sydney Law Review* 565

Posner RA, 'Judicial Self-Restraint' (1983) 59 *Indiana Law Journal* 1

Protocol (No 3) on the Statute of the Court of Justice of the European Union, Annexed to the Treaties [2010] OJ C83/210, as amended

Rackley E, *Women, Judging and the Judiciary: From Difference to Diversity* (Routledge 2013)

Recommendation 96/694/EC of 2 December 1996 on the Balanced Participation of Women and Men in the Decision-making Process [1996] OJ L319/11

Regulation (EU, Euratom) 2015/2422 of the European Parliament and of the Council of 16 December 2015 Amending Protocol No 3 on the Statute of the Court of Justice of the European Union [2015] OJ L341/14

Särmä S, 'Congrats, You Have an All-Male Panel!' (2016) 18(3) *International Feminist Journal of Politics* 470 doi:10.1080/14616742.2016.1189671
Sen M, 'Diversity, Qualifications, and Ideology: How Female and Minority Judges Have Changed, or Not Changed, Over Time' (2017) 2 *Wisconsin Law Review* 367
Siebert D, *Die Auswahl der Richter am Gerichtshof der Europäischen Gemeinschaften: zu der erforderlichen Reform des Art 167 EGV* (Peter Lang 1997)
Solanke I, 'Diversity and Independence in the European Court of Justice' (2009) 15 *Columbia Journal of European Law* 91
Sotomayor S, 'A Latina Judge's Voice' (2002) 13 *Berkeley La Raza Law Journal* 87
Sumption (Lord), 'Home Truths About Judicial Diversity' (Bar Council Law Reform Lecture, London, 15 November 2012) <www.supremecourt.uk/docs/speech-121115-lord-sumption.pdf> accessed 12 December 2017
Treaty of Lisbon Amending the Treaty on European Union and the Treaty Establishing the European Community [2007] OJ C306/1
Treaty on the Functioning of the European Union [2012] OJ C 326/47
Turenne S, *Fair Reflection of Society in Judicial Systems: A Comparative Study* (Springer 2015)
———, 'Institutional Constraints and Collegiality at the Court of Justice of the European Union: A Sense of Belonging?' (2017) 24(4) *Maastricht Journal of European and Comparative Law* 565
Voeten E, 'The Politics of International Judicial Appointments' (2008) 9(2) *Chicago Journal of International Law* 387
Zhang AH, 'The Faceless Court' (2016) 38 *University of Pennsylvania Journal of Int'l Law* 71

4 How the court works and why it matters

> Repeated litigation is the only way to define the problem from every angle and reveal the interior of hypocritical sexless agreements, the differences in classification, the excuses that motivate them and the poorly paid jobs that basically only women are allowed to do.[1]

Having considered the composition of the Court of Justice of the European Union (CJEU) in Chapter 3, we are now interested in procedural questions of how cases get to the CJEU and what happens once they get there. By considering the process and thus the possible choices or options available at each stage, we are able to ask questions about the extent to which gender impacts on the processes and *vice versa*. As outlined in the previous chapter, the CJEU is currently made up of two separate courts, namely the General Court and the Court of Justice. These courts have distinct jurisdictions and do not form an appeal structure the way in which national legal systems generally do, although appeals are possible from the General Court to the Court of Justice. The work of the Court of Justice encompasses all areas of EU law, such as constitutional cases involving free movement, fundamental rights, tax, environment, intellectual property, competition, state aid, and social policy.[2] The General Court deals principally with specific types of actions, namely cases brought against the Commission by Member States as well as direct actions brought against the EU institutions by natural or legal persons. It also has jurisdiction in cases relating to fact-intensive cases involving competition, state aid, trade, agriculture and trademarks.[3] The principal difference between the Court of Justice and the General Court is that, although the Court of Justice acts as the Court of first instance for certain matters, it is also the highest court for the EU, whereas the General Court forms the lower level of the

1 Eliane Gubin, *A Woman of Conviction: Eliane Vogel-Polsky* (Institute for the Equality of Women and Men 2008) (with Catherine Jacques) 84 citing Éliane Vogel-Polsky, 'Le travail des femmes et l'arrêté royal n°40 du 24 octobre 1967' (1968) *Socialisme* 2, 11.

2 Angela Huyue Zhang, 'The Faceless Court' (2016) 38 *University of Pennsylvania Journal of International Law* 71, 78.

3 ibid 78.

CJEU. Additionally, cases heard at the first instance by the General Court may be subject to appeal to the Court of Justice on points of law only. As the jurisdiction and type of cases and therefore, complainants or claimants are different in the two courts, it stands to reason that the issues arising from a gender perspective are also different. Since dealing with all these issues is beyond the scope of a single chapter, we focus in this chapter on the preliminary reference procedure as the main mechanism by which cases dealing with most of the substantive law in a number of key areas discussed in the later chapters have reached the Court of Justice. As part of this discussion we must also briefly examine the important role legal mobilisation has played in the development of EU equality law in particular. At the end of this chapter we offer some brief remarks on the workings of the General Court, focusing predominantly on the rules of standing for individuals hoping to bring a direct action to the Court and their implications.

The Court of Justice deals with cases which are brought before it in two distinct ways. First, cases are referred to it by national courts via the preliminary reference procedure under Article 267 TFEU and, second, the Commission may initiate infringement proceedings against Member States for alleged failure to fulfil their Treaty obligations. It also has jurisdiction to hear actions for annulment of EU law measures initiated by legal or natural persons, and actions for failure to act on the part of an EU institution, body, office or agency. In this chapter we do not intend to deal with all these types of actions in detail. Instead, we focus predominantly on procedural issues involved in the preliminary reference procedure. We do so because, from an EU citizen's perspective, this is probably the most important and significant way to bring EU law concerns before the Court and because preliminary references are likely to have the most obvious and direct impact on EU citizens. Indeed, preliminary references arise when a private litigant brings their case to a national court which subsequently determines whether EU law is relevant to the case and asks the Court of Justice for an interpretation of EU law. Once the Court's judgement is passed back down to the national court, the national court makes a final ruling. We have also chosen this focus because the preliminary reference procedure highlights well the way in which there are opportunities for gender as a consideration to be written in or written out of a case at every stage of the process.

The preliminary reference procedure

The preliminary reference procedure links domestic and European legal orders through an ongoing dialogue between national judges and the Court of Justice. The importance of this procedure is widely recognised as it was primarily through the early case law that the Court began to develop and construct its expansive constitutional doctrines of supremacy and direct effect.[4] Although the Court has

4 Rachel A Cichowski, 'Women's Rights, the European Court, and Supranational Constitutionalism' (1995) 38 *Law and Society Review* 489, 490–491 doi:10.111

been criticised for creating these doctrines to enhance its own power relative to the governments of Member States in addition to using Article 267 TFEU to strengthen its own authority, Rachel Cichowski has argued that the ability to refer questions of EU law to the Court has also empowered national judges and stimulated national legal action by private individuals and interest groups.[5] The existence of the procedure has been particularly useful for those women who have experienced gender discrimination by their employers but have enjoyed little or no protection under domestic law. Hence, Article 267 TFEU has enabled women to rely on general EU gender equality laws to bring claims before the national courts.[6] She concludes that this way the existence of this mechanism has been extremely beneficial for women and women's rights advocates because it has enabled the Court to develop a growing body of rights protecting women throughout Europe.[7]

Article 267 TFEU sets out the procedure:

> The Court of Justice of the European Union shall have jurisdiction to give preliminary rulings concerning:
>
> (a) the interpretation of the Treaties;
> (b) the validity and interpretation of acts of the institutions, bodies, offices or agencies of the Union;
>
> Where such a question is raised before any court or tribunal of a Member State, that court or tribunal may, if it considers that a decision on the question is necessary to enable it to give judgment, request the Court to give a ruling thereon.
>
> Where any such question is raised in a case pending before a court or tribunal of a Member State against whose decisions there is no judicial remedy under national law, that court or tribunal shall bring the matter before the Court.
>
> If such a question is raised in a case pending before a court or tribunal of a Member State with regard to a person in custody, the Court of Justice of the European Union shall act with the minimum of delay.

This looks relatively straightforward in that any court can refer a question and the courts of last instance must refer a question which arises in relation to the interpretation of the Treaties or the validity and interpretation of other acts. The boundaries of how this operates in practice have been established through case

1/j.0023-9216.2004.00055. See also Jessica Guth, 'Transforming the European Legal Order: The European Court of Justice at 60+' (2016) 12(1) *Journal of Contemporary European Research* 455.

5 Cichowski (n 4) 491 and 493.

6 ibid 507–508.

7 ibid 508.

law. There must be a genuine dispute[8] to which the interpretation of EU law is relevant and important,[9] and the national court must put a precise and clearly phrased question to the Court.[10] In the context of Article 267 TFEU, the term 'any court or tribunal of a Member State', which may refer a question on the interpretation of EU law, is fairly widely defined to include tribunals and bodies with judicial decision-making powers.[11] As per principles established by the Court of Justice in *CILFIT*,[12] the court or tribunal 'against whose decisions there is no judicial remedy'[13] must refer the case to the Court of Justice.[14] This is unless the question raised by the national court is 'irrelevant', the EU law provision has already been interpreted by the Court or 'the correct application of Community law was so obvious as to leave no scope for any reasonable doubt as to the manner in which the question raised is to be resolved'.[15] The basic tenet of this *acte clair* principle relates to the need to ensure consistent application of EU law across all the EU Member States, 'in the light of the specific characteristics of [EU] law, the particular difficulties to which its interpretation gives rise and the risk of divergences in judicial decisions within the [EU]'.[16]

In essence, the procedure under Article 267 TFEU was developed as a mechanism that allows any national court to refer a question of EU law to the Court of Justice and ask them for interpretative guidance. Therefore, the Court simply interprets the law and answers the questions referred to it, rather than apply the law to the facts. In effect, the Court does not deliver a judgement in which it rules for or against the parties. It is for the national courts referring the specific questions to the Court to resolve the case by applying EU and national law to the factual situation before them in light of the Court's guidance. There are a number of issues arising out of this which have significant implications when viewed using a gender lens. The rules contained in Article 267 are concerned with when and what sort of questions are to be referred and, as such, they may

8 Case C-244/80 *Pasquale Foglia v Mariella Novello* [1981] ECR 3045, para 3.

9 Case C-292/04 *Wienand Meilicke, Heidi Christa Weyde and Marina Stöffler v Finanzamt Bonn-Innenstadt* [2007] ECR I-1835, para 25: it is not the Court's task to deliver advisory opinions on general or hypothetical questions. See also Case C-508/16 *Boudjellal* (2017) not published, EU:C:2017:6, para 32; Joined Cases C-297/88 and C-197/89 *Massam Dzodzi v Belgian State* [1990] ECR I-3763.

10 Joined Cases C-320/90, C-321/90 and C-322/90 *Telemarsicabruzzo SpA and Others v Circostel, Ministero delle Poste e Telecomunicazioni and Ministero della Difesa* [1993] ECR I-393, para 6: 'it [is] necessary that the national court define the factual and legislative context of the questions it is asking or, at the very least, explain the factual circumstances on which those questions are based'.

11 Case T-184/95 *Dorsch Consult Ingenieurgesellschaft mbH v Council and Commission* [1997] ECR II-351.

12 Case 283/81 *Srl CILFIT and Lanificio di Gavardo SpA v Ministry of Health* [1982] ECRI-3415 (CILFIT).

13 ibid para 21.

14 ibid.

15 *CILFIT* (n 12) paras 16 and 21.

16 ibid para 21.

have significant impact on the type of cases which reach the Court and therefore the type of cases the Court has the opportunity to rule on.

There is also a new procedure called an 'urgent procedure for preliminary rulings', or '*procédure préjudicielle d'urgence*' in French, which is commonly abbreviated as PPU. The new procedure was introduced by the EU institutions and the Court in 2008 by amending[17] the procedural rules of the Court.[18] The PPU enables the Court to answer questions in the area of freedom, security and justice,[19] within a much shorter time than under the general procedural rules for preliminary rulings.[20] A considerable proportion of the rulings delivered thus far under the PPU have involved sensitive matters concerning the parent–child relationship under the Brussels II bis Regulation.[21] As far as possible, the PPU proceedings abstain from written statements and translations.[22] The ability to submit written statements or observations is reserved exclusively to the parties to the main proceedings, the government of the Member State of the referring court, the Commission and the EU institution, which adopted the contested act.[23] Other Member States are only able to plead at the hearing.[24] Under Article 104b of the Court's Rules of Procedure the matter which is subject to the PPU must be urgent. Although the Court has used the PPU in a number of decisions concerning minors,[25] it does not appear be too pedantic when it comes to assessing the urgency of a matter. Instead, it has made clear that the PPU is especially appropriate in cases of child abduction.[26] However, the PPU does not have to be requested by the referring court.[27] Instead, based on Article 104b § 1(3)24 of its Rules of Procedure, the Court of Justice can submit the reference to its urgent

17 Amendment of the Rules of Procedure of the Court of 15 January 2008 [2008] OJ L24/39. See also Council Decision of 20 December 2007 amending the Protocol on the Statute of the Court of Justice [2008] OJ L24/42.

18 Rules of Procedure of the Court of 19 June 1991 [1991] OJ L176/7, as amended.

19 Treaty on the Functioning of the European Union [2008] OJ C115/47 (TFEU), arts 67 et seq.

20 Anatol Dutta and Andrea Schulz, 'First Cornerstones of the EU Rules on Cross-Border Child Cases: The Jurisprudence of the Court of Justice of the European Union on the Brussels IIa Regulation From C to Health Service Executive' (2014) 10(1) *Journal of Private International Law* 1, 2 doi:10.5235/17441048.10.1.1

21 Council Regulation (EC) No 2201/2003 of 27 November 2003 concerning jurisdiction and the recognition and enforcement of judgements in matrimonial matters and the matters of parental responsibility, repealing Regulation (EC) No 1347/2000. See Geert De Baere and Kathleen Gutman, 'The Impact of the European Union and the European Court of Justice on European Family Law' (2015) 1 *European Family Law* 5, 32.

22 Dutta and Schulz (n 20) 2.

23 ibid.

24 ibid.

25 Case C-195/08 *PPU Inga Rinau* [2008] ECR I-5271; Case C-403/09 *PPU Jasna Detiček v Maurizio Sgueglia* [2009] ECR I-12193; Case C-211/10 *PPU Doris Povse v Mauro Alpago* [2010] ECR I-6669; Case C-400/10 *PPU J McB v LE* [2010] ECR I-8965; Case C-92/12 *PPU Health Service Executive v SC and AC* [2012] EU:C:2012:255.

26 See eg *Rinau* (n 25) para 44; *McB* (n 25) para 27.

27 Dutta and Schulz (n 20) 4.

procedure *ex officio*, if it comes to the conclusion that a swift answer is necessary upon request of the Court's President. This happened in *Aguirre Zarraga*[28] where the referring German court had explicitly asked the court not to apply the PPU. The application of PPU in this case was perhaps unsurprising as it concerned the removal of a child to Germany from Spain by her mother who resided in Germany. The child's father in this case had sole custody, and a delay would have risked deterioration in the child's relationship with her father.

Child abduction cases are likely to have visible gendered implications. Beaumont, Walker and Holliday have found, perhaps rather surprisingly, that in the vast majority of the non-return cases under the Brussels IIa Regulation the abducting parent was the child's primary carer, most of whom are mothers.[29] Although this could indicate an increase in female abductors in the recent decade, most probably this is a result of the fact the court in the State of Refuge is more likely to issue a non-return order in cases where the abducting parent is the primary carer-mother.[30] A feasible alternative theory may be that mothers are likely to have less financial stability than fathers, and hence they might not have the resources available to begin Article 11(6)-(8) Brussels IIa proceedings, especially if legal aid is not available.[31] Additionally, Peter McEleavy has noted that these mothers often appear to be vulnerable, whether through having experienced domestic violence or being in an economically weak position.[32] Having a procedure in place which can expedite these cases is therefore welcomed.

The preliminary reference procedure and gender

We argue that the preliminary reference procedure provides countless opportunities for gender to be written in or written out of the proceedings, as much of the content of the judgements depends on the actors involved in the individual cases. Leaving aside difficulties around access to justice more generally, the particular problems faced in accessing legal advice and the courts in an era of austerity and the disappearing legal aid across the EU,[33] this section is concerned with

28 Case C-491/10 PPU *Joseba Andoni Aguirre Zarraga v Simone Pelz* [2010] ECR I-14247, paras 38–41.

29 Paul Beaumont, Lara Walker, and Jayne Holliday, 'Conflicts of EU Courts on Child Abduction: The Reality of Article 11(6)-(8) Brussels IIa Proceedings Across the EU' (2016) 12(2) *Journal of Private International Law* 211, 215 doi.10.1080/17441048.2016.1206708.

30 ibid.

31 ibid.

32 Peter McEleavy, 'The European Court of Human Rights and the Hague Child Abduction Convention: Prioritising Return or Reflection?' (2015) 62(3) *Netherlands International Law Review* 365.

33 See eg Emma Hitchings, 'Official, Operative and Outsider Justice: The Ties That (May Not) Bind in Family Financial Disputes' (2017) *Child and Family Law Quarterly* 359; Lorna McGregor, 'Alternative Dispute Resolution and Human Rights: Developing a Rights-Based Approach Through the ECHR' (2015) 26(3) *European Journal of International Law* 607;

examining the various aspects of the preliminary reference process from a gendered perspective.

The ability of any court to refer a question of EU law has the potential to increase the chances of gender issues being considered by the Court. As a result of lower court referrals, cases which deal with what we might term everyday concerns of citizens are far more likely to reach the Court and those everyday concerns may well be gendered. The higher the case gets in the court hierarchy, the more likely it is that the issues under consideration are distilled to purely legal and eventually constitutional issues in which gender becomes less and less visible. If only supreme courts or equivalent could refer, referral would be dependent on cases negotiating the appeal structure in a given Member State first. Consequently, the number of cases actually being referred would be much smaller. In addition, the types of cases referred would also be different in that they would only be cases of constitutional importance or dealing with significant legal developments. In such cases, unless gendered issues are the focus of the case, they are less likely to be considered than in lower courts because the focus is likely to lie elsewhere. By allowing lower courts to refer questions, the EU ensures that the consistent interpretation, implementation and enforcement of EU law is placed in the hands of those who have most to gain from it, namely EU citizens. Gendered issues can thus, and have been, brought to the Court of Justice from a variety of courts across Member States.[34]

It may also be argued that lower courts, which often include more female judges, may be more open to gendered arguments.[35] As we have argued in Chapter 3, who the judge is matters and the presence of a female judge can influence what arguments are brought and how those arguments are framed. The presence of a female judge may therefore also lead to the parties to a case petitioning her

---

Andrew Higgins, 'The Costs of Civil Justice and Who Pays?'(2017) 37(3) *Oxford Journal of Legal Studies* 687; Richard Nash, 'Financing Access to Justice: Innovating Possibilities to Promote Access for All' (2013) 5 *Hague Journal on the Rule of Law* 96.

34 See eg Chapter 5 where cases dealing with equal pay and pensions as well as the protection of women before and during maternity leave has been deliberated by the Court. For equal pay and pension related cases, see specifically Case C-43/75 *Defrenne v Sabena* [1976] ECR 00455 (*Defrenne II*); Case 170/84 *Bilka-Kaufhaus GmbH v Karin Weber von Hartz* [1986] ECR 01607; Case 12/81 *Eileen Garland v British Rail Engineering Ltd* [1982] ECR 359; Case C-262/88 *Douglas Harvey Barber v Guardian Royal Exchange Assurance Group* [1990] ECR I-01889. For maternity leave related cases, see Case C-177/88 *Elisabeth Johanna Pacifica Dekker v Stichting Vormingscentrum voor Jong Volwassenen (VJV-Centrum) Plus* [1991] IRLR 27; Case C-32/93 *Carole Louise Webb v EMO Air Cargo (UK) Ltd* [1994] ECR I-3567; Case 394/96 *Mary Brown v Rentokil* [1998] IRLR 445; Case C-438/99 *Maria Luisa Jiménez Melgar v Ayuntamiento de Los Barrios* [2001] ECR I-06915; Case C-109/00 *Tele Danmark A/S v Handels- og Kontorfunktionærernes Forbund i Danmark (HK)* [2001] ECR I-06993; Case C-507/12 *Jessy Saint Prix v Secretary of State for Work and Pensions* [2014] EU:C:2014:2007.

35 For a discussion as to whether female judges indeed make a difference, see Rosemary Hunter, 'More Than Just a Different Face? Judicial Diversity and Decision-making' (2015) *Current Legal Problems* 1.

to refer a question, which takes note of gendered issues, or to ask for gendered considerations to be included in the questions to be referred. It is perhaps more likely that the female judges will accept the relevance of such submissions and act accordingly. If it is accepted that female judges are more likely to acknowledge that questions arising are gendered,[36] or that gender is relevant to the questions being addressed, she might also be more willing to recognise the need to refer questions where other (male) judges may not see a gender issue, which needs to be addressed, and be less willing to engage with EU law to address the question. While this is positive for those cases that are heard by sympathetic and gender aware judges, it also presents somewhat of a lottery – the judge hearing the case determines the likelihood of gender being seen as a relevant consideration. In fact, the lawyer or legal team presenting a female client also plays a role here and we return to this point in the section on legal mobilisation below. In conclusion, the effectiveness of this process depends very much on the individual judge's willingness to engage with gendered issues as well as the extent to which judges in national courts are willing to engage with the EU system and the extent to which that is accepted within the Member State. Sabrina Tesoka has noted in the context of discussion of judicial politics and their impact on national equality structures that '[d]espite the presence of equality litigation procedures in all EU Member States, it seems that certain national systems are more "open" than others and better equipped to provide effective and easy access to justice'.[37]

The guidance issued to Member States' courts and tribunals on the preliminary reference procedure makes clear that it is the national courts' and not the parties' decision as to whether or not to refer a question. It states:

> The jurisdiction of the Court to give a preliminary ruling on the interpretation or validity of EU law is exercised exclusively on the initiative of the national courts and tribunals, whether or not the parties to the main proceedings have expressed the wish that a question be referred to the Court.[38]

This means that, even where parties raise an EU law issue, which they think requires interpretation, the national court may disagree and the question will remain unanswered by the Court.

The extent to which gender questions are seen as relevant as well as the extent to which EU law is seen as a way to help address gender questions will also vary from one Member State to another. Since the Recommendations make clear that

36 There is some evidence to suggest that this is the case. See eg OECD, *Women, Government and Policy Making in OECD Countries: Fostering Diversity for Inclusive Growth* (OECD Publishing 2014) <http://dx.doi.org/10.1787/9789264210745-en> accessed 5 April 2018.

37 Sabrina Tesoka, 'The Differential Impact of Judicial Politics in the Field of Gender Equality: Three National Cases Under Scrutiny' (1999) *European University Institute Working Paper* RSC 99/18, 14.

38 Recommendations to National Courts and Tribunals in Relation to the Initiation of Preliminary Ruling Proceedings [2016] OJ 439/01, 3.

the relevance of the question to be referred is also for the national court to determine, this means that if a national court is able to phrase a question which addresses or even acknowledges gendered considerations, the Court of Justice cannot deem the question irrelevant to the proceedings. It has also probably hitherto meant however that if the national court ignores gender issues, the Court of Justice will not write those issues in its judgement. This is because established case law has indicated that if the Court is not asked a precise and clearly phrased question concerning gender, it has no way of answering the question it might want to answer, at least not officially.

Remarkably, however, in some of the more recent case law[39] the Court has noted that since the procedure laid down by Article 267 TFEU provides for 'cooperation between national courts and the Court of Justice' and it is the Court's task to provide the national court with an answer which 'will be of use to it and enable it to determine the case before it',[40] the role of the Court has become perhaps much more enabling than in the past. This argument is supported by the fact that the Court has noted in recent decisions that, with its ability to answer the questions put forward by the national court in mind, 'the Court may, where necessary, have to reformulate the questions referred to it'.[41] Additionally, it has noted that it 'may decide to take into consideration rules of EU law to which the national court has made no reference in the wording of its question'.[42] This is good news for gender equality advocates since it is a far cry from the rather inflexible and somewhat arrogant approach which became apparent in *Foglia* where the Court noted that:

> The fact that it requires the Court of Justice to distinguish between fictitious and genuine actions, a problem of Byzantine complexity, the occasion of futile theoretical speculation and a source of legal uncertainty, all the more so as most of the cases which have hitherto been submitted to the Court have been not so much fictitious disputes as test cases.[43]

Jo Shaw has characterised the preliminary reference procedure as 'an organic connection' between the national courts and the Court of Justice,[44] and it has been said to be essential for the preservation of the Community character of the law because it has the object of ensuring that in all circumstances the law is the same

39 Case C-111/17 *PPU OL v PQ* [2017] EU:C:2017:436 (Mother's decision not to return to the Member State where the couple had been habitually resident).

40 ibid para 34. See also Case C-233/15 *SIA "Oniors Bio" v Valsts ieņēmumu dienests* [2016] EU:C:2016:305, para 30; Case C-303/15 *Naczelnik Urzędu Celnego I w Ł v GM and MS* [2016] EU:C:2016:771, para 16 (*GM and MS*).

41 ibid.

42 *GM and MS* (n 40) para 16; Case C-456/15 *BASF SE v Bundesrepublik Deutschland* [2016] EU:C:2016:567, para 15.

43 *Foglia* (n 8) para 3.

44 Jo Shaw, *Law of the European Union* (3rd edn, Palgrave Macmillan 2000).

in all Member States.[45] While this does mean that if the Court is, indeed, gender aware, this gender awareness will filter through to national courts in preliminary rulings and may therefore have an impact on the experience of claimants and ultimately the implementation of EU law at national level. It also means though that where individual judges or panels in national courts are not gender aware they may not realise the importance or relevance of particular provisions and may therefore not refer a question. As Tesoka noted in 1999:

> The judicial transformation of gender equality politics in a supranational direction is uneven, incremental and patchy. It is the locus of an ongoing interplay between favourable conditions and incentives for the expansion of judicial politics in the field of gender equality, on the one hand, and adverse impulses and conflicting structures, on the other.[46]

This has not changed in the nearly two decades since Tesoka made her arguments and is perhaps even more so the case in areas where the gender implications are less obvious and gendered consequences are unintended. It seems then that the way the majority of cases arrive at the Court presents somewhat of a lottery for a gender-aware conduct of the case. The parties are reliant on their lawyers – assuming they can access lawyers in the first place and their lawyers are willing and able to engage with both gender equality and with EU law. Additionally, the lawyers must be able to persuade the national court to make a reference to the Court of Justice and frame the reference in a way that allows, if not forces, a gendered consideration. Lastly, the litigants must hope that the Court does indeed take gender into consideration in their interpretation of the questions referred and the law relevant to those questions. Those are not great odds. However, the Court has been very influential in areas where gender obviously plays a key role, such as equality law and in some areas where gender is relevant but less obvious such as in EU citizenship rights and we return to those substantive law areas in Chapters 5, 6 and 7. This influence is not accidental or the result of a win in the case law lottery. Many of the judgements, which have significantly advanced women's rights, have been strategic litigations supported by interest groups or by particularly engaged lawyers. We turn to this next.

The importance of legal mobilisation

Lawyers have a tendency to focus on the purely legal issues – both in substance and procedure – when thinking about how law works and how cases are decided. This, however, ignores the realities of how cases come to be, make their way through national legal systems and find their way into the EU system. Cases

45 Case 166–73 *Rheinmühlen-Düsseldorf v Einfuhr- und Vorratsstelle für Getreide und Futtermittel* [1974] ECR 33.
46 Tesoka (n 37) 26.

do not just happen. There are thousands of disputes concerning potential legal matters with EU relevance, most of which never reach a courtroom and out of those that do reach the legal arena fewer still end up anywhere near the CJEU. Cichowski has written persuasively about legal mobilisation in the context of the CJEU,[47] and although we do not intend to go over the arguments in detail in this chapter, we think it is worth noting the importance of non-governmental organisations (NGOs), lobbying and interest groups as well as particularly engaged, and maybe ambitious, lawyers in the process.

One early example highlights the importance of activism in this context. We consider the series of cases in more detail in later chapters for their contribution to equality law. Here we are concerned with how those cases got to the Court of Justice. The series of cases brought by Gabrielle Defrenne was taken on and driven by Belgian lawyer, Eliane Vogel-Polsky, who had been looking for a test case to argue that what was then Article 119 EEC (now Article 157 TFEU) on equal pay should allow individuals to utilise the provision before national courts.[48] She said

> In 1967 I was still alone in believing in the direct application of this article. I'd written so many articles that I sent to all my European colleagues in the legal profession, but they just smiled and replied good-humouredly . . . I was seen as the duty feminist who was blinded by my feminism! I was furious.[49]

The literature suggests that Vogel-Polsky searched for a possible test case from the trade unions but found little success. She was looking for a case because

> by virtue of its dynamism, jurisprudence can lead to the harmonization of individual contracts and collective agreements with the principle of equal pay between male and female workers. To be successful, we need to hope that all workers that are the victim of pay discrimination are not afraid to go to court. They have this right; will they dare claim it?[50]

No cases were forthcoming until eventually Vogel-Polsky represented Gabrielle Defrenne. It is thanks to her that Article 119 EEC was held to be directly effective and that equal pay law took giant leaps forward across the EU. Without Vogel-Polsky's tenacity, legal acumen, experience of EU law and vision as to how EU law could be utilised as a tool, the entire *acquis communautaire*, the body of

47 Cichowski (n 4).

48 Catherine Hoskyns, *Integrating Gender: Women Law and Politics in the European Union* (Verso 1996). Treaty establishing the European Economic Community (Rome, 25 March 1957) (EEC Treaty); Treaty of the Functioning of the European Union [2012] OJ C 326/47 (TFEU).

49 Gubin (n 1) 73 citing Anonymous, 'Agir pour les droits des femmes: Entretien avec Éliane Vogel-Polsky' (2003) 10(2) *Raisons politiques* 139.

50 Gubin (n 1) 84 citing Éliane Vogel-Polsky, 'Le travail des femmes et l'arrêté royal n°40 du 24 octobre 1967' (1968) *Socialisme* 2, 11.

EU law, and not just gender equality law at EU level, could look very different today. In the *Defrenne* trilogy, Vogel-Polsky eventually got her test case.[51]

Lawyers have not diminished in importance when it comes to selecting cases and pushing them onto the EU stage. Lisa Vanhala has observed similar mobilisation in the context of disability rights.[52] We can also see mobilisation working in similar ways in other areas of EU law including in relation to the rights of lesbian, gay, bisexual, and transgender (LGBT)[53] persons which we discuss further in Chapter 6. The International Lesbian, Gay, Bisexual, Trans and Intersex Association[54] has been influential in lobbying for LGBT rights along with its many member organisations. One such organisation is the Austrian Rechtscommitte Lambda whose president is prominent gay rights lawyer Dr Helmut Graupner. The organisation specialises in litigating gay rights claims with several notable victories in Austrian courts, the European Court of Human Rights and the Court of Justice.[55] The influence of such organisations should not be underestimated, and it is worth remembering that many of the big (equality) cases might not have been heard without it.

Court of Justice procedure

Once a case reaches the Court of Justice, it is assigned one judge who acts as the 'judge-rapporteur' and one Advocate General (AG), if it is necessary to obtain an Opinion from the latter. Cases are processed in two stages which consist of the written stage and the public hearing.[56] During the written stage, the parties to the dispute provide written statements to the Court. Observations can also be submitted by national authorities, EU institutions and sometimes private individuals. The statements and observations of the interested parties are subsequently summarised by the judge-rapporteur and then discussed at the Court's general meeting during which the justices decide on the size of a chamber dealing with the case.

The usual composition of the chambers is three, five or 15 judges, the latter which essentially means the whole Court, depending on the importance and

51 Case C-80/70 *Defrenne v Belgian State* [1971] ECR 00445 (*Defrenne I*); Case C-43/75 *Defrenne v Sabena* [1976] ECR 00455 (*Defrenne II*); Case C-149/77 *Defrenne v Sabena* [1978] ECR 01365 (*Defrenne III*).

52 Lisa Vanhala, *Making Rights a Reality? Disability Rights Activists and Legal Mobilization* (Cambridge University Press 2010).

53 The acronym LGBT can be used for the entire same-sex oriented community. Other terms used in literature include LGBTI where the letter I stands for 'intersex' and LGBTQ where the letter Q stands for either 'queer' or 'questioning'.

54 ILGA, <https://ilga.org> accessed 9 April 2018.

55 For a list of the successes of Rechtscommitte Lambda by year, see <www.rklambda.at/index.php/de/groesste-erfolge> accessed 9 April 2018. For the purposes of this book, see Case C-267/06 *Tadao Maruko v Versorgungsanstalt der deutschen Bühnen* (2008) I-1757; Case C-147/08 *Jürgen Römer v Freie und Hansestadt Hamburg* [2011] ECR I-03591.

56 Europa, 'Court of Justice of the European Union (CJEU)' <https://europa.eu/european-union/about-eu/institutions-bodies/court-justice_en> accessed 27 November 2017.

complexity of the case. The composition of the chambers changes periodically and the presidency of the chambers rotates on an annual basis.[57] Most cases are dealt with by five judges, and it is very rare for the whole Court to hear a case. The general meeting of the Court also decides whether a hearing needs to be held and whether an official Opinion from an AG is necessary. Laure Clément-Wilz has argued that the Opinions of the AGs have contributed to improving the coherence of legislation and case law.[58] Although the Treaty and the procedures of the Court firmly place the AGs at the same time within the Court, they are still outside the Court because the justices do not have to follow their Opinions and not every case will have a pre-judgement Opinion.

During the public hearing, lawyers from both parties to the dispute are able to put their case to the judges and AG, who can ask questions addressed to the lawyers. If the Court has decided that an Opinion of the AG is necessary, this will be delivered some weeks after the hearing. However, the justices take longer to deliver their judgement, and their verdict can follow anything up seven months on average after the Opinion of the AG. For instance, the French AG Yves Bot delivered his Opinion in *Lounes*,[59] which concerned the right of an Algerian national husband of a dual English and Spanish citizen to reside in the United Kingdom (UK) under EU law on 30 May 2017, whereas the justices took their time to deliberate their case and provided their verdict on 14 November 2017.[60] Angela Zhang has argued that since the AG alongside the judge acting as the rapporteur in a given case assumes most of the drafting responsibilities they will be most closely involved in the case.[61] Consequently, they also gain the 'first mover advantage' in influencing other judges on the chamber in terms of the conclusions on how the case will be decided.[62]

A distinctive feature of the decisions delivered by the CJEU as opposed to, for instance, the Member State courts, such as those in the UK, is that the CJEU are not required to provide an exhaustive account of the parties' arguments in their judgements. Hence, the way in which the Court reaches its conclusion in disputes before it is often unclear. In the appeal case seeking the annulment of the General Court's judgement in *ITK*,[63] the Court of Justice noted that the way in which the conclusion was reached did not matter, at least to the parties to the dispute anyway. It specifically referred to the decision by

57 Zhang (n 2) 78.

58 Laure Clément-Wilz, 'The Advocate General: A Key Actor of the Court of Justice of the European Union' (2012) 14 *Cambridge Yearbook of European Legal Studies* 587 doi:10.1017/S1528887000002391

59 Case C-165/16 *Toufik Lounes v Secretary of State for the Home Department* [2017] EU:C:2017:407, Opinion of AG Bot.

60 Case C-165/16 *Toufik Lounes v Secretary of State for the Home Department* [2017] EU:C:2017:862.

61 Zhang (n 2) 79.

62 Ibid.

63 Case C-583/11 *P Inuit Tapiriit Kanatami v Parliament and Council* [2013] EU:C:2013:625 (*ITK*).

the General Court which was criticised by the appellants on the grounds that the General Court did not state reasons concerning its interpretation of Article 263(4) TFEU in the light of the Charter of Fundamental Rights[64] and the European Convention on Human Rights,[65] whereas the appellants argued that the General Court had an obligation to do so.[66] The Court of Justice merely noted that the General Court 'was not required to provide an account which follows exhaustively all the arguments' raised, but that the reasoning could be implicit, provided that it 'enables the parties to know why the measures in question were taken and provides the competent court with sufficient material for it to exercise its power of review'.[67] Therefore, it was sufficient for the General Court to state that it would exceed its jurisdiction, if it interpreted Article 263(4) TFEU 'in a way which has the effect of setting aside the conditions . . . expressly laid down by the Treaty', even if this meant that, in the light of the principle of effective judicial protection, the outcome would have otherwise been different.[68] However, clearly, the General Court could not overstep its jurisdiction under the Treaties.

In addition to there being no requirement to set out extensive reasoning, the Court delivers only one judgement with no dissents being permitted.[69] The Court follows the French tradition of issuing 'a single, collective, and unanimous judgement without dissents' and the resulting 'obscurity' of its judgements is perpetuated by the requirement that the Court's judges are prohibited from revealing how the Court reached its decision in a particular case.[70] Furthermore, judges are bound by Article 2 of the Statute of the Court[71] which stipulates: 'Before taking up his duties each Judge shall, before the Court of Justice sitting in open court, take an oath to perform his duties impartially and conscientiously and to preserve the secrecy of the deliberations of the Court.' The deliberations in the courts making up the CJEU are therefore secret. Another overwhelming challenge in understanding the working of the Court is the secrecy of the decision-makers themselves.[72] While judges' profiles are disclosed by the Court, no information can be found publicly about the over 200 law clerks working for the Court. However, Zhang conducted interviews with the justices of the Court and found out information about their role within the Court as well as their linguistic, educational and professional background. She has argued that,

64 Charter of Fundamental Rights of the European Union in Nice [2000] OJ C364/1 (the Charter).
65 European Convention for the Protection of Human Rights and Fundamental Freedoms, signed in Rome on 4 November 1950 (European Convention of Human Rights, amended) (ECHR).
66 *ITK* (n 63) para 85.
67 ibid para 82.
68 ibid.
69 Zhang (n 2) 79. See also David Edward, 'How the Court of Justice Works' (1995) 20 *European Law Review* 539, 555–557.
70 Zhang (n 2) 75.
71 Statute of the Court of Justice of the European Union [2012] OJ C326/201.
72 Zhang (n 2) 75.

although the clerks play an important, and sometimes even crucial, role in the decision-making process of the Court,[73] they are barred from participating in the process under the Court's rules of the procedure.[74] Hence, the parties, their lawyers, the general public and we as researchers are not privy to the discussions, debates, considerations, arguments and possibly rows which ultimately form the final decision. Because of the secrecy we cannot know the compromises made or the power dynamics in the room as the deliberations take place. We do not know the extent to which the process is collegiate or confrontational, we cannot know the extent to which some judges acquiesce even while disagreeing or how different personalities play out. We therefore cannot know the impact gender has in the forming of individual judgements but we can, based on some of the work outlined above and in Chapter 3, suggest that there is an impact.

One example where a different way of working might help highlight gendered issues is if the CJEU allowed dissenting judgements, even anonymous dissenting judgements, to highlight where there have been disagreements, alternative interpretations of facts or law and different ways of approaching the question raised. As we argued in Chapter 3, this would strengthen rather than weaken the CJEU's legitimacy and could go some way to highlight that the Court is, at least to a certain extent, not gender blind. Dissents can be powerful and can help advocates and lobbyists build arguments which can, over time, have a significant impact on the development of the law.[75]

The CJEU has been subject to criticisms for its practice of issuing a single judgement without dissenting judgements.[76] While the practice of issuing a single judgement is common in civil law countries, the CJEU is the only court among supranational and international courts and the majority of national supreme courts and constitutional courts in Europe in prohibiting the publication of separate opinions.[77] A 2012 report by the Commission noted that only seven out of the current Member States do not allow the publication of dissenting opinions.[78] The main arguments in favour of separate opinions include, *inter alia*, preserving the judges' integrity and moral independence and their freedom

73 ibid.

74 Rules of Procedure of the Court of Justice [2012] OJ L265/1, as amended, art 32.

75 Although a detailed examination of the role of dissenting judgements in legal developments is beyond the scope of this chapter, see, eg, Robert H George, 'In Defence of Dissent: R (McDonald) v Royal Borough of Kensington and Chelsea' (2011) *Family Law Journal* 1097; Melvyn Urofsky, *Dissent and the Supreme Court: Its Role in the Court's History and the Nation's Constitutional Dialogue* (Knopf Doubleday 2015); John Alder, 'Dissents in Courts of Last Resort: Tragic Choices?' (2000) 20(1) *Oxford Journal of Legal Studies* 221 doi:10.1093/ojls/20.2.221

76 Zhang (n 2) 108. See also Henry Schermers and Denis Waelbroeck, *Judicial Protection in the European Union* (6th edn, Kluwer 2001) 736 (showing the different arguments utilised to support the use of dissenting and concurring opinions).

77 Vlad Perju, 'Reason and Authority in the European Court of Justice' (2009) 49 *Virginia Journal of International Law* 307, 309. See also Zhang (n 2) 108.

78 Rosa Raffaelli, 'Dissenting Opinion in the Supreme Court of the Member States' (European Union 2012) 7 <www.europarl.europa.eu/document/activities/cont/201304/20130423ATT64963/20130423ATT64963EN.pdf> accessed 12 December 2017.

of speech; improving the quality of judgements and their persuasiveness; promoting transparency; and improving dialogue with future and lower courts.[79]

One powerful argument in favour of permitting the publication of individual opinions is, indeed, that dissents can 'play an essential role in the future development of the law' and, in some cases, they may eventually become the majority opinion, or influence it.[80] While most dissenting opinions may never find their way into a subsequent final judgement, they 'can play a positive role even in such a case, since they ensure that the decision-making process does not become rigid by infusing different ideas and methods into it and by pointing to the existence of alternatives'.[81] The function of dissenting judgements is particularly valuable because they guarantee that the decision-making process leads the judges to take the most convincing decision, rather than the 'one where old decisions are confirmed without paying much attention to their rationale and persuasiveness'.[82] Thus, dissents ensure that judgements are periodically reviewed and deal with the same issues of law in a new way where different interpretations might be warranted.[83] Hence, it is possible to argue that were the Court permit the publication of individual opinions of its judges, which take into account gender of the applicant, this could well influence future decisions of the Court as a whole. Thus, if the justices were to deal with cases where the gender of the applicant was of relevance, the judges may actually become more gender aware.

In their current form the judgements do not reveal which one of the judges thought what and why. Zhang has criticised the outcome of Court's judgements in the absence of dissenting opinions by observing that a single judgement 'inevitably tends to blur distinctions and resorts to qualifications, reducing the clarity of the judgement. Sometimes ambiguity and unequivocal language are used to cloak disagreement.'[84]

This is in contrast to, for instance, the UK Supreme Court where some suggestions about the influence of Lady Hale, who up until October 2017 was the only female judge at that level, can be made based on analysis of her dissenting judgements as well as by reading her judgements together with those of her colleagues in the same cases.[85] However, due to the lack of possibility to identify which of the Court's justices said what in the decisions of the Court of Justice it is not possible to conduct an analysis of similar quality in the CJEU. We can begin to draw some comparisons between judgements and AG Opinions which do tell

79 ibid 7.
80 ibid 15.
81 William J Brennan, 'In Defense of Dissent' (1986) 37 *Hastings Law Journal* 427, 437.
82 Raffaelli (n 78) 15.
83 ibid.
84 Zhang (n 2) 112.
85 Lady Hale was sworn-in officially as the President of the UK Supreme Court on 2 October 2017. At the same time, the appointment of another female judge, Lady Justice Black, was made to the UK Supreme Court. See Supreme Court, 'Lady Hale Appointed Next President of Supreme Court, Alongside Three New Justices' (21 July 2017) <www.supremecourt.uk/news/lady-hale-appointed-next-president-of-supreme-court-alongside-three-new-justices.html> accessed 21 July 2017.

us something. Even though AGs do not participate in the deliberation of cases, their role is 'a quasi-decision-maker'[86] since their position is similar to judges as they are officially members of the Court and enjoy status equal to judges.[87] As stipulated by Article 252 TFEU, the role of the AGs is 'acting with complete impartiality and independence, to make, in open court, reasoned submissions on cases which, in accordance with the Statute of the Court of Justice of the European Union, require. . . [their][88] involvement'. However, given the general lack of women on the Court, it is impossible to distil the impact the gender of the AG might have had on their opinion.

Comparative law or politics of judging?

It is worth remembering that the Court does not make its decisions in a vacuum or legal bubble. It is not isolated from political events in the EU or from the mood of the general public, national government or indeed other institutions. The political climate must and does have some bearing on the judges. This awareness of politics can be couched in purely legal terms of course. The European Court of Human Rights jurisprudence refers to the State Parties' margin of appreciation for example. The CJEU instead refers to the common legal traditions of the EU Member States. The current president of the Court of Justice, Koen Lenaerts of Belgium, argued in 2003 that '[e]ach time the Court of Justice is asked to rule on the compatibility of a provision or "solution" of national law with the Community legal order, it will adopt a comparative approach' which means that it looks at the specific legal order and its respective priorities and requirements.[89] According to him, when looking for the interpretation of a given concept which suits best the interests of the EU legal order the CJEU frequently compares the national legal systems.[90] After ensuring that the chosen interpretation is unlikely to meet serious opposition by Member States unfamiliar with such interpretation, the Court is not hesitant to 'import' this interpretation in EU law.[91] Taking into account the observations made by the Member States and the Commission, the Court 'gauge[s] the temperature' of the national legal systems in order to ascertain the credibility and 'acceptability' of its decision for the whole of the EU.[92] Through a comparative analysis the CJEU can either confirm the compatibility of

86 Zhang (n 2) 77.

87 Court of Justice of the European Union, *Annual Report 2014* (European Union 2015) 67–89. See also Zhang (n 2) 77.

88 The original provision states 'his'. However, considering the subject matter of the book, we found the use of gendered language highly inappropriate as the default position of the drafters appears to suggest that the AGs of the Court are men.

89 Koen Lenaerts, 'Interlocking Legal Orders in the European Union and Comparative Law' (2003) 52 *International and Comparative Law Quarterly* 873, 898.

90 ibid 897.

91 ibid.

92 ibid 898.

the national provision with EU law, set aside a rule of national law which is considered to be incompatible with the requirements of EU law, or take note of the choice made by the national legal system concerned and confront the latter with the consequences of this choice as regards the EU legal order. While Lenaerts make this process sound very legal, it is actually political. When taking the temperature of a national legal system, the Court also gauges the political willingness to accept its approach and decision. We can see how this plays out very obviously in cases surrounding sexual-orientation discrimination and perhaps also religious discrimination, which we examine in more detail in Chapter 6. In addition, this sort of approach has arguably led to a particular conceptualisation of women in the EU which characterises them as mothers and carers while at the same time privileging market citizenship. We return to this issue in Chapter 7.

The General Court and direct actions

Clifford Carrubba and his colleagues have argued that the CJEU are fairly unusual for an international regulatory regime, considering that most international regimes hear only cases brought by Member States against one another.[93] In contrast, in the EU, a variety of parties can challenge EU law and Member State compliance with the law before the CJEU.[94] Whereas the Commission is the primary source of direct actions against the EU Member States, Member States and private applicants can bring actions for annulment and actions for inactivity against the acts of EU institutions, or absence thereof.[95] Consequently, the Court has the opportunity to rule on a large number of cases where the Member State compliance and the interpretation of EU law are in question.[96] Direct actions by private applicants (ie companies, NGOs and individuals) can only be brought to the Court in cases where these applicants fulfil the strict standing requirements under Article 263 TFEU. The lack of adequate access to justice for private applicants directly before the Court has been an issue surrounding the CJEU for some decades. Commentators have criticised the Court for denying private applicants legal protection due to the strict application of the legal test[97] governing legal challenges against the acts of institutions.[98] Despite criticism, the Court has maintained the same approach for over five decades. It was anticipated that the standing rules would be relaxed

93 Clifford Carrubba, Matthew Gabel, and Charles Hankla, 'Judicial Behavior Under Political Constraints: Evidence from the European Court of Justice' (2008) 102(4) *American Political Science Review* 435, 437 doi:10.1017/S0003055408080350
94 ibid 437.
95 ibid.
96 ibid.
97 The test was initially established in the Court's 1963 decision in Case 25/62 *Plaumann and Co v Commission* [1963] ECR 95.
98 See eg Case C-50/00 P *Unión de Pequeños Agricultores v Council* [2002] ECR 1-6677 (*UPA*), Opinion of AG Jacobs. Under art 252 TFEU, the role of the AGs is to propose to the Court of Justice, in complete independence, a legal solution to the cases for which they are responsible. However, their Opinions are non-binding on the Court. See also Mariolina

by the Treaty of Lisbon. However, although the Treaty revision changed the rules slightly, this has not benefited most applicants. Due to the restrictive standing rules, direct actions have created very little case law which has contributed to development of a growing body of rights protecting women throughout Europe.

The preliminary reference procedure discussed above has been far more prolific in this area. Therefore, the importance of direct actions for gender equality remains minimal because most private applicants, who are natural persons, are unable to fulfil the standing rules. Although Cichowski has argued that 'women, as legal experts, group activists, and individual litigants' who may otherwise be excluded from EU policy making, have made a use of the preliminary reference procedure to achieve significant policy reform and inclusion and that the Court's jurisprudence has shifted the distribution of gains away from dominant political interests, such as the business community, to less powerful individuals,[99] the same cannot be said for direct actions. In conclusion, not very much has changed in this area since the Court's 1963 decision in *Plaumann*.[100]

Very briefly, the standing rules are as follows. Under Article 263 TFEU the CJEU has jurisdiction to review the legality of acts of the institutions. Because the institutions are privileged or semi-privileged applicants, generally their *locus standi* is not controversial. Natural or legal persons are, however, more complicated and can challenge any acts 'addressed directly to them', an act addressed to another person which is of 'direct and individual concern' to the applicant, or a regulatory act which is 'direct concern to the applicant' and which 'does not entail implementing measures'. The concept of 'direct concern' relates to being able to show an unbroken line establishing causation between the EU measures and any damage suffered. The concept of 'individual concern' relates to the applicant being affected 'by reason of certain attributes which are peculiar to them or by reasons of circumstances in which they are differentiated from all other persons' as set out in *Plaumann*.[101] This has been interpreted strictly ever since and, in fact, the Court of Justice rejected a less restrictive test in *UPA*[102] and in *Jego-Quere*.[103] Once standing has been established – which is near to impossible for natural or legal persons – an EU measure can be annulled because of lack of

---

Eliantonio and Nelly Stratieva, 'From Plaumann, Through UPA and Jégo-Quéré, to the Lisbon Treaty: The locus standi of Private Applicants Under Article 230(4) EC Through a Political Lens' (2009) *Maastricht Working Papers Faculty of Law* 2009/13; Mariolina Eliantonio and Betül Kas, 'Private Parties and the Annulment Procedure: Can The gap in the European System of Judicial Protection Be Closed?'(2010) 3(2) *Journal of Politics and Law* 121; Steve Peers and Mario Costa, 'Judicial Review of EU Acts After the Treaty of Lisbon' (2012) 8(1) *EuConst* 82. See also Treaty of Lisbon Amending the Treaty on European Union and the Treaty Establishing the European Community [2007] OJ C306/01.

99 ibid.

100 *Plaumann* (n 97).

101 ibid 107.

102 Case C-50/00 P *Unión de Pequeños Agricultores v Council* [2002] ECR I-06677 (*UPA*).

103 Case C-263/02 P *Commission v Jégo-Quéré* [2004] ECR I-3425, para 36.

competence, the infringement of an essential procedural requirement or of the Treaty or any rule relating to its application or the misuse of powers.

The 2013 decision in *ITK*[104] is a prime example of how little has changed in the area of private litigation against the EU institutions with the amendment of the Treaty in 2009. In her Opinion, the German AG Julianne Kokott indicated that the absence of easier direct legal remedies available to individuals against legislative acts adopted by the EU institutions could be explained principally by the 'particularly high democratic legitimation of parliamentary legislation'.[105] She noted that similarly in many national legal systems in Europe individuals had either limited direct legal remedies, or no remedies at all, against parliamentary laws.[106] She also observed that the General Court had failed to acknowledge that there was one female applicant amongst the Inuit applicants, Ms Karliin Aariak, who herself both processed and placed products containing seal fur on the EU market.[107] It appears that Ms Aariak fulfilled the requirements of less stringent standing rules under Article 263(4) TFEU:

> If it is assumed, however, as the General Court seems to have in mind, that Ms Aariak actually places seal products on the European internal market herself, (49) it can hardly be denied that the contested regulation is of direct concern to her. Ms Aariak's business activity is then directly subject to the rules concerning the placing on the market of seal products established by Regulation No 1007/2009.[108]

Indeed, according to AG Kokott, the fact that the Commission had made the Regulation subject to implementing measures, which had not yet been adopted at the time of the Opinion, was not relevant. Therefore, she noted that Ms Aariak was directly concerned,[109] whereas the General Court had rejected direct concern in her case because she did not 'claim to be active in the placing on the market of products other than those covered by the [Inuit] exception'.[110]

However, AG Kokott did not consider that the error made by the General Court was significant enough to set aside the General Court's whole judgement. Therefore, it appears that the existence of one female applicant, who fulfilled the *locus standi* rules under Article 263, was wholly irrelevant. In other words, Ms Aarik's small-scale business activity of 'the design and sale of sealskin garments'[111] from which she made living was entirely insignificant, as was the fact

104 *ITK* (n 63).
105 Case C-583/11 P *Inuit Tapiriit Kanatami and Others v Parliament and Council* [2013] EU:C:2013:21, Opinion of AG Kokott, para 38.
106 ibid.
107 ibid paras 76–84.
108 *ITK v Parliament and Council*, Opinion of AG Kokott (n 105) para 79.
109 ibid para 80.
110 ibid para 76.
111 ibid para 76.

that she was an indigenous woman. Although AG Kokott noted that Ms Aariak 'herself belongs to the Inuit community',[112] the Court's subsequent decision was gender blind, and we may argue that the fact that Ms Aariak was directly concerned by the EU legislation made absolutely zero difference in the end. This is despite the fact that the whole case revolved around the alleged impractical nature of the specific exemption for the placing on the EU's internal market of seal products which originate 'from hunts traditionally conducted by Inuit and other indigenous communities and contribute to their subsistence' in the contested EU Regulation.[113] Hence, the EU's outwardly inclusive approach in providing an exemption for indigenous peoples but narrow interpretation making that exemption fairly meaningless in practice tells us very much, not only about the Court's decision processes and priorities in terms of direct actions, but also the Court's dismissive approach towards small-scale female entrepreneurs who also happen to be indigenous. Although it should not come as a surprise to anyone that there are plenty of companies which are owned by women and by non-white, non-heterosexual entrepreneurs, who 'do not compete in the market as the canons of the for-profit enterprise dictate',[114] research has shown that an entrepreneur is usually considered to be a man.[115] Additionally, there is evidence that the woman's role and competence in her work domain is easily questioned.[116]

The decisions by the Court in Ms Aariak's case also highlight the Court's and, more generally, the European legislators' unfamiliarity concerning the individual circumstances of this particular indigenous female applicant. By ignoring her gender and her indigeneity the Court maintains deeply rooted hierarchies, societal norms and practices within which inequalities are embedded and which systematically discriminate women because of the intersections between inequalities such as race and gender.[117] In fact, the tradition of intersectionality, which is mentioned elsewhere in this book, is rooted in the history of Black feminist writing, indigenous feminism, queer theory as well as postcolonial theory.[118] Because not all women share similar experiences, visions, locations and cultural, linguistic and social needs,[119] we cannot argue that our interpretation that EU law

112 ibid.

113 Regulation (EC) No 1007/2009 of the European Parliament and of the Council of 16 September 2009 on trade in seal products [2009] OJ L286/36, art 3(1).

114 Attila Bruni, Silvia Gherardi, and Barbara Poggio, 'Entrepreneur-Mentality, Gender and the Study of Women Entrepreneurs' (2004) 17(3) *Journal of Organizational Change Management* 256, 261.

115 ibid 257.

116 Suvi Välimäki, Anna-Maija Lämsä, and Minna Hiillos, 'The Spouse of the Female Manager: Role and Influence on the Woman's Career' (2009) 24(8) *Gender in Management: An International Journal* 596, 597 doi:10.1108/17542410911004867.

117 Petra Debusscher, 'Analysing European Gender Equality Policies Abroad: A Reflection on Methodology' (2016) 23(3) *European Journal of Women's Studies* 265, 267.

118 Gemma Hunting, Simon Fraser, Daniel Grace, and Olena Hankivsky, 'Taking Action on Stigma and Discrimination: An Intersectionality-Informed Model of Social Inclusion and Exclusion' (2015) 4(2) *Intersectionalities* 101, 103.

119 Myrna Cunningham, 'Indigenous Women's Visions of an Inclusive Feminism' (2006) 49(1) *Development* 55, 57.

limited Ms Aariak's access to the enjoyment of her rights as a result of a number of factors, such as race, indigeneity and gender, is necessarily correct, or the only one. Since indigenous women can draw from a model of gender justice, egalitarian ethic, which contains an idea that indigenous women's struggles are against the patriarchal systems, which grew out of colonialism,[120] we can argue that the 'indigenous exemption' in the contested EU Regulation is entirely meaningless for Ms Aarik, who is unable to benefit from that exemption – despite fulfilling its conditions. Even though the Court may have not meant its decision to be dismissive and belittling of Ms Aarik, the decision sends a loud and clear message that only those applicants who have significant business interests, which have been affected by the contested legislation, can contest the acts of EU institutions. Others, especially small-scale entrepreneurs, should not bother.

In its decision the Court of Justice deliberated the role of the newly established legal status of the Charter of Fundamental Rights, and specifically whether the provisions of the Charter could be seen to create new rights for private applicants. Article 47 of the Charter, which was invoked by the Inuit applicants, stipulates that:

> Everyone whose rights and freedoms guaranteed by the law of the Union are violated has the right to an effective remedy before a tribunal in compliance with the conditions laid down in this Article. Everyone is entitled to a fair and public hearing within a reasonable time by an independent and impartial tribunal previously established by law.

The Court noted that, as established in case law, and reaffirmed in Article 19(1) TEU, it was the Member States' responsibility 'to establish a system of legal remedies and procedures which ensure respect for the fundamental right to effective judicial protection'.[121] This was because 'the national courts and tribunals, in collaboration with the Court of Justice, fulfil a duty entrusted to them both of ensuring that in the interpretation and application of the Treaties the law is observed'.[122] However, according to the Court, neither Article 47 of the Charter nor Article 19(1) TEU required that an individual should be entitled to bring actions against EU acts, as their primary subject matter, before the national courts or tribunals.[123] Further, the protection conferred by Article 47 of the Charter did 'not require that an individual should have an unconditional entitlement to bring an action for annulment' directly before the Court of Justice.[124] Referring to the highly criticised decisions in *UPA*[125] and *Jégo-Quéré*, the Court noted that although the conditions of admissibility under Article 263(4) TFEU had to be interpreted in the light of the fundamental right to effective

120 ibid.
121 *ITK* (n 63) paras 99–101. See also Treaty on European Union [2012] OJ C326/13 (TEU), art 19(2).
122 *ITK* (n 63) paras 99–101.
123 ibid para 105.
124 ibid.
125 *UPA* (n 102).

judicial protection, such an interpretation could not have the effect of setting aside the conditions expressly laid down in the Treaty.[126] Further, the protection conferred by Article 47 of the Charter was not intended to change the system of judicial review established by the Treaties, specifically under Article 263(4) TFEU.[127] The implication of *ITK* is that how the adequate protection of the applicants in question is to be implemented depends on the Member States since the Court does not have the jurisdiction to amend the standing rules under Article 263(4) TFEU.

The rules on standing appear gender blind but precisely because they are gender blind there is a real risk that they will be interpreted based on stereotypes and assumptions and without taking into consideration the lived experience of women, particularly minority women. If direct actions which concern issues which might have gendered impacts cannot even make it to the Court for a full consideration then there is little hope that even a gender-aware court could make a difference in those areas. Much is therefore being left to Member States in these cases.

Conclusion

This chapter has outlined some of the issues arising from the way in which the Court works. Our focus has been on the preliminary reference procedure as this is the process most likely to impact on EU citizens in the enforcement of their rights. In some ways the odds are stacked against gendered questions being addressed by the Court. There are opportunities for gender to be written in or kept out of the cases and much depends on the parties, or rather their legal teams, and the referring courts. Whether or not the way the Court works impacts differently on men and women therefore depends very much on the personalities involved in each case, the parties, the lawyers, the referring court and the CJEU personnel. However, there are some issues which could be addressed to help. For instance, the use of clearer reasoning and the allowing of dissenting opinions might make the decisions of the Court more transparent as well as allowing for more detailed research into the impact of gender. Further, allowing the Court of Justice to reformulate the questions referred to it would also allow it to write gender into cases where it has not been included in the reference. However, this would, of course, also allow the Court to ignore gendered questions even where they have been specifically asked where it considers them irrelevant. We are therefore back to the importance of who our judges are which we outlined in Chapter 3.

126 *ITK* (n 63) para 98.

127 This was apparent from the Explanation on Charter Article 47, which must, in accordance with art 6(1), (3) TEU and Charter art 52(7), be taken into consideration for the interpretation of the Charter. *ITK* (n 63) para 97.

Bibliography

Alder J, 'Dissents in Courts of Last Resort: Tragic Choices?' (2000) 20(1) *Oxford Journal of Legal Studies* 221 doi:10.1093/ojls/20.2.221

Amendment of the Rules of Procedure of the Court of 15 January 2008 [2008] OJ L24/39

Brennan WJ, 'In Defense of Dissent' (1986) 37 *Hastings Law Journal* 427

Bruni A, Gherardi S and Poggio B, 'Entrepreneur-mentality, Gender and the Study of Women Entrepreneurs' (2004) 17(3) *Journal of Organizational Change Management* 256

Carrubba C, Gabel M and Hankla C, 'Judicial Behavior Under Political Constraints: Evidence from the European Court of Justice' (2008) 102(4) *American Political Science Review* 435, 437 doi:10.1017/S0003055408080350

Charter of Fundamental Rights of the European Union in Nice [2000] OJ C364/1

Cichowski RA, 'Women's Rights, the European Court, and Supranational Constitutionalism' (1995) 38 *Law and Society Review* 489–491 doi:10.1111/j.0023-9216.2004.00055

Clément-Wilz L, 'The Advocate General: A Key Actor of the Court of Justice of the European Union' (2012) 14 *Cambridge Yearbook of European Legal Studies* 587 doi:10.1017/S1528887000002391

Council Decision of 20 December 2007 Amending the Protocol on the Statute of the Court of Justice [2008] OJ L24/42

Cunningham M, 'Indigenous Women's Visions of an Inclusive Feminism' (2006) 49(1) *Development* 55

De Baere G and Gutman K, 'The Impact of the European Union and the European Court of Justice on European Family Law' (2015) 1 *European Family Law* 5

Debusscher P, 'Analysing European Gender Equality Policies Abroad: A Reflection on Methodology' (2016) 23(3) *European Journal of Women's Studies* 265

Dutta A and Schulz A, 'First Cornerstones of the EU Rules on Cross-Border Child Cases: The Jurisprudence of the Court of Justice of the European Union on the Brussels IIa Regulation from C to Health Service Executive' (2014) 10(1) *Journal of Private International Law* 1 doi:10.5235/17441048.10.1.1

Edward D, 'How the Court of Justice Works' (1995) 20 *European Law Review* 539

Eliantonio M and Kas B, 'Private Parties and the Annulment Procedure: Can the Gap in the European System of Judicial Protection Be Closed?' (2010) 3(2) *Journal of Politics and Law* 121

Eliantonio M and Stratieva N, 'From Plaumann, Through UPA and Jégo-Quéré, to the Lisbon Treaty: The locus standi of Private Applicants Under Article 230(4) EC Through a Political Lens' (December 2009) *Maastricht Working Papers Faculty of Law* 2009/13

Europa, 'Court of Justice of the European Union (CJEU)' <https://europa.eu/european-union/about-eu/institutions-bodies/court-justice_en> accessed 27 November 2017

European Convention for the Protection of Human Rights and Fundamental Freedoms, signed in Rome on 4 November 1950 (European Convention of Human Rights, amended)

George RH, 'In Defence of Dissent: R (McDonald) v Royal Borough of Kensington and Chelsea' (2011) *Family Law Journal* 1097

Gubin E, *A Woman of Conviction: Eliane Vogel-Polsky* (Institute for the Equality of Women and Men 2008) (with Catherine Jacques)

Guth J, 'Transforming the European Legal Order: The European Court of Justice at 60+' (2016) 12(1) *Journal of Contemporary European Research* 455

Higgins A, 'The Costs of Civil Justice and Who Pays?' (2017) 37(3) *Oxford Journal of Legal Studies* 687

Hitchings E, 'Official, Operative and Outsider Justice: The Ties That (May Not) Bind in Family Financial Disputes' (2017) *Child and Family Law Quarterly* 359

Hoskyns C, *Integrating Gender: Women Law and Politics in the European Union* (Verso 1996)

Hunter R, 'More Than Just a Different Face? Judicial Diversity and Decision-making' (2015) *Current Legal Problems* 1

Hunting G, Fraser S, Grace D and Hankivsky O, 'Taking Action on Stigma and Discrimination: An Intersectionality-Informed Model of Social Inclusion and Exclusion' (2015) 4(2) *Intersectionalities* 101

Lenaerts K, 'Interlocking Legal Orders in the European Union and Comparative Law' (2003) 52 *International and Comparative Law Quarterly* 873

McGregor L, 'Alternative Dispute Resolution and Human Rights: Developing a Rights-Based Approach Through the ECHR' (2015) 26(3) *European Journal of International Law* 607

Nash R, 'Financing Access to Justice: Innovating Possibilities to Promote Access for All' (2013) 5 *Hague Journal on the Rule of Law* 96

OECD, *Women, Government and Policy Making in OECD Countries: Fostering Diversity for Inclusive Growth* (OECD Publishing 2014) doi:10.1787/9789264210745-en

Peers S and Costa M, 'Judicial Review of EU Acts After the Treaty of Lisbon' (2012) 8(1) *EuConst* 82

Perju V, 'Reason and Authority in the European Court of Justice' (2009) 49 *Virginia Journal of International Law* 307

Raffaelli R, 'Dissenting Opinion in the Supreme Court of the Member States' (2012) *European Union* 7 <www.europarl.europa.eu/document/activities/cont/201304/20130423ATT64963/20130423ATT64963ENpdf> accessed 12 December 2017

Rechtscommitte Lambda, Größte Erfolge <www.rklambda.at/index.php/de/groesste-erfolge> accessed 9 April 2018

Recommendations to National Courts and Tribunals in Relation to the Initiation of Preliminary Ruling Proceedings [2016] OJ 439/01

Regulation (EC) No 1007/2009 of the European Parliament and of the Council of 16 September 2009 on Trade in Seal Products [2009] OJ L286/36

Rules of Procedure of the Court of 19 June 1991 [1991] OJ L176/7, as amended

Rules of Procedure of the Court of Justice [2012] OJ L265/1, as amended

Schermers H and Waelbroeck D, *Judicial Protection in the European Union* (6th edn, Kluwer 2001)

Shaw J, *Law of the European Union* (3rd edn, Palgrave 2000)

Statute of the Court of Justice of the European Union [2012] OJ C326/201

Supreme Court, 'Lady Hale Appointed Next President of Supreme Court, Alongside Three New Justices' (21 July 2017) <www.supremecourt.uk/news/lady-hale-appointed-next-president-of-supreme-court-alongside-three-new-justices.html> accessed 21 July 2017

Tesoka S, 'The Differential Impact of Judicial Politics in the Field of Gender Equality: Three National Cases Under Scrutiny' (1999) *European University Institute Working Paper* RSC 99/18

Treaty of Lisbon Amending the Treaty on European Union and the Treaty Establishing the European Community [2007] OJ C306/01

Treaty on European Union [2012] OJ C326/13

Treaty on the Functioning of the European Union [2008] OJ C115/47

Urofsky M, *Dissent and the Supreme Court: Its Role in the Court's History and the Nation's Constitutional Dialogue* (Knopf Doubleday 2015)

Välimäki S, Lämsä A-M and Hiillos M, 'The Spouse of the Female Manager: Role and Influence on the Woman's Career' (2009) 24(8) *Gender in Management: An International Journal* 596 doi:10.1108/17542410911004867

Vanhala L, *Making Rights a Reality? Disability Rights Activists and Legal Mobilization* (Cambridge University Press 2010)

Zhang AH, 'The Faceless Court' (2016) 38 *University of Pennsylvania Journal of International Law* 71

5 Gendering EU gender equality case law

> Gender equality law has played a pivotal – in many respects pioneer – role in the field of enforcement of Community law in general and in particular for the protection of rights, which individuals derive from that law.[1]

The manner in which equality between women and men entered the European agenda in 1957, when equal pay was included in Article 119 of the Treaty establishing the European Economic Community (EEC),[2] is indicative of the economic rationale that has guided of the European Union (EU) gender equality policies.[3] The French government, which had already introduced legislation on equal pay, was afraid that countries using low-wage female labour might undermine the competitiveness of French industry.[4] Gender equality has come a long way since the signing of the EEC Treaty in 1957. It is no longer a factor that harmonised conditions on the common market, but a fundamental right enshrined in the Treaties. Additionally, the scope of the EU's gender equality policies has extended from the sphere of employment to issues covering reconciliation of work and family life as well as violence against women.[5] We argue that gender equality has been pivotal in the development of EU law in that 'sex equality law was part of Community Law from the very beginning'.[6] This chapter begins with

1 Sacha Prechal, 'Achievements and Trends in EU Gender Equality Law' (2005) 35 <www.euroinfo.ee/malta/pdf/c4.pdf> accessed 12 December 2017. Sacha Prechal has been a judge at the Court of Justice of the European Union since 2010.

2 Treaty establishing the European Economic Community (Rome, 25 March 1957) (Treaty of Rome).

3 Anna Elomäki, 'The Economic Case for Gender Equality in the European Union: Selling Gender Equality to Decision-makers and Neoliberalism to Women's Organizations' (2015) 22(3) *European Journal of Women's Studies* 288, 290.

4 ibid. See also Johanna Kantola, *Gender and the European Union* (Palgrave Macmillan 2010) 27–28.

5 Elomäki (n 3) 290.

6 Ann Numhauser-Henning, 'EU sex equality law post-Amsterdam' in Helen Meenan (ed), *Equality in an Enlarged European Union: Understanding the Article 13 Directives* (Cambridge University Press 2007) 147.

a brief outline of EU equality law before considering key cases in gender equality law. The section analysing gender equality case law is split into an examination of cases dealing with equal pay and equality of employment terms and conditions on the one hand, and pregnancy and maternity discrimination and other gender-related issues on the other hand.

EU equality law

The development of European non-discrimination and equality law provisions is well rehearsed in the existing literature. Hence, we do not intend to provide a detailed analysis of the Treaty and legislative provisions here, nor do we have scope to rehearse the development of EU policy in this area.[7] It is however useful to briefly examine the evolution of the rationale underpinning European non-discrimination and equality law in order to set the context for our discussion.

The principle of non-discrimination can be found in the EEC Treaty, essentially in relation to nationality. The original Article 6 EEC offered a general aspiration statement that 'within the scope of application of [the] Treaty, and without prejudice to any special provisions contained therein, any discrimination on grounds of nationality shall be prohibited'. This so-called equal treatment principle is now codified in Article 18 of the Treaty in the Functioning of the European Union[8] (TEFU). Article 48 EEC (now Article 45 TFEU), which was further elaborated by Regulation 1612/68[9] on freedom of movement for workers, in turn offered more specific protection for Community workers in the sphere of employment by guaranteeing, *inter alia*, equal access to employment. Additionally, Article 119 EEC (now Article 157 TFEU) concerned itself with equal pay for men and women. However, there were no provisions on non-discrimination based on particular characteristics in the EEC Treaty, and these have been added later. The aims of the early Treaty provisions and the 1970s Directives on equal pay[10] and equal treatment in employment[11] were clearly economic in nature. As Catherine

7 For the development of Treaty and legislative provisions, see, eg, Catherine Barnard, *EU Employment Law* (4th edn, Oxford University Press 2012). For an insightful analysis of gender equality policy in the EU see eg Petra Ahrens, *Actors, Institutions, and the Making of EU Gender Equality Programs* (Palgrave MacMillan 2018).

8 Treaty of the Functioning of the European Union [2012] OJ C 326/47 (TFEU).

9 Regulation (EEC) No 1612/68 of the Council of 15 October 1968 on freedom of movement for workers within the Community [1968] OJ L257/2. This Regulation was recast as Regulation (EU) No 492/2011 of the European Parliament and of the Council of 5 April 2011 on freedom of movement for workers within the Union [2011] OJ L141/1.

10 Directive 75/117/EEC on equal pay for male and female workers [1975] OJ L45/19.

11 Directive 76/207/EEC on the implementation of the principle of equal treatment for men and women as regards access to employment, vocational training and promotion and working conditions [1976] OJ L39/40 (Equal Treatment Directive). This Directive has been recast as Directive 2006/54/EC of the European Parliament and of the Council of 5 July 2006 on the implementation of the principle of equal opportunities and equal treatment of men and women in matters of employment and occupation (recast) [2006] OJ L204/23.

Barnard notes, 'equal opportunities were acceptable so long as they did not interfere significantly with the operation of the Single Market'.[12]

Barnard further comments that the 1990s saw a shift in the rationale underpinning non-discrimination law with a focus on promoting efficiency and reducing inefficiency associated with statistical discrimination.[13] Hence, the economic emphasis remained alive and well for a number decades. However, at the same time social considerations in relation to non-discrimination provisions were coming to the fore and in its 2000 decision in *Deutsche Post*[14] the Court of Justice remarked that:

> the economic aim pursued by Article 141[15] of the [EC] treaty, namely the elimination of distortion of competition between undertakings established in different Member States is secondary to the social aim pursued by the same provision, which constitutes the expression of a fundamental human right.[16]

Hence, the aim of promoting equal pay for women and men from a social perspective started to receive well-deserved attention before the Court. The same period also saw the inclusion of Article 13 in the Treaty establishing the European Community[17] (now Article 19 TFEU) which soon gave rise to two new Directives: firstly, the Race Directive,[18] prohibiting discrimination on the grounds of race and ethnic origin; and, secondly, the Framework Directive,[19] covering discrimination on the grounds of sex, disability, sexual orientation, religion and belief and age. The inclusion of Article 13 in the Treaty along with the introduction of the two Directives was justified noticeably more on moral and social grounds than previous provisions and we deal with these provisions in more detail in the next chapter.

Undoubtedly European non-discrimination provisions have come a long way since the late 1950s, but nonetheless gender equality has not been achieved across the EU. Empirical studies continue to show the existence of a gender pay gap and sex discrimination in the workplace and more generally.[20] Eurostat's gender

12 Barnard (n 7) 299.
13 ibid.
14 Joined Cases C-270/97 and C-271/97 *Deutsche Post AG v Elisabeth Sievers and Brunhilde Schrage* [2000] ECR I-799.
15 Now TFEU, art 157.
16 *Deutsche Post* (n 14) para 57.
17 Treaty establishing the European Community [2002] OJ C325/33 (EC Treaty).
18 Council Directive 2000/43/EC of 29 June 2000 implementing the principle of equal treatment between persons irrespective of racial or ethnic origin [2000] OJ L180/22.
19 Council Directive 2000/78/EC of 27 November 2000 establishing a general framework for equal treatment in employment and occupation [2000] OJ L303/16.
20 Jolanta Maj, *Gender Equality in the European Union: A Comparative Study of Poland and Germany* (Nomos 2017); Anna van der Vleuten, *The Price of Gender Equality: Member States and Governance in the European Union* (Routledge 2016); Veronika Hedija, 'Sector-specific Gender Pay Gap: Evidence from the European Union Countries' (2017) 30(1) *Economic Research-Ekonomska Istraživanja* 1804 doi:10.1080/1331677X.2017.1392886.

pay gap statistics reveal that there is a clear pattern of male pay advantage.[21] In 2016, women's gross hourly earnings were on average 16.2% below those of men in EU-28. Additionally, the age of employees had an impact on lower earnings, especially for older women. The gaps in average pay were found to be much lower for younger employees, whereas the gap tended to increase with age, in all probability due to career interruptions experienced by women during their working life.

The existence of male advantage when it comes to gender equality in general is supported by the 2017 report compiled by the European Institute for Gender Equality, which noted that significant improvements were still 'needed in all Member States in order to attain gender-equal societies where both women and men can enjoy equal levels of well-being in all domains of life'.[22] A gendered reading of the case law of the Court of Justice can thus help us understand why this is so and what can be done to promote equality and avoid discrimination. This can help us conceptualise non-discrimination and equality in a different way which is more likely to lead to better decisions and ultimately better policies and practices in the Member States.

The equal pay case law

Simon Hix has suggested that gender equality policy is perhaps the only policy area where EU law and policy has set a higher standard than the lowest common denominator,[23] and this standard setting is to a large extent due to Court action in this area. Between 1971 and 1996 the Court received 90 cases relating to gender equality in some way and over half of them referred directly to what was then Article 119 EEC.[24] Perhaps the most high-profile series of cases is the one brought in the 1970s by Belgian lawyer Eliane Vogel-Polsky,[25] who introduced us to one of the (reluctant?) heroines of EU equality Law: Gabrielle Defrenne. Ms Defrenne was a flight attendant for the Belgian state airline Sabena. In a series of three cases the Court considered her situation in relation to equal pay, equal terms and conditions and State pensions. Not only was Gabrielle Defrenne paid

21 Eurostat, 'Gender Pay Gap Statistics' (March 2018) <http://gldr.co/1LcrZai> accessed 4 April 2018.

22 The Index is aimed at facilitating the planning and implementation of more targeted and efficient policy measures through monitoring gender equality while unmasking explicit differences within groups of women and men by accounting for several relevant social factors, including 'age, (dis)ability, migrant background (measured by the country of birth), education and family composition'. See Davide Barbier and others, *Gender Equality Index 2017: Measuring Gender Equality in the European Union 2005–2015* (European Institute for Gender Equality 2017) 1 and 7.

23 Simon Hix, *The Political System of the European Union* (Palgrave MacMillan 2005).

24 Uta Klein, *Geschlechterverhaeltnisse und Gleichstellungspolitk in der Europaeischen Union* (Springer VS 2013).

25 We have considered the importance of lawyers and legal teams in Chapter 4 where we discuss the importance of legal mobilisation in bringing cases to the Court.

less than her male counterparts, she also received a lower pension and a lower lump sum on retirement, which was mandated at 40 years of age for women. While the second *Defrenne* action is, in EU law and equality law terms, perhaps the most important, her story is worth telling in its entirety.

Ms Defrenne worked as an air hostess, performing the same work as the male air stewards. However, between February 1963 and February 1966 she was being paid less for that work than her male colleagues. While her employers did not dispute the fact that she was paid less for the same work, there was no remedy for Ms Defrenne in national law. The first case, *Defrenne I*,[26] is perhaps a little technical. It concerned the definition of 'pay' in EU law and, in particular, whether or not certain pension provisions, which operated essentially as a social security scheme, or which were governed by legislation rather than agreement between employer and employee, could be considered pay. The Court decided that this was not the case, noting that: '[t]he part due from the employer in financing such schemes does not constitute a direct or indirect payment to the worker; the latter receives the benefits legally prescribed by reason of the fact that [s]he fulfils the legal conditions required for their being granted'.[27] While the gender implications of this decision are less obvious, it raises questions about how pension and social security schemes impact on women and men and whether there is a difference in that impact. As Camila Arza notes '[s]ince women's lifecourses are different from men's, pension systems also often have different outcomes for women and men'.[28] Her discussion paper produced for the United Nations (UN) suggests that in all types of pension men do better than women and that there is a significant gap in coverage between men and women in many EU countries. Different aspects of pension provisions, such as length of service required, benefit calculations and indexing, also have gendered consequences and none of these considerations were taken into account in *Defrenne I*.[29]

As far as we know, these issues were not part of the deliberations in *Defrenne I* because the gendered implications, or dimensions of the question referred, were not deemed visible or important throughout the proceedings. The gender dimension was clearly obvious to the lawyers involved, with Vogel-Polsky herself noting that 'equality of pay, taken in isolation, does not exist. It's a myth. It can only have significance in the wider context of the recognition of equal

26 Case C-80/70 *Defrenne v Belgian State* [1971] ECR 00445 (*Defrenne I*).

27 ibid Summary. See also paras 9–10.

28 Camila Arza, 'The Gender Dimensions of Pension Systems: Policies and Constraints for the Protection of Older Women' (2015) UN Women Discussion Paper 1.

29 For more information on the impact of pensions and related social security systems, see eg Commission, *The Gender Gap in Pensions in the EU* (European Union 2013); Bernd Marin and Eszter Zólyomi, *Women's Work and Pensions: What Is Good, What Is Best? Designing Gender-Sensitive Arrangements* (Ashgate 2010); Manuela Samek Lodovici, Serena Drufuca, Monica Patrizio, and Flavia Pesce, *The Gender Pension Gap: Differences Between Mothers and Women Without Children* (EU 2016); Fran Bennett, *Megatrends and Social Security: Family and Gender* (International Social Security Association 2017).

treatment.'[30] However, it seems that the Court was not yet ready to embrace that wider context and engage with it in a way that could make a significant positive difference to women's lives. It is worth noting that the Court has since this decision been prepared to interpret 'pay' more broadly in cases such as *Garland*,[31] *Barber*,[32] and *Bilka-Kaufhaus*.[33]

The most famous and perhaps also most influential case in the *Defrenne* trilogy is the first challenge brought against the Belgian national airline Sabena, *Defrenne II*,[34] which concerned Ms Defrenne's equal pay claim. The first question for the Court involved establishing whether or not the provisions on equal pay contained in what was then Article 119 EEC (now Article 157 TFEU) were directly effective in this situation. The Court held that they were. This is the first example of direct effect of a Treaty provision being applied in this way between an individual and a private entity (the airline), and it is, indeed, for this reason that the case is discussed and analysed in the law school curriculum rather than because it represents a significant win for women. Vogel-Polsky herself noted the importance of the decision in these terms:

> The Court of Justice accepted that Article 119 was self-executing, that the State and the employers had to implement it by 31 December 1961. . . The Court accepted . . . that Article 119 had to be applied. It even accepted that this was a fundamental right. So it was a fantastic ruling.[35]

Defrenne II led the way to consistent enforcement of equal pay across the Member States and is undoubtedly a landmark decision which has changed the face of equality law at EU level and in the Member States. However, the Court's underpinning economic outlook and instrumentalism are hard to miss in the judgement. As Gerard Conway notes, the Court

> has played an important role not in establishing a principle of equality of treatment, which was set out in the treaty, but in broadly interpreting it and in strengthening the institutional structure of the EU in this area and its own capacity to influence the law.[36]

30 Eliane Gubin, *Eliane Vogel-Polsky: A Woman of Conviction* (Institute for the Equality of Women and Men 2008) (with Catherine Jacques) 90 citing Eliane Vogel-Polsky, 'Les facteurs d'extranéité; le rôle du droit et de la jurisprudence communautaires' (1978) (1–3) *Revue de l'Université libre de Bruxelles, À l'enseigne du droit social belge* 283, 301.

31 Case 12/81 *Eileen Garland v British Rail Engineering Ltd* [1982] ECR 359.

32 Case C-262/88 *Douglas Harvey Barber v Guardian Royal Exchange Assurance Group* [1990] ECR I-01889.

33 Case 170/84 *Bilka-Kaufhaus GmbH v Karin Weber von Hartz* [1986] ECR 01607.

34 Case C-43/75 *Defrenne v Sabena* [1976] ECR 00455 (*Defrenne II*).

35 Gubin (n 30) 92 citing Vogel-Polsky.

36 Gerard Conway, *EU Law* (Routledge Spotlights 2015) 657.

Defrenne II did not make reference to equal pay as a good thing *per se*; it noted that the intention of the Treaty was to avoid Member States from suffering competitive disadvantage:

> First, in the light of the different stages of the development of social legislation in the various member states, the aim of Article 119 is to avoid a situation in which undertakings established in states which have actually implemented the principle of equal pay suffer a competitive disadvantage in intra-community competition as compared with undertakings established in states which have not yet eliminated discrimination against women workers as regards pay.[37]

Before then acknowledging the

> social objectives of the community, which is not merely an economic union, but is at the same time intended, by common action, to ensure social progress and seek the constant improvement of the living and working conditions of their peoples.[38]

However, this is subtly different from acknowledging that equal pay is a fundamental cornerstone of equality. Partly, of course, we must remember the context and time in which *Defrenne II* was decided. Equality law was far less established across the majority of Member States in the mid-1970s. It is easy to forget how important this decision is with hindsight and to criticise the Court for not being more explicit about the importance of equal pay for its own sake and simply the right thing to do, rather than as a means for improving working and living conditions. The judgement is couched in terms of ensuring the implementation of (then) EC law and concerned with establishing direct effect of the Treaty provisions far more than with reaffirming equal pay as an important legal principle. Arguably, *Defrenne II* would have been all the more powerful if it had been able to do both. It was further weakened by the time limit put on the effect of the decision which limited claims based on it to after the ruling rather than from the date of Article 119 EEC having to be applied and also by the fact that it limited itself to the application of direct discrimination as set out in Article 119 EEC rather than also engaging with the possibility of indirect discrimination which was prohibited by the Equal Treatment Directive[39] albeit in a rather less precise manner. According to Gubin, 'Éliane Vogel-Polsky was indignant that the Court of Justice had so easily trampled over the law. *"In reality it's an entirely political ruling, taken under very strong pressure from the United Kingdom. But I remained bitter"*.'[40]

37 *Defrenne II* (n 34) para 9.
38 ibid para 10.
39 Directive 76/207.
40 Gubin (n 30) 93 (emphasis in original).

Although the third (and last) decision in the trilogy, *Defrenne III*,[41] has received less attention than *Defrenne II*, it is nonetheless significant. It dealt with Ms Defrenne's claim that the requirement for women to retire at the age of 40 where her male counterparts were not required to do so was discriminatory under Article 119 EEC. Ms Defrenne argued that the requirement to retire early meant that she could receive less pay over her career than her male colleagues. However, the claim in *Defrenne III* was stretching the scope of Article 119 EEC too far. The Court held that:

> [a]s regards to the relationships of employer and employee which are subject to national law, the community had not, at the time of the events now before the Belgian courts, assumed any responsibility for the supervising and guaranteeing the observance of the principle of equality between men and women in working conditions other than remuneration.[42]

Therefore, Ms Defrenne's third and final claim for equal pay failed. While that is disappointing, it is not surprising, given the legal framework in place at the time.[43] However, there are other aspects in this decision which could be applauded for advancing gender equality. For instance, the Court noted that the 'respect for fundamental personal human rights is one of the general principles of community law, the observance of which it has a duty to ensure', and that 'there can be no doubt that the elimination of discrimination based on sex forms part of those fundamental rights'.[44] The assertion that the protection from sex discrimination is important from the fundamental human rights point of view is significant in itself because the general principles allow 'liberal interpretation of what might otherwise seem to be a narrow rule'.[45] Unfortunately, the Court was not willing to engage in a liberal interpretation in this case in spite of making important claims for the future development of the law in this area.

The Court returned to the issue of equal pay in its 1980 decision in *Macarthys v Smith*,[46] which concerned a claim for equal pay with an employee's predecessor in the same job. While this case is a leading example of a decision which forced change in national legislation,[47] its implications are more significant than

41 Case C-149/77 *Defrenne v Sabena* [1978] ECR 01365 (*Defrenne III*).
42 ibid para 30.
43 The disadvantages experienced by women in terms of remuneration and pensions are widely acknowledged. See, eg, International Labour Organization, 'Rights, Jobs and Social Security: New Visions for Older Women and Men' (30 September 2008) <www.ilo.org/gender/Events/Campaign2008-2009/WCMS_098840/lang—en/index.htm> accessed 14 December 2017; Karel Neels, David De Wachter and Hans Peeters, 'The Effect of Family Formation on the build-up of Pension Rights Among Minority Ethnic Groups and Native Women in Belgium' (2017) *Ageing and Society* 1, 2 doi:10.1017/S0144686X17000010.
44 *Defrenne III* (n 41) paras 26–27.
45 Evelyn Ellis and Phillipa Watson, *EU Anti-Discrimination Law* (Oxford University Press 2012) 101.
46 Case 129/79 *Macarthys Ltd v Wendy Smith* [1980] ECR-01275.
47 This case concerned the English Equal Pay Act 1970.

that because the decision forced other Member States to examine their equal pay laws. The Court acknowledged that an equal pay claim could be based on a comparison between current pay and the pay of a predecessor in the same role. It further noted when determining pay for an employee that, regardless of their gender, the decisive test lay in establishing whether there was 'a difference in treatment between a man and a woman performing "equal work" within the meaning of article 119'.[48] The scope of the concept of equal work was entirely qualitative in character because it exclusively concerned the nature of the services performed and 'may not be restricted by the introduction of a requirement of contemporaneity'.[49] This is crucial because it precludes employers from thinking that they can save money by employing women in roles previously occupied by men. Significantly, the decision also changed the conversation about the value of women in the workplace. While there are, of course, evidential difficulties in cases where a claim is made on the basis of a predecessor's remuneration, it is conceptually an important step forward. However, if the Court had really wanted to increase protection for women and drive the notion of equal pay forward both at EU and national level, it could have gone further.

In the context of the proceedings in *Macarthys*, the national court referred another question for the consideration of the Court, which in essence concerned a query whether the principle of equal pay applied in circumstances where a female worker could show that she received less pay in respect of her employment than she would have received 'if she were a man doing equal work for the employer'.[50] The existence of a 'hypothetical male employee' is significant because it could have revolutionised equal pay law had it been accepted by the Court. Instead, it recognised the evidential difficulties and concluded that the national court's question was an example of 'indirect and disguised discrimination'.[51] The Court referred to its decision in *Defrenne*, stating that the identification of indirect discrimination implied comparative studies of entire branches of industry and the elaboration of criteria of assessment by the EU and national legislative bodies. Therefore, in cases concerning:

> actual discrimination falling within the scope of the direct application of article 119, comparisons are confined to parallels which may be drawn on the basis of concrete appraisals of the work actually performed by employees of different sex within the same establishment or service.[52]

This means that even where a woman could show that she would have been paid more had she been male, she cannot bring a claim if there is no actual male

48 *Macarthys v Smith* (n 46) para 11.
49 ibid.
50 ibid para 7.
51 ibid para 20.
52 ibid.

comparator – either past or present – with whom she can compare her remuneration package. In other words, if establishing equal treatment appears too complex or involves disproportionate effort then the Court is not prepared hold that equality is more important and that Member States must find a way of assessing such claims. However, there is some evidence that what is 'too complex' has perhaps changed over time. In *Enderby*,[53] the Court was prepared to conclude that there was sex discrimination, if the salaries in two comparable professions, at an equivalent professional level, were lower in the profession which consisted of primarily women. It held that:

> if the pay of speech therapists is significantly lower than that of pharmacists and if the former are almost exclusively women while the latter are predominantly men, there is a prima facie case of sex discrimination, at least where the two jobs in question are of equal value . . . Where there is a prima facie case of discrimination, it is for the employer to show that there are objective reasons for the difference in pay.[54]

Although the economic rationale of putting business needs first is still apparent in this case, the Court is at least willing to accept that equality is of importance and places the onus on the employer to prove that a difference in pay is justified. However, due to the nature of the preliminary reference procedure it is for the national court to make the finding of fact in relation to that justification.[55] Hence, the Court places the power as to how to balance equality with business needs back into national courts' hands.

There are further examples of the Court resorting to economic rationales rather than putting equality at the forefront of its decision making. For example, in its 1986 decision in *Bilka-Kaufhaus*,[56] the Court concluded that withholding pension contributions from part-time workers was unlawful because it breached the provisions on equal pay. The Court established its decision on the basis that more women than men were part-time workers. However, it noted that the measures could be justified by 'objective economic grounds relating to the management of the undertaking'[57] and that:

> article 119 does not have the effect of requiring an employer to organize its occupational pension scheme in such a manner as to take into account the particular difficulties faced by persons with family responsibilities in meeting the conditions for entitlement to such a pension.[58]

53 Case C-127/92 *Dr Pamela Mary Enderby v Frenchay Health Authority and Secretary of State for Health* [1993] ECR I-05535.
54 ibid paras 17–18.
55 For more details about the preliminary reference procedure, see chapter 4.
56 *Bilka-Kaufhaus* (n 33).
57 ibid para 36.
58 ibid para 43.

The Court thus concluded that discrimination against women was acceptable if there were good economic reasons for that discrimination. It saw no issue with allowing companies to pursue a policy of seeking to employ as few part-time workers as possible,[59] or with allowing the employers to disregard responsibilities relating to taking care of one's family which still continue to fall predominantly onto women. In 1989 the Court decided in *Achterberg*[60] that Article 119 EEC and relevant EU law on equal pay 'implement equal treatment between men and women not generally but only in their capacity as workers'.[61] This decision appears to again suggest a narrow reading of the Treaty. The Court could have been much bolder in its decisions in *Bilka-Kaufhaus* and *Achterberg*. It could have concluded that since the pension provisions in question in *Bilka-Kaufhaus* constituted pay, they should have to apply equally to men and women, including having access to the scheme. However, the Court was seemingly conscious of possible future legislation and of blurring the lines between existing provisions on equal pay and those on promotion of employment and living and working conditions which were to be adopted under Article 117 EEC.[62] This may explain why the Court was careful to confine itself very clearly to matters of pay and matters relating to the workforce while leaving other issues, such as access to employment, terms and conditions once in employment, or social security provisions for further legislative developments. We now turn to some of those other issues in more detail.

Access to employment

Access to employment is often the most difficult hurdle for women seeking entry to the labour market particularly in sectors which are traditionally male dominated. Detailed discussions of employment practices and difficulties in defining merit and setting criteria which do not inadvertently discriminate against women are beyond the scope of this chapter. However, the Court's case law suggests that employers can take positive action to increase the number of women in areas where they are under-represented. They must not, however, positively discriminate. *Kalanke*[63] and *Marschall*[64] highlight this difference. In both cases complaints of sex discrimination were brought by men because of employment policies requiring women to be hired over men. The relevant provisions read as follows. In *Kalanke*:

> (1) In the case of an appointment (including establishment as a civil servant or judge) which is not made for training purposes, women who have the

59 ibid para 37.

60 Joined cases 48/88, 106/88 and 107/88 *JEG Achterberg-te Riele and others v Sociale Verzekeringsbank* [1989] ECR 01963.

61 ibid para 12.

62 *Bilka-Kaufhaus* (n 33) paras 40–41. Article 117 EEC (now art 151 TFEU) has been amended significantly over time to include reference to fundamental social rights.

63 Case C-450/93 *Eckhard Kalanke v Freie Hansestadt Bremen* [1995] ECR I-03051.

64 Case C-409/95 *Hellmut Marschall v Land Nordrhein-Westfalen* [1997] ECR I-06363.

> same qualifications as men applying for the same post are to be given priority in sectors where they are under-represented. (2) In the case of an assignment to a position in a higher pay, remuneration and salary bracket, women who have the same qualifications as men applying for the same post are to be given priority if they are under-represented. This also applies in the case of assignment to a different official post and promotion.[65]

And in *Marschall*:

> Where, in the sector of the authority responsible for promotion, there are fewer women than men in the particular higher grade post in the career bracket, women are to be given priority for promotion in the event of equal suitability, competence and professional performance, unless reasons specific to an individual [male] candidate tilt the balance in his favour.[66]

Although the provisions look similar, the Court treated them very differently. In *Kalanke*, the provision was unlawful because it required women to be hired in all circumstances where the qualifications and circumstances were similar. In *Marschall*, all other things being equal, employers could find a specific reason which tilted the balance in the male applicant's favour and therefore the provision could stand as one which was non-discriminatory. Jessica Guth has noted that '[w]hile *Kalanke* was seen as a major setback for equality across the EU, *Marschall* restored some of the balance'.[67] However, both decisions are detrimental for gender equality. *Kalanke* ignores the historical gender bias and discrimination in employment and misses an opportunity to correct that by mandating that were candidates are equally qualified, women must be hired instead of men. By holding that the provision was discriminatory, the Court simply upheld existing structures of discrimination against women which lead to them being under-represented in that sector in the first place.

Marschall looks more promising. It appears to require the hiring of women where candidates are equally qualified and experienced, unless there is something which tips the balance in favour of the male applicant. The Court held in cases where there were fewer women at the level of the relevant post in a sector of the public service, promoting the hiring of female candidates was not precluded by Article 2(1) and (4) of the Equal Treatment Directive,[68] provided that the candidates were to be the subject of an objective assessment which took into account of all criteria specific to the individual candidates. In cases where one or more of those criteria tilted the balance in favour of the male candidate, an employer

65 *Kalanke* (n 63) para 3.
66 *Marschall* (n 64) para 3.
67 Jessica Guth, 'Law as the object and agent of integration: Gendering the Court of Justice of the European Union, its decisions and their impact' in Gabriele Abels and Heather MacRae (eds), *Gendering European Integration Theory: Engaging New Dialogues* (Barbara Budrich Publishers 2016).
68 Directive 76/207/EEC.

could override the priority accorded to female candidates. However, the criteria could not be such as to discriminate against female candidates.[69] If the applicants are equally competent, qualified and experienced, the reason which tips the balance appears rather vague. Given the wording of the provision, candidates will be of 'equal suitability, competence and professional performance' for the job for which they are applying. Therefore, any reason must relate to factors which do not impact on the ability to carry out the job. However, it is precisely those reasons which are routinely used to exclude women, or favour men, for positions and promotions. It is not hard to imagine recruitment or promotions panels which prefer a male candidate on what they think is 'merit' when, in reality, the panel has given the concept of 'merit' very little thought.[70] Colm O'Cinneide has argued convincingly that 'a lingering attachment to "formal" equality concepts has resulted in a confusing, incoherent and complex case law that has a "chilling effect" on the use of positive action'.[71]

Pregnancy discrimination in recruitment

Although European societies have advanced well beyond the view that continued participation in the paid workforce is incompatible with motherhood, women continue to face gender discrimination in the workplace on grounds of pregnancy or maternity leave.[72] Applying the principle of non-discrimination, the Court has firmly established through its case law that pregnant workers require protection against unfair dismissal throughout the period of pregnancy. In the long line of relevant cases, *Dekker*[73] and *Webb*[74] which were decided in early 1990s highlight some of the issues well. The Court's early approach dictates that temporary absences of pregnant women cannot be equated to those of men who are temporarily unable to work because of illness. This stance has been confirmed in the Court's later case law, lastly in the 2014 decision in *Saint Prix*.[75] There are nevertheless some who criticise this approach on the grounds that it is essential that women's protection is equivalent to that of ill men, in order to prevent

69 *Marschall* (n 64) para 35.

70 See Chapter 3 for a discussion about merit in the context of judicial appointments. The same arguments can be made here.

71 Colm O'Cinneide, 'Positive Action and the Limits of Existing Law' (2006) 13 *Maastricht Journal of European and Comparative Law* 351–364, 351.

72 Sandra Fredman, 'Reversing Roles: Bringing Men into the Frame' (2014) 10(4) *International Journal of Law in Context* 442, 444 doi:10.1017/S1744552314000214; Roberta Guerrina, *Mothering the Union: The Politics of Gender, Equality and Maternity Rights in the EU* (Manchester University Press 2005).

73 Case C-177/88 *Elisabeth Johanna Pacifica Dekker v Stichting Vormingscentrum voor Jong Volwassenen (VJV-Centrum) Plus* [1991] IRLR 27.

74 Case C-32/93 *Carole Louise Webb v EMO Air Cargo (UK) Ltd* [1994] ECR I-3567.

75 Case C-507/12 *Jessy Saint Prix v Secretary of State for Work and Pensions* [2014] EU:C:2014:2007.

discrimination against pregnant women.[76] For the critics, the failure to compare pregnancy to an illness is not an equality approach, but an approach that highlights the difference between sexes.[77] They also argue that, while this approach might be important in relation to pregnancy, it does not make any clear provision for maternity rights or parental rights which include fathers.

In *Dekker*, the Court held that discrimination of female workers due to their pregnancy could not be defended on the basis that a sick male absent for the same amount of time would have been treated in the same way. Carole Dekker applied for employment as an instructor in a youth training centre and, while the employer considered her as the best candidate for job, the selection committee declined the offer of employment because of her pregnancy. The employer justified their decision on the grounds that if Ms Dekker were employed, they would have to pay her the percentage of her salary as determined by Dutch law (in the region of 80–100%) whilst she was on maternity leave. The employer believed that as Ms Dekker informed the company about her pregnancy at the application stage, they would be unable to claim any potential costs of her maternity leave salary from their insurance company. Consequently, the employer would be short-staffed because they could not employ cover for Ms Dekker. Although the Member States' parental leave systems provide women a strong incentive to participate in the labour force, employers frequently argue that the availability of generous maternity leave encourages women to take long periods of parental leave and to be less flexible with respect to hours once they return to work.[78] These extended absences and lack of flexibility have been argued to be particularly costly for employers when employees hold 'top jobs'.[79] However, there is an inherent gender bias in such argument because very few women hold executive positions in organisations.[80] In fact, there has been not a single case before the Court involving sex discrimination on the grounds of pregnancy concerning women in executive or board of director positions. In fact, most cases concern women holding part-time and full-time positions at the level of an employee in non-male dominated industries, working as a (nursery) nurse, clerk, driver and youth worker. Indeed, Sandra Fredman has argued that discrimination due to pregnancy disproportionately affects low-paid female workers, who have less economic bargaining power and are more likely to be in precarious employment

76 Fredman (n 72) 446 citing *Daniel Coleman v Court of Appeals of Maryland* 132 S Ct 1327 (2012) (US Supreme Court) (Ginsburg J) citing S Rep No 101-77, 32 (1989).

77 Fredman (n 72) 446.

78 James Albrecht, Peter Skogman Thoursie and Susan Vroman, 'Parental Leave and the Glass Ceiling in Sweden' (European Society of Population Economics conference, Braga, Portugal, June 2014).

79 ibid.

80 Madeline Heilman, Francesca Manzi and Susanne Braun, 'Presumed incompetent: Perceived lack of fit and gender bias in recruitment and selection' in Adelina Broadbridge and Sandra Fielden (eds), *Handbook of Gendered Careers in Management: Getting in, Getting on, Getting out* (Edward Elgar 2015).

and therefore out of the reach of statutory employment protection.[81] Hence, the protection from sex discrimination and the enforcement of such protection is likely to have most significant impact on low-paid female workers. There is evidence that, for instance, the vast majority of employees in the UK on so called 'zero-hour contracts', where the employees are not guaranteed any hours in a given week, are women.[82]

The questions referred to the Court in *Dekker* concerned the issue whether an employer directly or indirectly was in breach of the principle of equal treatment laid down in Articles 2(1) and 3(1) of the Equal Treatment Directive if it refused to enter into an employment contract with a suitable candidate because of the anticipated adverse consequences for the employer due to the applicant's pregnancy. The public authorities in the Netherlands had adopted rules on unfitness for work which equated the inability to work on account of pregnancy and confinement to the inability to work on account of illness. The national court further asked whether the fact that there were no male candidates for the same post made any difference. The Court held that the employer was in direct contravention of the principle of equal treatment embodied in Articles 2(1) and 3(1) if it refused to enter into an employment contract with a suitable candidate where such refusal was based on the possible adverse consequences for the employer of employing a pregnant woman. Further, the Court held that the application of the Equal Treatment Directive would not differ where no male candidates had applied for a post. The importance of *Dekker* for women claiming discrimination due to pregnancy cannot be overstated because the Court made it clear that it was always discriminatory to refuse employing a woman due to matters relating to her sex, for example pregnancy. Hence, treating women unfavourably because of pregnancy or maternity leave was direct sex discrimination. Accordingly, it was not necessary for the woman to identify a non-pregnant comparator in similar circumstances to demonstrate discrimination. This means that there is no need for a comparison with another person who is not pregnant or does not have children.[83]

81 Fredman (n 72) 444.

82 Workers on zero-hours contracts 'are more likely to be young, part-time, women, or in full-time education when compared with other people in employment'. See Office for National Statistics, 'People in Employment on a Zero-hours Contract: Mar 2017' 2 <www.ons.gov.uk/employmentandlabourmarket/peopleinwork/earningsandworkinghours/articles/contractsthatdonotguaranteeaminimumnumberofhours/mar2017> accessed 26 November 2017.

83 See Fredman who notes that direct discrimination on grounds of pregnancy can be established independently of the need to find a comparator by using the words 'unfavourably' rather than 'less favourably'. Fredman (n 72) 445–446. Additionally, this principle has been implemented at the national level, eg, in the Equality Act 2010 (England and Wales) c 15, s 4 which sets out 'pregnancy and maternity' as one of the nine protected characteristics. Rather than outlawing 'less favourable treatment' of women, the 2010 Act prohibits 'unfavourable treatment' because of pregnancy, childbirth, maternity or breastfeeding. Section 18(2)(a)–(b) prohibits unfavourable treatment at work during the protected period because of

Dismissal while pregnant

The 1994 decision in *Webb* concerned an employee who was dismissed after becoming pregnant while being employed on an indefinite term during the maternity leave of another employee.[84] Ms Webb was hired as an import operations clerk and, while she was initially covering for maternity leave of another employee, she expected to stay on after the end of the period.[85] Several weeks after starting work she informed her employer of her pregnancy. The employer took the view that it had no alternative but to dismiss her. The fundamental issue was therefore whether the dismissal was unlawful.[86] Ms Webb claimed that the dismissal amounted to discrimination contrary to section 1 of the Sex Discrimination Act 1975 which should be interpreted subject to the Equal Treatment Directive. In its response to the national court, the Court of Justice made it clear that it was contrary to Articles 2(1) and 5(1) of the Equal Treatment Directive to dismiss a woman who, shortly after her recruitment, was found to be pregnant.

According to the Court, no comparison could be made between the situation of a woman incapable of working due to pregnancy and a man similarly incapable for working due to medical or other reasons. This was because pregnancy was not a pathological condition comparable to non-availability for work on non-medical grounds, which would otherwise justify dismissal without discrimination on grounds of sex. The judgement made it clear that dismissing an employee recruited for an indefinite period could not be justified on grounds related to her inability to fulfil a fundamental condition of her employment contract due to her pregnancy. The wording appeared to provide a loophole allowing dismissal in circumstances where a worker became pregnant having been engaged for a definite period of time (eg as a maternity leave replacement). This anomaly was resolved by Article 10 of the 1992 Pregnancy Directive,[87] which was aimed at improving health and safety and protection against 'unfavourable'[88] treatment at work for female workers who are pregnant, have recently given birth or are breastfeeding. Article 10 provides that Member States should take the necessary measures to

---

the pregnancy or pregnancy-related illness. Section 17(2)–(5) protects women against unfavourable treatment because of a pregnancy, childbirth (in the period of 26 weeks beginning with the day of giving birth), breast-feeding, as well as miscarriage after 24 weeks of the pregnancy in other non-work related cases (eg provision of services, education; associations).

84 *Webb* (n 74) para 14.

85 Case C-32/93 *Carole Louise Webb v EMO Air Cargo (UK) Ltd* [1994] ECR I-3569, Opinion of AG Tesauro, point 4.

86 *Webb* (n 74) para 14.

87 Council Directive 92/85/EEC of 19 October 1992 on the introduction of measures to encourage improvements in the safety and health at work of pregnant workers and workers who have recently given birth or are breastfeeding [1992] OJ L/348.

88 By using the words 'unfavourably' rather than 'less favourably', direct discrimination on grounds of pregnancy can be established independently of the need to find a male comparator. See Fredman (n 72) 445–446.

prohibit the dismissal of such workers during the period from the beginning of their pregnancy to the end of the maternity leave.

Although the Pregnancy Directive did not explicitly cover refusal to employ a pregnant woman, in *Mahlburg*[89] a regional government's refusal to appoint a pregnant woman for an indefinite period in line with a national prohibition was in breach of Articles 2(1) and (3) of the Equal Treatment Directive.[90] The Court held that since there was a vacant post, which Silke-Karin Mahlburg was qualified to hold, she could not be turned down on the grounds that she could not from the outset and for the duration of her pregnancy be employed in the post. This was because the application of provisions concerning the protection of pregnant women could not result in unfavourable treatment regarding access to employment.[91] The Court also disproved Member States' arguments that a refusal to employ Ms Mahlburg on account of her pregnancy could be justified on grounds relating to the financial loss, which specifically small and medium-sized undertakings would suffer due to the employee's maternity leave.[92] As a result of this judgement the prohibition to discriminate against recruitment of pregnant workers is now codified in Article 14(1) of the Recast Equal Treatment Directive[93] which specifically stipulates that: '[t]here shall be no discrimination on grounds of sex either directly or indirectly in the public or private sectors, including public bodies'.

Cases involving dismissal of pregnant workers have similarly been decided in the favour of the worker, rather than the employer. In the 1990 decision in *Brown*,[94] Mary Brown, who was employed by Rentokil as a driver, informed her employer that she was pregnant. Because her work involved heavy lifting, she submitted to her employer a series of four-week certificates regarding various pregnancy-related disorders from which she was suffering. Three months later representatives of Rentokil informed Mrs Brown that, following an independent medical examination, her contract would be terminated pursuant to a term of her contract entitling the company to do so if she took more than 26 weeks' continuous sick leave. Since Mrs Brown did not return to work by the date given by the employer, she was accordingly dismissed while pregnant. The importance of this decision on the protection of pregnant workers under national legislation cannot be emphasised enough, since the Court's case law has had profound influence on Member States' employment law. It can be effectively argued that, as a result of *Brown* and many other decisions of the Court, all women working in the EU are able to benefit from their rightfully earned EU law protection as employees in the territory of the Member States.

89 Case C-207/98 *Silke-Karin Mahlburg v Land Meckleburg-Vorpommern* [2000] ECR I-00549.
90 ibid para 30.
91 ibid para 27.
92 *Mahlburg* (n 89) paras 28–29.
93 Directive 2006/54/EC.
94 Case 394/96 *Mary Brown v Rentokil* [1998] IRLR 445.

In *Melgar*[95] and *Tele Danmark*[96] the Court held that the prohibition on the dismissal of pregnant women applies also to fixed-term and part-time appointments. Maria Luisa Jiménez Melgar was an employee who had been recruited by the municipality of Los Barrios in Spain for three months over the spring months and, during that short period of time, her contract was renewed twice. After signing her fourth contract for a fixed term on a part-time basis in May 1999 Ms Melgar was issued with a letter stating that her contract would terminate in June 1999. Her pregnancy had advanced to the second trimester at the time since she gave birth in September 1999. *Tele Danmark* concerned a dismissal of an employee on a six months fixed-term contract who was dismissed during the first two months of her employment contract on account of pregnancy. Ms Brandt-Nielsen's contract required her to follow a training course for the first two months during which she also informed her employer of her pregnancy and that she was expected to give birth in early November.[97] She was dismissed shortly after the notification on the ground that she had not informed the employer that she was pregnant when she was recruited.[98] Her employer also claimed that Ms Brandt-Nielsen should have informed them that she was due to give birth before the end of the six-month period. The Court confirmed that a refusal of an employment on account of pregnancy could not be justified by financial loss which the employer may suffer, if the employer had recruited an employee during her maternity leave or because employee could not occupy the post during her pregnancy.

In *Paquay*[99] the Court held that the Pregnancy Directive prohibited the notification of a decision to dismiss an employee of an architect's firm on grounds of a pregnancy and birth of a child during the period of protection provided in Article 10(1) of the Directive, which is the period from the beginning of the pregnancy to the end of the maternity leave. According to the Court, such a dismissal constituted direct discrimination on the grounds of sex because it could affect only women.[100] It held that it was:

> precisely in view of the harmful effects which the risk of dismissal may have on the physical and mental state of women who are pregnant, have recently given birth or are breastfeeding, including the particularly serious risk that pregnant women may be prompted voluntarily to terminate their pregnancy, that, pursuant to Article 10 of Directive 92/85, the EU legislature provided

95 Case C-438/99 *Maria Luisa Jiménez Melgar v Ayuntamiento de Los Barrios* [2001] ECR I-06915.
96 Case C-109/00 *Tele Danmark A/S v Handels- og Kontorfunktionærernes Forbund i Danmark (HK)* [2001] ECR I-06993.
97 ibid paras 11–12.
98 ibid para 12.
99 Case C-460/06 *Nadine Paquay v Société d'architectes Hoet + Minne SPRL* [2007] ECR I-08511.
100 ibid para 29.

for special protection for women, by prohibiting dismissal during the period from the beginning of pregnancy to the end of maternity leave.[101]

The approach taken by the Court in case law involving pregnant workers' access to employment and dismissal is very proactive. The focus on economic rationales appears to have been pushed aside in order to make way for comprehensive protection of pregnant workers. Hence, the Court demonstrates awareness that this is an area which impacts exclusively on women. This is perhaps obvious though. Pregnancy is a gendered issue, only women can be pregnant and less favourable treatment of pregnant workers only impacts on women. Hence, the discrimination could not be more obvious. However, the protection of pregnant workers also fits the EU's ideal of full labour market participation. In protecting the rights of female workers during and after pregnancy the Court can showcase its commitment to EU integration and the EU's desire to encourage all EU citizens to take part in the labour market. It challenges the notion of women as only mothers and carers and thus fits well into the economic rationale of the EU and the Court's approach to EU citizens. Since economic activity is privileged in the EU, protecting the rights of female workers supports that particular category of EU citizens to be economically active.[102] We therefore argue that the Court does so only to enable mothers to stay attached to the labour market during temporary interruptions of employment such as maternity.[103] For instance, in *Saint Prix*, the Court made it clear that an EU citizen, who stopped working due to difficult pregnancy, would retain a status of a worker in the period of temporary absence from work, if she returned to work 'within a reasonable period after confinement'. Worryingly for women, the UK decided to deprive Jessy Saint Prix of the status of 'worker' despite having returned to work three months after having given birth. Therefore, the case revealed lack of any protection for a French woman who was temporarily unemployed, because Article 7(3) of the Citizens' Rights Directive[104] does not afford any protection against the loss of right of residence due to temporary inability to work as the result of pregnancy, whereas it covers temporary absence from work due to an illness or accident. Additionally, the Court decided that the period of absence from work due to pregnancy should be very brief, a mere few months, in order not to impact the retention of worker

101 ibid.

102 We explore economic activity further in Chapter 7 on EU citizenship.

103 Claudia Olivetti and Barbara Petrongolo, 'The Economic Consequences of Family Policies: Lessons from a Century of Legislation in High-Income Countries' (2017) 31(1) *Journal of Economic Perspectives* 205, 212.

104 Directive 2004/38/EC of the European Parliament and of the Council of 29 April 2004 on the right of citizens of the Union and their family members to move and reside freely within the territory of the Member States amending Regulation (EEC) No 1612/68 and repealing Directives 64/221/EEC, 68/360/EEC, 72/194/EEC, 73/148/EEC, 75/34/EEC, 75/35/EEC, 90/364/EEC, 90/365/EEC and 93/96/EEC [2004] OJ L158/77 (CRD).

status under Article 45 TFEU, and subsequently the period of residency under the Directive, negatively.

Rachel Cichowski has noted that 'the Court recognises that pregnancy and maternity may require re-organization of the workplace'.[105] However, the Court has not shied away from requiring Member States and employers to do so even where it may prove expensive to them. She highlights the importance of case law in expanding and clarifying the rights of pregnant women under the Treaty, Equal Treatment Directive and Pregnancy Directive, but also notes that the rulings around pregnancy, particularly in relation to payment or remuneration received during pregnancy are immensely problematic. For instance, the cases of *Gillespie*,[106] *Lewen*[107] and *Abdoulaye*[108] all concerned payments made in relation to maternity leave. The Court held firm that where there was differential treatment because of pregnancy or maternity, sex discrimination was automatically established and there was no need for a comparator. *Abdoulaye* is illustrative of the deeply entrenched sexism women face in their working lives. Ms Abdoulaye's male colleagues alleged that a lump sum of FRF 7,500 made for pregnant women going on maternity leave under the collective agreement violated the principle of equal pay. The Court noted that the Treaty did not preclude employers from making certain payments available exclusively to female workers where such payments were 'designed to offset the occupational disadvantages which arise for those workers as a result of their being away from work'.[109]

While the differential treatment makes some sense, for example in dismissal cases, it also reinforces stereotypes of parenthood, mothering and men's and women's roles. The reality seems to be that even if most heterosexual couples' pre-parenting relationship had been relatively egalitarian, the birth of a child results in a gendered division of labour where women take on the bulk of the unpaid labour, particularly childcare and related matters, while fathers serve as helpers when needed and asked.[110] Catherine Verniers and Jorge Vala have argued that the assumption that women, by their very nature, have specific abilities for domestic and parental work is used as a justification of sex discrimination in the

105 Rachel Cichowski, *The European Court and Civil Society: Litigation, Mobilization and Governance* (Cambridge University Press 2007) 107. See also Eugenia Caracciolo di Torella, 'Recent Developments in Pregnancy and Maternity Rights' (1999) 28 *Industrial Law Journal* 276.

106 Case C-342/93 *Joan Gillespie and others v Northern Health and Social Services Boards and Others* [1996] ECR I-00475.

107 Case C-333/97 *Susanne Lewen v Lothar Denda* [1999] ECR I-07243 (maternity pay and Christmas bonus).

108 Case C-218/98 *Oumar Dabo Abdoulaye and Others v Régie nationale des usines Renault SA* [1999] ECR I-05723, paras 4–5: Additionally, during the duration of maternity leave a female employee received 100% of her net salary, less the daily allowances paid by social security.

109 ibid para 23.

110 See eg Erin M Rehel, 'When Dad Stays Home Too: Paternity Leave, Gender, and Parenting' (2014) 28(1) *Gender and Society* 110-111.

workplace.[111] Hence, the views that women possess specific parenting abilities and ability to provide their children with 'unrivalled nurturing surroundings' are used to ensure that the traditional distribution of gender roles continues.[112]

Thus, although the attempt to secure maternity rights has been a major focus of decades of campaigning for women's equality, concerns have been raised that maternity rights might reinforce the assumption that women should be responsible for childcare.[113] Whereas all new mothers take temporary absence from the workforce to recover from birth and to adjust to their new role for varying lengths of time, fathers typically maintain their employment ties in the post-birth period.[114] A different interpretation would arguably be more helpful in furthering gender equality. The Court could equally have employed reasoning based on payments and other benefits available to parents rather than just mothers. Cichowski questions whether entitlements paid only to women in connection with parenthood help or hinder in promoting equality in the long term in the workplace and society.[115] So while the case law clearly advanced women's rights, it also plays to the stereotypes of women as mothers and carers and men as workers and breadwinners. However, it is worth noting the dilemmas women face with maternity because the reality is that whether maternity leave enforces gendered stereotypes, as the Court has noted it also disadvantages women in relation to men. Additionally, it has been argued that extended maternity leave may encourage women to stay out of work for lengthy or repeated periods, which in turn may hinder women from re-entering employment on the same pre-maternity track.[116] The law as it has developed appears to require women to do it all – have children, care for them and participate in the labour market. We will return to this theme in Chapter 7 on EU Citizenship.

The impact of remedies and sanctions

Alexandra Timmer and Linda Senden have noted that the degree to which EU gender equality law will impact the eradicating sex discrimination depends on the type of remedies and sanctions provided for by Member States.[117] While the

111 Catherine Verniers and Jorge Vala, 'Justifying Gender Discrimination in the Workplace: The Mediating Role of Motherhood Myths' (2018) 13(1) *PLoS ONE* doi:10.1371/journal.pone.0190657.

112 ibid.

113 Fredman (n 72) 442.

114 Rehel (n 110) 111.

115 Cichowski (n 105) 106. See Clare McGlynn, 'Pregnancy, Parenthood and the Court of Justice in Abdoulaye' (2000) 25 *European Law Review* 654; Eugenia Caracciolo di Torella and Annick Masselot, 'Pregnancy, Maternity and the Organisation of Family Life: An Attempt to Classify the Case Law if the Court of Justice' (2001) 26 *European Law Review* 239.

116 Olivetti and Petrongolo (n 103) 212.

117 eg financial compensation, reinstatement, criminal sanctions, administrative fines. Alexandra Timmer and Linda Senden, *A Comparative Analysis of Gender Equality Law in Europe 2016* (European Union 2016).

Member States remain responsible for determining the choice of sanctions for breaches of EU gender equality law, Articles 18 and 25 of the Recast Equality Directive stipulate that violations must be met by effective, proportionate and dissuasive sanctions. Further, possible financial compensation or reparation must also be proportionate to the damage suffered. Although in principle, the fixing of an upper limit on the amount of compensatory award is not inconsistent with the requirements of the Directive, the award of compensation has to 'guarantee real and effective judicial protection, have a real deterrent effect on the employer and must in any event be adequate in relation to the damage sustained'.[118] Hence, purely nominal compensation would not satisfy the requirements of an effective transposition of the Directive. This was the central issue in *Marshall*[119] where the Court deliberated whether or not it was valid for the Sex Discrimination Act 1975 to have an upper limit on the amount of compensation that could be awarded for discriminating against a female employee. Although the tribunal wanted to award Helen Marshall almost £20,000 for sex discrimination, her compensation was subject to a limit.[120] Ms Marshall challenged the compensation limit as being contrary to EU law. The Court held that Member States could not fix an upper limit on compensation for loss and damage suffered as a result of sex discrimination. As a result, both the Sex Discrimination Act 1975 and Race Relations Act 1976 were amended to remove the cap on discrimination awards. Due to the lack of such cap, discrimination claims on grounds of sex and race are feared by employers precisely because compensation is potentially unlimited. The record award was made in the 2011 English Employment Tribunal decision in *Michalak*,[121] in which a former NHS doctor was awarded £4.5 million for sex and race discrimination. *Marshall* may therefore be significant for bringing sex discrimination cases before national courts. However, compared to *Michalak*, the amount of compensation sought in *Marshall* is very modest and it is therefore worth asking whether the level of compensation available in sex discrimination cases has meant that employers are more likely to settle cases outside the courts instead. This would obviously result in an inability to find out the extent of such cases initiated before the national courts.

Conclusion

Suzanne Goldberg has acknowledged the limitations of the law as articulated by the courts by emphasising the fact that the courts are only one source for remedying gender discrimination and that the courts' version of law is only one among

118 Case 14/83 *Sabine von Colson and Elisabeth Kamann v Land Nordrhein-Westfalen* [1984] ECR 1891, paras 23–24.
119 Case C-271/92 *M Helen Marshall v Southampton and South-West Hampshire Area Health Authority* [1993] ECR I-4397.
120 £8,500 at the time.
121 *Michalak v Mid Yorkshire Hospitals NHS Trust* [2011] ET 1810815 (Employment Tribunal).

many.[122] Therefore, enforcement of anti-discrimination law by the courts cannot respond fully to the complex ways in which often unconscious biases manifest themselves, shape individuals' participation into discrimination and challenge the ways in which individuals perceive and react to identity traits designated for protection.[123] Therefore, the courts do not solely contribute to the achievement of gender equality, or the principle of non-discrimination, in workplaces or society in general, even if they have the power to shape the direction or scope of equality law. This is worth keeping in mind when trying to evaluate the achievements of the Court of Justice in this area.

The equal pay cases suggest that the economic rationale underpinning the EU law provisions remains the key driver and that equality remains a secondary consideration even though the Court has introduced some safeguards such as applying equal pay for equal work also to work of higher value so that employers cannot assign additional duties and then pay an employee less because the work is not actually equal.[124] However, at the same time the approach taken by the Court in its case law involving pregnant workers' access to employment or dismissal of pregnant workers appears to be very proactive. The focus on economic rationales appears to have been pushed aside in cases involving pregnant workers in order to make way for comprehensive protection of pregnant workers. In these cases, it is easier to see that the Court considers that the economic aim is secondary to the social aim.[125]

EU equality law has developed from the economic beginnings of Article 119 EEC with the principle of equality between men and women slowly gaining traction in Community and later EU law.[126] According to Ann Numhauser-Henning, '[t]his background implies a double aim, still inherent in EU sex equality law, one linked to internal market arguments and one linked to the discourse on fundamental rights'.[127] It is this double aim that the Court has tried to negotiate, sometimes favouring the one, sometimes the other. The Court has undoubtedly driven gender equality forward through its case law and subjected both national and EU legal provisions to scrutiny in order to ensure compliance with measures which protect women in the labour market. However, the economic underpinnings are never far away. The law is framed in relation to labour market participation rather than equality generally and the Court has not taken opportunities to expand the equality agenda or to challenge stereotypes which define women's roles and perhaps form some of the strongest barriers to equality.

122 Suzanne B Goldberg, 'Identity-based discrimination and the barriers to complexity' in Dagmar Schiek and Anna Lawson (eds), *European Union Non-Discrimination Law and Intersectionality: Investigating the Triangle of Racial, Gender and Disability Discrimination* (Taylor and Francis 2011) 179.

123 ibid.

124 See, eg, Case C-157/86 *Mary Murphy and others v An Bord Telecom Eireann* [1988] ECR 673.

125 Case C-50/96 *Deutsche Telekom AG, formerly Deutsche Bundespost Telekom v Lilli Schröder* [2000] ECR I-743, para 57.

126 Meenan (n 6).

127 Numhauser-Henning (n 6) 147.

Bibliography

Ahrens P, *Actors, Institutions, and the Making of EU Gender Equality Programs* (Palgrave MacMillan 2018)

Albrecht J, Skogman Thoursie P and Vroman S, 'Parental Leave and the Glass Ceiling in Sweden' (European Society of Population Economics Conference, Braga, Portugal, June 2014)

Arza C, 'The Gender Dimensions of Pension Systems: Policies and Constraints for the Protection of Older Women' (2015) *UN Women Discussion Paper* No 1

Barbier D and others, *Gender Equality Index 2017: Measuring Gender Equality in the European Union 2005–2015* (European Institute for Gender Equality 2017)

Barnard C, *EU Employment Law* (4th edn, Oxford University Press 2012)

Bennett F, *Megatrends and Social Security: Family and Gender* (International Social Security Association 2017)

Caracciolo di Torella E, 'Recent Developments in Pregnancy and Maternity Rights' (1999) 28 *Industrial Law Journal* 276

Caracciolo di Torella E and Masselot A, 'Pregnancy, Maternity and the Organisation of Family Life: An Attempt to Classify the Case Law if the Court of Justice' (2001) 26 *European Law Review* 239

Cichowski R, *The European Court and Civil Society: Litigation, Mobilization and Governance* (Cambridge University Press 2007)

Commission, *The Gender Gap in Pensions in the EU* (European Union 2013)

Conway G, *EU Law* (Routledge Spotlights 2015) 657

Council Directive 2000/43/EC of 29 June 2000 Implementing the Principle of Equal Treatment Between Persons Irrespective of Racial or Ethnic Origin [2000] OJ L180/22

Council Directive 2000/78/EC of 27 November 2000 Establishing a General Framework for equal Treatment in Employment and Occupation [2000] OJ L303/16

Council Directive 92/85/EEC of 19 October 1992 on the Introduction of Measures to Encourage Improvements in the Safety and Health at Work of Pregnant Workers and Workers Who Have Recently Given Birth or Are Breastfeeding [1992] OJ L/348

Directive 2006/54/EC of the European Parliament and of the Council of 5 July 2006 on the Implementation of the Principle of Equal Opportunities and Equal Treatment of Men and Women in Matters of Employment and Occupation (Recast) [2006] OJ L204/23

Directive 75/117/EEC on Equal Pay for Male and Female Workers [1975] OJ L45/19

Directive 76/207/EEC on the Implementation of the Principle of Equal Treatment for Men and Women as Regards Access to Employment, Vocational Training and Promotion and Working Conditions [1976] OJ L39/40

Ellis E and Watson P, *EU Anti-Discrimination Law* (Oxford University Press 2012)

Elomäki A, 'The Economic Case for Gender Equality in the European Union: Selling Gender Equality to Decision-makers and Neoliberalism to Women's Organizations' (2015) 22(3) *European Journal of Women's Studies* 288

Eurostat, 'Gender Pay Gap Statistics' (March 2018) <http://gldr.co/1LcrZai> accessed 4 April 2018

Fredman S, 'Reversing Roles: Bringing Men into the Frame' (2014) 10(4) *International Journal of Law in Context* 442, 444 doi:10.1017/S1744552314000214

Goldberg SB, 'Identity-based Discrimination and the Barriers to Complexity' in Schiek D and Lawson A (eds), *European Union Non-Discrimination Law and Intersectionality: Investigating the Triangle of Racial, Gender and Disability Discrimination* (Taylor and Francis 2011)

Guerrina R, *Mothering the Union: The Politics of Gender, Equality and Maternity Rights in the EU* (Manchester University Press 2005)

Guth J, 'Law as the Object and Agent of Integration: Gendering the Court of Justice of the European Union, Its Decisions and Their Impact' in Abels G and Macrae H (eds), *Gendering European Integration Theory Engaging New Dialogues* (Barbara Budrich 2016)

Hedija V, 'Sector-Specific Gender Pay Gap: Evidence from the European Union Countries' (2017) 30(1) *Economic Research-Ekonomska Istraživanja* 1804 doi:10.1080/1331677X.2017.1392886

Heilman M, Manzi F and Braun S, 'Presumed Incompetent: Perceived Lack of Fit and Gender Bias in Recruitment and Selection' in Broadbridge A and Fielden S (eds), *Handbook of Gendered Careers in Management: Getting in, Getting on, Getting out* (Edward Elgar 2015)

Hix S, *The Political System of the European Union* (Palgrave MacMillan 2005)

International Labour Organization, 'Rights, Jobs and Social Security: New Visions for Older Women and Men' (30 September 2008) <www.ilo.org/gender/Events/Campaign2008-2009/WCMS_098840/lang – en/index.htm> accessed 14 December 2017

Kantola J, *Gender and the European Union* (Palgrave Macmillan 2010)

Klein U, *Geschlechterverhaeltnisse und Gleichstellungspolitk in der Europaeischen Union* (Springer VS 2013)

Maj J, *Gender Equality in the European Union a Comparative Study of Poland and Germany* (Nomos 2017)

Marin B and Zólyomi E, *Women's Work and Pensions: What Is Good, What Is Best? Designing Gender-Sensitive Arrangements* (Ashgate 2010)

McGlynn C, 'Pregnancy, Parenthood and the Court of Justice in Abdoulaye' (2000) 25 *European Law Review* 654

Meenan H, 'Introduction' in Meenan H (ed), *Equality Law in an Enlarged European Union* (Cambridge University Press 2007)

Neels K, De Wachter D and Peeters H, 'The Effect of Family Formation on the Build-up of Pension Rights Among Minority Ethnic Groups and Native Women in Belgium' (2017) *Ageing and Society* 1-2 doi:10.1017/S0144686X17000010

Numhauser-Henning A, 'EU Sex Equality Law Post-Amsterdam' in Meenan H (ed), *Equality in an Enlarged European Union: Understanding the Article 13 Directives* (Cambridge University Press 2007)

O'Cinneide C, 'Positive Action and the Limits of Existing Law' (2006) 13 *Maastricht Journal of European and Comparative Law* 351–364

Office for National Statistics, 'People in Employment on a Zero-hours Contract: Mar 2017' 2 <www.ons.gov.uk/employmentandlabourmarket/peopleinwork/earningsandworkinghours/articles/contractsthatdonotguaranteeaminimumnumberofhours/mar2017> accessed 26 November 2017

Olivetti C and Petrongolo B, 'The Economic Consequences of Family Policies: Lessons from a Century of Legislation in High-Income Countries' (2017) 31(1) *Journal of Economic Perspectives* 205

Prechal S, 'Achievements and Trends in EU Gender Equality Law' (2005) 35 <www.euroinfo.ee/malta/pdf/c4.pdf> accessed 12 December 2017

Regulation (EEC) No 1612/68 of the Council of 15 October 1968 on Freedom of Movement for Workers Within the Community [1968] OJ L257

Regulation (EU) No 492/2011 of the European Parliament and of the Council of 5 April 2011 on Freedom of Movement for Workers Within the Union [2011] OJ L141/1

Rehel EM, 'When Dad Stays Home Too: Paternity Leave, Gender, and Parenting' (2014) 28(1) *Gender and Society* 110

Samek Lodovici M, Drufuca S, Patrizio M and Pesce F, *The Gender Pension Gap: Differences Between Mothers and Women Without Children* (European Union 2016)

Timmer A and Senden L, *A Comparative Analysis of Gender Equality Law in Europe 2016* (European Union 2016)

Treaty Establishing the European Economic Community (Rome 25 March 1957)

Treaty of the Functioning of the European Union [2012] OJ C 326/47

van der Vleuten A, *The Price of Gender Equality: Member States and Governance in the European Union* (Routledge 2016)

Verniers C and Vala J, 'Justifying Gender Discrimination in the Workplace: The Mediating Role of Motherhood Myths' (2018) 13(1) *PLoS ONE* doi:10.1371/journal.pone.0190657

6 It's not just gender that's gendered

Equality case law more broadly

> There is a theory behind the culture of victimhood: It's called 'intersectionality'. This theory posits that racism, sexism, classism, ableism, etc. are interconnected, overlapping and mutually reinforcing. Together they form a 'matrix of oppression'.[1]

The previous chapter has outlined the role of the Court of Justice[2] in gender equality law at European Union (EU) level and has highlighted how it made a significant contribution but also missed opportunities. Those missed opportunities come predominantly from maintaining a traditional view of women as mothers and carers, by focusing on a labour market or economic rationale underpinning all decisions and by undervaluing roles traditionally and predominantly undertaken by women, such as caring work or domestic labour. In this chapter we continue the theme of looking at equality law but now broaden our scope to consider equality on grounds other than gender. In this chapter we examine the role the Court has played in interpreting and developing the law in relation to non-discrimination on the grounds of religion or belief, sexual orientation and disability. In doing so we are particularly interested in how a gendered reading can help us make sense of the case law and what it could add to our understanding in this area. As such, this chapter inevitably grapples with difficult and complex concepts such as intersectionality and multiple grounds of discrimination as we seek to understand whether adding gender to the mix can help us move towards a more holistic understanding of equality law.

The chapter begins with a very brief outline of the legislative framework in this area before then moving on to analyse selected cases on sexual orientation discrimination, religious discrimination and race discrimination and, in particular, issues with intersectionality. We cannot analyse these areas in full in a single

1 Christina Hoff Sommers.

2 While the Court of Justice of the European Union consists of the Court of Justice, the General Court and specialised courts, we refer exclusively to the Court of Justice in this Chapter. See Treaty on European Union [2012] OJ C326/13 (TEU), art 19(1).

chapter; so we have chosen sub-topics and cases which help us reflect on the difference a gendered reading can make and which allow us to best illustrate our argument overall. In the final part of the chapter we consider disability discrimination and associative discrimination which was introduced in relation to disability discrimination. The latter area of law allows us to consider how the idea of basing discrimination and equality law on the notion of human dignity might inform this area of law. We examine how a gendered reading can inform that concept and how gender awareness can be enhanced by putting human dignity at the centre of our thinking.

The EU legal framework

Prior to the Treaty of Amsterdam[3] the only equality or non-discrimination provisions were those which related specifically to nationality or those under what was Article 119 of the Treaty Establishing European Economic Community[4] (EEC) and what is now Article 157 of the Treaty on the Functioning of the European Union[5] (TFEU) on equal pay. The Treaty of Amsterdam saw the inclusion of what was then Article 13 of the Treaty establishing European Community[6] (TEC) (now Article 19(1) TFEU), which provides:

> Without prejudice to the other provisions of the Treaties and within the limits of the powers conferred by them upon the Union, the Council, acting unanimously in accordance with a special legislative procedure and after obtaining the consent of the European Parliament, may take appropriate action to combat discrimination based on sex, racial or ethnic origin, religion or belief, disability, age or sexual orientation.

Article 13 EC set the scene for a series of Directives prohibiting discrimination on various grounds and in various settings. We will not deal with those in relation to sex discrimination here as gender equality was the focus of the previous chapter but instead focus on the others.

The Race Equality Directive[7] prohibits discrimination on the ground of racial or ethnic origin in a broad range of fields, including employment, social protection and social advantages, education and goods and services available to the public, including housing. The Employment Equality or Framework Directive,[8]

3 ibid.
4 Treaty establishing the European Economic Community (Rome, 25 March 1957).
5 Treaty of the Functioning of the European Union [2012] OJ C 326/47.
6 Treaty establishing the European Community [2002] OJ C325/33.
7 Council Directive 2000/43/EC of 29 June 2000 implementing the principle of equal treatment between persons irrespective of racial or ethnic origin [2000] OJ L180/22.
8 Council Directive 2000/78/EC of 27 November 2000 establishing a general framework for equal treatment in employment and occupation [2000] OJ L303/16 (the Framework Directive).

however, is limited to the field of employment and occupation but covers the grounds of religion or belief, disability, age and sexual orientation.

The Directives prohibit direct and indirect discrimination as well as harassment and define those concepts as follows:

> 2 (a) direct discrimination shall be taken to occur where one person is treated less favourably than another is, has been or would be treated in a comparable situation. . .
> (b) indirect discrimination shall be taken to occur where an apparently neutral provision, criterion or practice would put persons having a particular [characteristic] at a particular disadvantage compared with other persons unless:
>
> (i) that provision, criterion or practice is objectively justified by a legitimate aim and the means of achieving that aim are appropriate and necessary, or
>
> 3 Harassment shall be deemed to be a form of discrimination within the meaning of paragraph 1, when unwanted conduct related to any of the grounds referred to in Article 1 takes place with the purpose or effect of violating the dignity of a person and of creating an intimidating, hostile, degrading, humiliating or offensive environment.
> 4 An instruction to discriminate against persons on any of the grounds referred to in Article 1 shall be deemed to be discrimination within the meaning of paragraph 1.[9]

It seems clear that social considerations were in the mind of the drafters. The Preamble to the Framework Directive contains the following statement:

> Discrimination based on religion or belief, disability, age or sexual orientation may undermine the achievement of the objectives of the EC Treaty, in particular the attainment of a high level of employment and social protection, raising the standard of living and the quality of life, economic and social cohesion and solidarity, and the free movement of persons.[10]

9 Directive 2000/78 and Directive 2000/43 both contain these definitions in Article 2. The definitions are the same although the wording in the Framework Directive is slightly more complex as it includes additional provisions on disability which have been removed in our reproduction above but which we deal with in more detail in the relevant section below.

10 Directive 2000/78, recital 11. Directive 2000/43 contains an almost identical statement in recital 9: Discrimination based on racial or ethnic origin may undermine the achievement of the objectives of the EC Treaty, in particular the attainment of a high level of employment and of social protection, the raising of the standard of living and quality of life, economic and social cohesion and solidarity. It may also undermine the objective of developing the European Union as an area of freedom, security and justice.

However, the non-discrimination provisions, though couched in fundamental rights and social terms, are still underpinned by a fundamentally economic rationale. For example, the Framework Directive applies exclusively to the employment sphere, and the Race Directive, though extended to matters that go beyond the employment relationship *per se*, only extends to market-related issues and is restricted in scope to matters relating to race or ethnic origin. As Catherine Barnard rightly points out, the Framework Directive prohibits discrimination on wide grounds but in narrow circumstances, whereas the Race Directive prohibits discrimination on narrow grounds but in slightly broader circumstances.[11] As well as impacting on the level and scope of protection offered to those directly affected by the Directives this may also have gendered implications and, of course, continues the narrative of equality as something good for the market rather than as something good *per se*. We will return to these issues as we consider the individual protected characteristics in turn below.

The EU, fundamental rights and the European Convention on Human Rights

One of the earliest mentions of fundamental rights in the Court's jurisprudence appears in *Internationale Handelsgesellschaft*,[12] more famous perhaps for reinforcing the supremacy of EU law than for establishing fundamental rights, where the Court declared:

> In fact, respect for fundamental rights forms an integral part of the general principles of law protected by the Court of Justice. The protection of such rights, whilst inspired by the constitutional traditions common to the Member States, must be ensured within the framework of the structure and objectives of the Community.[13]

In order to adjudicate matters falling within the scope of fundamental rights, the Court draws inspiration primarily from two sources, namely the Member States' common constitutional traditions and the guidelines supplied by international treaties for the protection of human rights to which the Member States are signatories or on which they have collaborated.[14]

More concretely the EU affirmed its commitment to fundamental rights with the inclusion of the Charter of Fundamental Rights and Freedoms[15] in the Treaty of Nice in 2000. However, the legal status of the Charter remained unclear and it

11 Catherine Barnard, *EU Employment Law* (4th edn, Oxford University Press 2012) 310.

12 Case 11/70 *Internationale Handelsgesellschaft mbH v Einfuhr- und Vorratsstelle für Getreide und Futtermittel* [1970] ECR 1125.

13 *Internationale Handelsgese* (n 11) para 3.

14 Opinion 2/13 [2014] EU:C:2014:2454, para 37.

15 Charter of Fundamental Rights of the European Union in Nice [2000] OJ C364/1 (the Charter).

did not become legally binding until the coming into force of the Treaty of Lisbon[16] in 2009. Nonetheless the Court did make reference to the Charter as well as fundamental rights enshrined elsewhere in its case law; always stressing that:

> Although respect for fundamental rights which form an integral part of those general principles of law is a condition of the legality of Community acts, those rights cannot in themselves have the effect of extending the scope of the Treaty provisions beyond the competences of the Community.[17]

There is some mention of the jurisprudence of the European Court of Human Rights in early decisions and in its 1991 decision in *ERT*[18] the Court explicitly states that the European Convention on Human Rights[19] (ECHR) has special significance in the area of fundamental rights in the EU.[20] However, it seems the ECHR is not significant enough to allow the EU to accede to the Convention. In *Opinion 2/94*[21] in which the Court held that as European Community law stood at the time, the Community had no competence to accede to the ECHR and act in the field of human rights.[22] That changed with the Lisbon Treaty which provided for the accession of the EU to the ECHR. Article 6(2) states:

> The Union shall accede to the European Convention for the Protection of Human Rights and Fundamental Freedoms. Such accession shall not affect the Union's competences as defined in the Treaties.

A draft accession agreement was prepared and the Court was asked for its opinion on it. It rejected it. It seems the Court of Justice considers that opening up the EU to scrutiny by the European Court of Human Rights (ECtHR) runs counter to the primacy, unity and effectiveness of EU law.[23] While a detailed analysis of the relationship between the two European jurisdictions is beyond the scope of this chapter,[24] we suggest that because of the tensions and different approaches

16 Treaty of Lisbon amending the Treaty on European Union and the Treaty establishing the European Community [2007] OJ C306/01.

17 Case C-249/96 *Lisa Jaqueline Grant v South-West Trains Ltd* [1998] ECR I-621, para 5.

18 Case C-260/89 *ERT* [1991] EU:C:1991:254, para 41.

19 Convention for the Protection of Human Rights and Fundamental Freedoms (European Convention on Human Rights, as amended).

20 See also Case C-402/05 P and C-415/05 *P Kadi and Al Barakaat International Foundation v Council and Commission* [2008] EU:C:2008:461, para 283; Anthony Arnull, *The European Union and its Court of Justice* (2nd edn, Oxford University Press 2006).

21 Opinion 2/94 [1996] ECR I-1759.

22 ibid para 36.

23 Benedikt Pirker and Stefan Reitemeyer, *Zum Gutachten 2/13 des EuGH über den Beitritt der EU zur EMRK*, Jusletter 23. März 2015 <http://jusletter.weblaw.ch/juslissues/2015/795/zum-gutachten-2-13-d_e6837ca053.html__ONCE> accessed 9 April 2018.

24 But see eg Paul Gragl, *The Accession of the European Union to the European Convention on Human Rights* (Hart 2013); Anthony Arnull, Piet Eeckhout and Takis Tridimas, *Continuity*

between the courts, fundamental rights in the EU context can appear disjointed and incoherent. Instead of focusing on ensuring its position as the highest arbiter in *all* things EU law, the Court of Justice should focus on effective fundamental rights protection and help shape accession to the ECHR in a meaningful way. Instead of effectively blocking the accession on primacy or autonomy of EU law grounds, the Court of Justice should be learning from the ECtHR as well as sharing its own practice in areas where it has had cause to develop protection going beyond that adjudicated on by the ECtHR. We highlight where these issues arise in the consideration of the protected grounds below.

Sexual orientation discrimination

The EU did not have a good start in terms of protecting the rights of lesbian, gay, bisexual, and transgender (LGBT)[25] persons.[26] Laurence Helfer and Erik Voeten have argued that since LGBT rights were not explicitly part of EU law in the 1990s, the EU has relied heavily on the case law of the ECtHR. Therefore, the dismantling of the restrictions on LGBT rights in Europe has been driven largely by Strasbourg, rather than the EU. The case law of the ECtHR has, in turn, been influenced by progressive shifts in European national laws and social policies regarding sexual minorities.[27] Although the ECtHR is now 'increasingly progressive

---

and Change in EU Law: Essays in Honour of Sir Francis Jacobs (Oxford University Press 2008), Part II which includes contributions from Antonio Tizzano, Robin Whit and Jacqueline Dutheil de la Rochere; Tobias Lock, 'EU Accession to the ECHR: Implications for the Judicial Review in Strasbourg' (2011) 35(6) *European Law Review* 777; Tobias Lock, 'Walking on a Tightrope: The Draft ECHR Accession Agreement and the Autonomy of the EU Legal Order' (2011) 48(4) *Common Market Law Review* 1025; Samantha Besson, 'Gender Discrimination Under EU and ECHR Law: Never Shall the Twain Meet?' (2008) 8(4) *Human Rights Law Review* 647 doi:10.1093/hrlr/ngn023; Tawhida Ahmed, 'The Opposition of the CJEU to the ECHR as a Mechanism of International Human Rights' (2017) 4(2) *Journal of International and Comparative Law* 1; Dimitry Kochenov (ed), *EU Citizenship and Federalism: The Role of Rights* (Cambridge University Press 2016); Gráinne de Búrca, 'After the EU Charter of Fundamental Rights: The Court of Justice as a Human Rights Adjudicator?' (2013) 13 *Maastricht Journal of European and Comparative Law* 168; Louise Halleskov Storgaard, 'EU Law Autonomy Versus European Fundamental Rights Protection: On Opinion 2/13 on EU Accession to the ECHR' (2015) 15(3) *Human Rights Law Review* 485; Ulf Bernitz, Stephen Weatherill, and Sybe De Vries (eds), *The Protection of Fundamental Rights in the EU After Lisbon* (Hart 2013).

25 The acronym LGBT can be used for the entire same-sex oriented community. Other terms used in literature include LGBTI where the letter I stands for 'intersex' and LGBTQ where the letter Q stands for either 'queer' or 'questioning'.

26 For the contribution that the general principles of EU law have made to the protection of the rights of LGBT individuals and same-sex couples under EU law, see Alina Tryfonidou, 'Discrimination on the grounds of sexual orientation and gender identity' in Stefan Vogenauer and Stephen Weatherill (eds), *General Principles of Law: European and Comparative Perspectives* (Hart 2017).

27 Laurence R Helfer and Erik Voeten, 'International Courts as Agents of Legal Change: Evidence from LGBT Rights in Europe' (2014) 68 *International Organization* 77, 85 doi:10.10170S0020818313000398.

on LGBT issues',[28] the change occurred incrementally over more than half a century.[29] Because the rulings against one Council of Europe member state have a tendency to influence policy changes also in other member states,[30] LGBT rights feature prominently in legal and social science debates about court-led social change and political backlashes against judges.[31] They further found that almost all LGBT rights litigation before the ECtHR has focused on a handful of States, namely Austria, Germany and the United Kingdom (UK) where attitudes towards sexual minorities are relatively progressive.[32]

The CJEU has, in matters of sexual orientation, remained conservative and careful. In 1998 the case of *Grant*[33] suggested that the Court was not prepared to jump the legislative gun and make a decision that would clearly have been in line with the soon to be introduced Framework Directive which made express provision for sexual orientation as a protected ground in Article 1. Thus, in its rather surprising decision in *Grant*, the Court held that it could not be sex discrimination where an employer limited travel concessions to a spouse or dependents even though at the time it was clear that same-sex partners would not be able to claim such concessions; there was no provision for equal marriage or even equivalent legal status in most Member States. The Court decided not to extend protection on the grounds of sex to protection on the grounds of sexual orientations – the argument presumably being that, as long as treatment of lesbians and gay men is equal (or equally bad), there is no discrimination between the sexes.

The approach is not entirely consistent with the Court's own reasoning in *P v S* which concerned discrimination on the grounds of gender reassignment. As Helfer and Voeten note, the UK has long recognised the right of transwomen and men to change their sex on driver's licences, passports and other official documents following gender reassignment surgery.[34] Discrimination against transwomen and men was initially prohibited via an amendment to the now repealed Sex Discrimination Act 1975, following the Court of Justice's 1996 decision in *P v S*.[35] P was dismissed from a post of a manager in an educational establishment after informing S, the Director of Studies, Chief Executive and Financial Director of the establishment of her intention to undergo gender reassignment.[36] P commenced action against her employer on the basis that the dismissal

28 ibid 79.
29 ibid 88.
30 ibid.
31 ibid 85.
32 ibid 88 and 90.
33 *Grant* (n 17).
34 Helfer and Voeten (n 26) 94.
35 Case C-13/94 *P v S and Cornwall County Council* [1996] ECR I-2143.
36 P was given three months' notice after undergoing minor surgical operations. Her final surgical operation to give P the physical attributes of a woman was performed before her dismissal took effect, but after she had been given notice. ibid paras 3–4.

amounted to sex discrimination.[37] When the case got to the Court of Justice, it held that:

> 'discrimination [arising, as in this case, from the gender reassignment] is based, essentially if not exclusively, on the sex of the person concerned'.[38] Hence, a person who was dismissed because they intended to undergo, was undergoing or had undergone gender reassignment was treated less favourably than persons of the sex to which they were deemed to belong before undergoing gender reassignment.[39]

It is unfortunate that the Court did not see fit to apply an equally expansive definition in *Grant*. However as Barry Fitzpatrick notes,

> P v S can be seen as an unusually progressive decision for the Court in the mid 1990s when much of the rest of its jurisprudence was consolidating the dramatic advances in sex equality law from the mid-to-late 1980s. In this sense Grant can be seen as a cautious judgement more in keeping with the judicial mood of the times.[40]

In addition, the Court was clearly aware of the inclusion of sexual orientation discrimination in Article 13 EC and the negotiations of the Framework Directive so this may simply be a case brought a little too early to a court that did not want to pre-empt legislative developments. It is also, of course, a case brought to a very politically aware Court which has again and again stressed Member States' sole competence to regulate matters of family law and legal status of relationships.

Since the introduction of the Framework Directive, the Court has not had the opportunity to consider a vast number of cases relating to sexual orientation discrimination and most of them have dealt with access to benefits for spouses and partners. In *D and Sweden*[41] the Court of Justice dismissed an appeal lodged against the judgement of the General Court[42] upholding a Council decision refusing an employee the benefit of the household allowance provided for in

37 ibid para 3: 'The gender reassignment began with a 'life test', a period during which P dressed and behaved as a woman, followed by surgery to give P the physical attributes of a woman'.

38 ibid paras 20–21.

39 ibid para 21.

40 Barry Fitzpatrick, 'The "mainstreaming" of sexual orientation into European Equality Law' in Helen Meenan (ed), *Equality Law in an Enlarged European Union* (Cambridge University Press 2007) 316.

41 Joined Cases C-122/99 P and C-125/99 P *D and Sweden v Council* [2001] ECR I-4319. This was a staff case so tells us something about how the EU considers these issues in relation to its own employees.

42 or Court of First Instance as it was known then.

the Staff Regulations[43] for married officials.[44] In his opinion in the same case, Advocate General (AG) Mischo had considered that, in light of the Court's 1986 decision in *Reed*,[45] 'the definition of marriage includes only traditional marriage between two people of the opposite sex'.[46] In *Reed*, the Court of Justice had concluded that:

> In the absence of any indication of a general social development which would justify a broad construction, and in the absence of any indication to the contrary in the regulation, it must be held that the term 'spouse' in Article 10 of the Regulation refers to a marital relationship only.[47]

AG Mischo also pointed out that the EU legislature had expressly decided not to adopt Sweden's request to modify the Staff Regulations to assimilate same-sex registered partnerships with marriage, but instead to engage in further study of the matter.[48] These points filtered into the Court's judgement upholding the General Court's interpretation of the Staff Regulations.[49] The Court further rejected D's plea regarding infringement of the principle of equal treatment, finding that the situation of an official in a registered partnership was not comparable to that of a married official, taking into account the existing situation in the Member States reflecting the absence of any general assimilation of marriage and other forms of statutory union.[50] The Court of Justice recalled that 'according to the definition generally accepted by the Member States, the term "marriage" means a union between two persons of the opposite sex'.[51] It then

43 Regulation No 30/65/EEC, 4/65/Euratom of the Councils of 16 March 1965 amending the Staff Regulations of Officials and the Conditions of Employment of Other Servants of the European Economic Community and the European Atomic Energy Community [1965] OJ 47/701 (Staff Regulations), annex VII, art 1(2): 'The household allowance shall be granted to: (a) a married official; (b) an official who is widowed, divorced, legally separated or unmarried and has one or more dependent children. . . .'

44 Case T-264/97 *D v Council* [1999] ECR-SC I-A-1 and II-1.

45 Case 59/85 *State of the Netherlands v Ann Florence Reed* [1986] ECR 1283. Ms Reed was the partner of a British citizen, legally residing in the Netherlands. The Dutch authorities had refused to grant her a residence permit on the grounds that she was not married to her partner. AG Lenz had already stressed in his Opinion in this case that 'companions can certainly not be treated in the same way as spouses in all Member States in view of the fact that their cultural, social and ethical traditions vary widely in some respects'. See Case 59/85 *State of the Netherlands v Ann Florence Reed* [1986] ECR I-1284, Opinion of AG Lenz.

46 Joined Cases C-122/99 P and C-125/99 P *D and Sweden v Council* [2001] ECR I-4329, Opinion of Advocate General Mischo, para 48.

47 *Reed* (n 45) para 15.

48 *D and Sweden* (n 41) paras 51–53.

49 ibid para 48.

50 ibid paras 47–52. See also Koen Lenaerts and Kathleen Gutman, 'The Comparative Law Method and the European Court of Justice: Echoes Across the Atlantic' (2016) 64(4) *The American Journal of Comparative Law* 841 doi:10.1093/ajcl/avw017.

51 *D and Sweden* (n 41) para 34.

considered that even if, since 1989, an increasing number of Member States have introduced statutory arrangements granting legal recognition to various forms of union between partners of the same sex or of the opposite sex (such as the registered partnership), such arrangements were regarded in the Member States concerned as being distinct from marriage.[52] In such circumstances, the Court concluded that the intention of the legislature was indeed to grant the benefit only to married couples.[53] However, it is worth noting that the Staff Regulations were amended following *D and Sweden* to include 'stable non-marital partners' as long as certain conditions are met.[54] The Civil Service Tribunal held in *W v Commission*[55] that those condition must be interpreted flexibly; in this case considering the applicant's right to marry his partner under Belgian law irrelevant because in doing so he would risk prosecution in Morocco as a dual Belgian–Moroccan national. Effectively therefore he should be treated as though he did not have the right to marry. The Court's decisions demonstrate an approach where it reacts to social science debates rather than actively leads social change and thus criticism against the increasing social conservativism of the justices of the Court of Justice may well be warranted.[56]

In two important decisions the Court held that spouses in certain circumstances where there is no equal marriage available the Member State in question must nonetheless provide equal access to same-sex partners to all the employment benefits open to heterosexual married couples. These circumstances are where same-sex partners have entered into a form of registered partnership which provides an equivalent legal status to marriage. Anything else is direct discrimination under the Framework Directive. These cases taken together with the decisions in *Hay*[57] and *Asociaţia Accept*[58] suggested that the Court was moving towards protecting LGBT rights and taking them seriously.

52 ibid paras 35–36.
53 ibid para 37.
54 Council Regulation (EC, Euratom) No 723/2004 of 22 March 2004 amending the Staff Regulations of officials of the European Communities and the Conditions of Employment of other servants of the European Communities [2004] OJ L124/1, particularly recitals 7–8, art 1(2)(c). The Staff Regulations have been further amended, most recently by Regulation (EU, Euratom) No 1023/2013 of the European Parliament and of the Council of 22 October 2013 [2013] OJ L287/15.
55 Case F-86/09 *W v Commission* [2010] EU:F:2010:125.
56 See eg Maxine David and Roberta Guerrina, 'Gender and European External Relations: Dominant Discourses and Unintended Consequences of Gender Mainstreaming' (2013) 39 *Women's Studies International Forum* 53, 60 doi:10.1016/j.wsif.2012.06.005.
57 Case C-267/12 *Frédéric Hay v Crédit agricole mutuel de Charente-Maritime et des Deux-Sèvres* [2013] EU:C:2013:823 (the French Association of Banks and Unions' collective agreement which restricted a benefit in respect of pay and working conditions to married employees, excluding partners entering into a civil solidarity pact).
58 Case C-81/12 *Asociaţia Accept v Consiliul Naţional pentru Combaterea Discriminării* [2013] EU:C:2013:275 (public statements ruling out the recruitment of a professional footballer presented as being homosexual).

However, more recently there have been a couple of disappointing decisions. In *Léger*[59] the Court decided that blanket bans on gay and bisexual men donating blood can be lawful in the absence of effective techniques for detecting severe infectious diseases that can be transmitted by blood, such as HIV. Rather encouragingly, AG Mengozzi noted that assuming that certain 'risk behaviour' occurred exclusively among the entire group of gay and bisexual men was wrong because risk taking was also 'possible for the rest of the population', and that the national court should ensure that the medical staff 'identify more precisely the type of behaviour presenting a risk for the health of recipients, in order to impose a less onerous contraindication than a permanent contraindication for the entire group of men'.[60] The Court's reasoning, however, suggests some rather deep-seated homophobia and, interestingly, asking some gendered questions helps reveal that homophobia. While the Court's decision initially looks promising in that it recognises that a blanket ban on blood donation for gay and bisexual men is discriminatory, the Court does go on to say that this discrimination can be justified in certain circumstances. The Court's reasoning is fundamentally flawed. Much of it turns on whether or not gay or bisexual men fall into the category of 'high risk' when it comes to potentially transmitting diseases through the blood they donate. The assumption underpinning the Court's reasoning suggests that they are. Asking a very simple gender question highlights the issue: Why ban men? The answer to that question suggests that the Court has a particular view of gay men and their lifestyle. The Court presumes promiscuity and unprotected sex with multiple partners and what might, therefore, in this context, be 'high risk' behaviour. The same is not presumed of lesbians, straight women or heterosexual men. In fact, there was no blanket ban of groups of persons who might be considered high risk such as sex workers or intravenous drug users. While the AG found it problematic that the ban under consideration by the Court drew a distinction between gay men and these other, perhaps more obviously, high-risk categories, the Court did not. Instead of making it clear that it is the behaviour of an individual that may render them a high risk for contracting serious diseases transmittable through blood, the Court played to stereotypes and reinforced fears held in some Member States. By not saying that banning gay and bisexual men from giving blood *per se* is unacceptable, the Court sanctioned discrimination. Sanctioning discrimination based on any stereotype is harmful and women have often felt the brunt of that sort of stereotyping.[61] The Court taking this approach is therefore disappointing.

59 Case C-528/13 *Geoffrey Léger v Ministre des Affaires sociales and others* [2015] EU:C:2015:288 (eligibility criteria for blood donors).

60 Case C-528/13 *Geoffrey Léger v Ministre des Affaires sociales and others* [2014] EU:C:2014:2112, Opinion of AG Mengozzi, points 66 and 70.

61 Patricia Pattison and Jessica Guth, 'The Road Less Travelled: Gender Identity Discrimination in the US and UK' (2015) 17 *Atlantic Law Journal* 85.

In *Parris*[62] the Court missed an opportunity to continue its line of cases protecting LGBT rights. University lecturer, David Parris, challenged Irish rules that precluded his civil partner from the survivor's benefit under his pension scheme because even though they had entered into a civil partnership, they had not done so before Dr Parris' 60th birthday, a requirement of the scheme. The German AG Juliane Kokott in her opinion suggests that while not directly discriminatory, the rules were clearly indirectly discriminatory as it was impossible for gay men or lesbians to enter into a civil partnership in Ireland until 2011 and therefore any homosexual person born before 1951 would not be able to do so before their 60th birthday. The provision therefore had a more severe negative impact on homosexual employees. She also noted that the only way to fully understand the discrimination suffered is to understand it as combined age and sexual orientation discrimination. She said:

> In the present case, particular attention will have to be given to the fact that any discrimination perpetrated against the person concerned is attributable to a combination of two factors, age and sexual orientation. The Court's judgment will reflect real life only if it duly analyses the combination of those two factors, rather than considering each of the factors of age and sexual orientation in isolation.[63]

The Court disagreed. It concluded that there was neither direct nor indirect discrimination on the grounds of sexual orientation under EU law. Its reasoning is based on the fact that Member States retain full competence in matters of family law and in particular the regulation of marital status and same-sex relationships. It concluded that there was no duty on Ireland to recognise civil partnerships and, if they chose to do so, no obligation to give the relevant law retrospective effect. The Court was more comfortable considering the age discrimination and concluded that while the rules in question did produce a difference in treatment based on age it fell within the exceptions in Article 6(2) of the Framework Directive which sets out an exception for provisions fixing an age for the entitlement of an old age benefit. The Court thus decided that there was no discrimination in this case and went on to say: 'Consequently, where a national rule creates neither discrimination on the ground of sexual orientation nor discrimination on the ground of age, that rule cannot produce discrimination on the basis of the combination of those two factors.'[64]

62 Case C-443/15 *Dr David L Parris v Trinity College Dublin and Others* [2016] EU:C:2016:897.
63 Case C-443/15 *Dr David L Parris v Trinity College Dublin and Others* [2016] EU:C:2016:493, Opinion of AG Kokott, point 4.
64 *Parris* (n 62) para 81.

At the time of writing, several Member States, as well as third States, have recognised same-sex marriage.[65] The question is no longer whether marriage should be limited to opposite sex couples and, hence, the Court's guarded approach towards the elaboration of these concepts is no longer warranted, if ever it was. Be that as it may, the Court's approach should arguably be situated within the particular context and time period in which the judgements were delivered. Clearly, judgements in *D and Sweden*[66] and *Reed*[67] have attracted criticism in scholarly literature on several grounds, such as privileging traditional marital relationships and discounting social developments taking place in the Member States.[68] Noticeably, both judgements were delicately framed against the background of the 'common rules' and principles shared by the majority of Member States at the time in which they were decided.[69] Furthermore, the Court's cautious approach in elaborating controversial concepts of family law is symptomatic of, and thus helps to expose, the differences in the treatment of family law issues among the Member States, which cannot be remedied by the Court alone.[70] It remains to be seen whether the Court will be inclined to revisit its position on the definition of family in future case law,[71] as it has done with respect to matters relating to the discrimination on grounds of sexual orientation since *Grant*, or in relation to the treatment of transwomen and men in light of the common consensus of the Member States.[72]

The Court has, it seems, had difficulty with sexual orientation discrimination. Its approach has been cautious and couched in terms of an emerging consensus

65 See eg Ian Curry-Sumner, 'Same-sex Relationships in a European Perspective' and Joanna Miles, 'Unmarried Cohabitation in a European Perspective' in Jens M Scherpe (ed), *European Family Law Vol III: Family Law in a European Perspective* (Edward Elgar 2016).

66 n 41.

67 n 45.

68 See, eg, Masha Antokolskaia, *Harmonisation of Family Law in Europe: A Historical Perspective* (Intersentia 2006) 429–434; Clare McGlynn, 'Challenging the European harmonisation of family law: Perspectives on "the family"' in Katharina Boelki-Woelki (ed), *Perspectives for the Unification and Harmonisation of Family Law in Europe* (Intersentia 2003) 219; Jule Mulder, 'Some More Equal Than Others? Matrimonial Benefits and the CJEU's Case Law on Discrimination on the Grounds of Sexual Orientation' (2012) 19 *Maastricht Journal of European and Comparative Law* 505; Jessica Guth, 'When Is a Partner Not a Partner? Conceptualisations of 'Family' in EU Free Movement Law' (2011) 33(2) *Journal of Social Welfare and Family Law* 193 doi:10.1080/09649069.2011.617078.

69 Geert De Baere and Kathleen Gutman, 'The Impact of the European Union and the European Court of Justice on European Family Law' (2015) 1 *European Family Law* 5, 43.

70 ibid.

71 See also Guth (n 67).

72 De Baere and Gutman (n 69) 43 referring to *P v S* (n 35). Cf Case C-249/96 *Lisa Jacqueline Grant v South-West Trains Ltd* [1997] EU:C:1997:449, Opinion of AG Elmer, who came to the opposite conclusion on the basis of the foregoing judgement. See further the judgements in Case C-117/01 *KB v National Health Service Pensions Agency and other* [2004] ECR I-541; Case C-423/04 *Sarah Margaret Richards v Secretary of State for Work and Pensions* [2006] ECR I-3585. But see Mark Bell, 'Gender Identity and Sexual Orientation: Alternative Pathways in EU Equality Law' (2012) 60 *AJCL* 127.

in the Member States. It has not used the provisions in the Framework Directive to drive forward an equality agenda in the same way that it has arguably done in relation to gender equality. Maybe this is the case because it really is concerned with the position in Member States where discrimination and non-acceptance of LGBTQ people are still the norm. Maybe this is the Court at its most politically aware with heightened awareness of a potential backlash to what might be perceived as judicial activism. However, the Directive clearly includes sexual orientation as a protected ground and the Court then perhaps needs reminding of the recital stating that discrimination in this area undermines the achievements of the Treaty.[73]

There have also simply been fewer opportunities to rule on sexual orientation issues and the issues which have been referred to the court have been of a particular type – they have been about spousal/partner benefits in some way rather than about discrimination relating to access to employment or employment terms and conditions. The cases reaching the Court appear to be about who the applicant is in a relationship with rather than about who the applicant themselves is. This is in itself interesting and gendered. Rosemary Auchmuty has noted that the experiences of women and men are not similar and that the laws applying to sexual minorities are experienced differently depending on one's gender.[74] According to her, because of the gendered differences and inequalities that still dominate society, LGBT women have more in common with heterosexual women than they have in common with LGBT men.[75] For instance, legislation such as the Civil Partnership Act 2004, which allow same-sex couples to register their partnership in England and Wales and acquire comparatively similar rights and responsibilities as heterosexual married couples, are of no practical use to the majority of women.[76] Although the 2004 Act seemingly treats sexual minorities equally, as a group LGBT women do not benefit from it in the same way as men as a group do.[77] This is because women often do not possess similar assets to men, who are more likely to have property they want to protect and pass on through inheritance and pensions.[78] Therefore, civil partnerships and same-sex marriage, with their legal and social privileges, do nothing for those in society who are already excluded from certain privileges, such as single mothers and uncoupled people.[79] When we look at the claimants who have brought cases against their employers for discrimination on the grounds of sexual orientation, it is possible to note that in contrast to sex discrimination cases involving, for instance, pregnant women discussed in Chapter 5, many of the claimants in sexual orientation discrimination

73 Directive 2000/78, preamble, recital 11.
74 Rosemary Auchmuty, 'Feminist Approaches to Sexuality and Law Scholarship' (2015) 15(1) *Legal Information Management* 4, 5.
75 ibid 5.
76 ibid.
77 ibid.
78 ibid.
79 ibid.

cases are gay or bisexual men,[80] in relatively well-paid positions, such as a university lecturer, manager working for an educational establishment, a male working in a bank, officials working for the EU institutions, and a professional footballer. This in itself tells us something about the gendered nature of access to justice and the ability to assert what type of rights.

Age discrimination

Age discrimination appears to be a well-litigated area. Dagmar Shiek has noted the unusually high volume of cases brought on grounds of age discrimination in the early days of the Framework Directive.[81] She makes reference to age as a protected ground offering the opportunity to bring white, straight, non-disabled men into the equality framework and perhaps this does go some way to explaining the popularity of the ground for litigation. In addition, though, age discrimination is something which can impact on all of us rather than on sections of the population, so this may also explain why the cases came thick and fast.

In this section we particularly focus on those cases dealing with compulsory retirement ages and maximum ages for beginning in a particular profession. The Court has not been entirely consistent. In *Mangold*[82] it held that 'permitting employers to conclude without restriction fixed-term contracts of employment with workers over the age of 52 constituted a difference of treatment on the grounds directly of age' and was not acceptable.[83] According to the Court, such rules would lead to a situation in which significant numbers of older workers could be excluded from the benefit of stable employment because employers could offer them fixed-term employment contracts which could be renewed an indefinite number of times.[84] In comparison, in *Palacios de la Villa*[85] the Court applied a rather more relaxed approach to scrutiny and allowed the Member State much more leeway to justify discriminatory provisions concerning compulsory retirement age.[86] The Court is still finding its way to a consistent interpretation of the Framework Directive in relation to the age provisions. However, what we can

80 with the exception of Ms Grant.

81 Dagmar Schiek, 'Age Discrimination Before the ECJ: Conceptual and Theoretical Issues' (2011) 48(3) *Common Market Law Review* 777.

82 Case C-144/04 *Werner Mangold v Rüdiger Helm* [2005] ECR I-09981. Mr Mangold, who was then aged 56, was employed as a lawyer by Mr Helm for a period of seven months on a fixed-term basis.

83 ibid para 57.

84 ibid para 64.

85 Case C-411/05 *Félix Palacios de la Villa v Cortefiel Servicios SA* [2007] ECR I-08531 (collective agreement providing for automatic termination of employment relationship where a worker had reached 65 years of age and was entitled to a retirement pension).

86 The Court held that the national provisions would be consistent with EU law if they were 'objectively and reasonably justified . . . by a legitimate aim relating to employment policy and the labour market' and were not 'inappropriate and unnecessary for the purpose'. ibid para 77.

learn from the cases is that Member States are likely to be able to justify compulsory retirement provisions as long as they are clearly based on economic policies such as allowing younger workers, entry into the labour market and sharing the burden of employment across generations. Provisions which require retirement at a certain age will almost always be allowed if that required retirement coincides with the possibility of being able to draw on a pension[87] – in other words, if the age set is relatively high. Similar human resource management or economic rationales have been offered alongside health and safety concerns, in relation to maximum age limits for starting a career in certain sectors. Fire fighters in Germany must therefore start their firefighting careers before age 30.[88]

In these cases, gender is mostly ignored. However, gender is actually a really important consideration in age discrimination cases and the decisions made do not impact on men and women equally. Retirement age might be a particularly powerful example. If we require employees to retire at a certain age when they are able to draw on a pension, we put women in a vulnerable position. As we have already seen in the previous chapter, women are less likely to have significant income from pension and may not have anywhere near enough to live on. The requirement to retire even when the employee is perfectly capable of carrying out her job may result in women in particular being pushed into poverty. This was the case in the Court's decision in *Rosenbladt*.[89] The flip side of the argument is, of course, that by not requiring employees to retire at a given point women may feel particular pressure to keep working to the detriment of their health, well-being and ability to enjoy their old age. What is clear is that the impact of age discrimination is inextricably linked to life course and the life courses of men and women are different. It therefore stands to reason that the experience of age and of discrimination on the grounds of age will be felt differently.[90] The Court has had the opportunity repeatedly to engage with these issues but has failed to do so. Looking at life course issues when considering age-discrimination claims would undoubtedly make for a more reasoned and holistic approach. For example, it would allow recognition of the fact that for some women beginning a professional career may be delayed by having children and for others childbearing will result in career breaks which impact on progression, earning savings and pensions.

87 Schiek (n 81). See Case C-388/07 *R, on the application of The Incorporated Trustees of the National Council for Ageing (Age Concern England) v Secretary of State for Business, Enterprise and Regulatory Reform* [2009] I-1569; Case C-341/08 *Domnica Petersen v Berufungsausschuss für Zahnärzte für den Bezirk Westfalen-Lippe* [2010] ECR I-47; Case C-555/07 *Seda Kücükdeveci v Swedex GmbH & Co KG* [2010] ECR I-00365, Case C-45/09 *Gisela Rosenbladt v Oellerking Gebäudereinigungsges mbH* [2010] ECR I-9391.

88 Case C-229/08 *Colin Wolf v Stadt Frankfurt am Main* [2010] ECR I 00001.

89 *Rosenbladt* (n 87) (termination of employment contract on reaching retirement age).

90 Anne-Marie Guillemard, 'The advent of a flexible life-course and the reconfiguration of welfare' in Jørgen Goul Andersen, Anne-Marie Guillemard, Per H Jensen and Birgit Pfau-Effinger (eds), *The Changing Face of Welfare: Consequences and Outcomes from a Citizenship Perspective* (Policy Press 2005) 132.

There is a glimmer of hope in *Kleist*,[91] which is not an age discrimination case, but notes that provisions which have different retirement ages for men and women must interpret exceptions allowing such a differentiation strictly. This case could have been framed in age discrimination terms given that it related to questions of pensionable age and a requirement to retire at pensionable age. However, the question for the Court to answer was, perhaps sensibly, constructed as a sex discrimination question,[92] and the Court took the opportunity to remind us that the question is up to the referring court, so it did not feel the need or ability to consider age discrimination:

> As regards, finally, the possibility that there is discrimination on the grounds of age within the meaning of Directive 2000/78, it should be recalled that, in proceedings under Article 234 EC, it is solely for the national court, before which the dispute has been brought and which must assume responsibility for the subsequent judicial decision, to determine in the light of the particular circumstances of the case both the need for a preliminary ruling in order to enable it to deliver judgment and the relevance of the questions which it submits to the Court.[93]

In this case the national court had written gender in, but as we have seen above and throughout this book, there is no guarantee that this will happen. However, by effectively hiding behind procedural issues such as this, the Court is missing an opportunity to make decisions rooted in the reality of people's lives and to genuinely be a proactive Court which drives forward equality, and in particular gender equality, in a meaningful way.

Religious discrimination

A further area of case law where the Court has seemingly chosen not to see gender is in relation to discrimination on the grounds of religion or belief. The banning of the wearing religious symbols is one such area. While the legal provisions and cases at national and EU level are often couched in language of religious symbols or dress, it seems fairly clear that in the majority of cases what Member

91 Case C-356/09 *Pensionsversicherungsanstalt v Christine Kleist* [2010] ECR I-11939 (equal treatment of men and women in matters of employment and occupation under Directive 76/207/EEC, art 3(1)(c)). The case concerned dismissal of workers, who had acquired the right to draw their retirement pension. National rules set the age conferring entitlement to a retirement pension at 60 years for women and 65 years for men. The justification was the objective of promoting employment of younger persons. Mrs Kleist, who was employed as a chief physician by the pension insurance institution, had no intention to retire at the age of 60 but wished to work until she was 65.

92 Schiek (n 81) has noted the importance of picking the 'right' ground and the implications of picking age as a ground when others might have been available.

93 *Kleist* (n 91) para 44.

States are actually concerned with is the dress of Muslim women.[94] The debates on this issue as well as the Court's treatment of these cases reveal an approach that sees women as victims, who must be saved from oppression, rather than as women who are choosing to express their religious beliefs in a particular way. In this debate, as in many others, what women wear, or where they wear headscarves, seems to be something that is legitimately the subject of regulation in a way that what men wear simply is not. In its 2017 decision in *Bougnaoui*, the Court concluded that although an employer could not require their employee not to wear an Islamic headscarf at work because the company's customers did not like the scarf,[95] the judgement is nevertheless seemingly weak as it appears to give leeway to the employer to argue that there was a seemingly 'neutral' rule in place, which prohibited the wearing of any visible sign of political, philosophical or religious beliefs and which the employee failed to comply with. It asked the national court to ascertain whether Ms Bougnaoui's dismissal was based on non-compliance with such a rule.[96] Although the Court noted that if the compliance with this rule resulted in placing Ms Bougnaoui at a particular disadvantage because of her religion, there was indirect discrimination on grounds religion in accordance with Article 2(2)(b) of the Framework Directive,[97] indicating that her dismissal was unlawful.[98]

In relation to discrimination on the grounds of wearing a headscarf or a veil, the argument often suggested is that the dismissal of a female employee is not direct discrimination on grounds of religion, but only indirect discrimination. This is because of a criterion or practice which requires, for example, that an employee's face is not covered, is likely to have a more significant impact on Muslims. However, this reasoning, though widely employed, misses the point because gender is taken out of the equation. Essentially, such a requirement does not have a more significant impact on a religious group, but it impacts almost exclusively on one group, namely Muslim women. Women of other faiths, or those not having any religion, are not affected, neither are Muslim men or men of any other faith. Requiring employees not to cover their hair or face directly

94 The Court of Justice addressed the issue of employee's headscarf in *Bougnaoui*, which concerned a dismissal of a French design engineer, Asma Bougnaoui. The Court concluded that the company's customer's wish not to have the IT services provided by an employee wearing an Islamic headscarf was not a 'genuine and determining occupational requirement' for performing the job within the meaning of Directive 2000/78/EC, art 4(1). See Case C-188/15 *Asma Bougnaoui and Other v Micropole SA* [2017] EU:C:2017:204, para 27.

95 ibid paras 40–41.

96 ibid para 32.

97 ibid. See also Case C-157/15 *Samira Achbita and Other v G4S Secure Solutions NV* [2017] EU:C:2017:203, paras 30 and 34.

98 However, the Court also noted that indirect discrimination under art 2(2)(b)(i) did not exist, if the dismissal was objectively justified by a legitimate aim, such as the implementation of a policy of neutrality *vis-à-vis* its customers by her employee, and if the means of achieving that aim were appropriate and necessary. *Bougnaoui* (n 94) para 33. See also *Achbita* (n 97) paras 35–43.

discriminates against one group of women and indirectly discriminates against others who might need or want to cover their face because of, for instance, a disability. By not engaging with gender in relation to these cases, the Court again misses the reality of claimants' lives.

The same is true for the ECtHR which also has a poor track record of protecting Muslim women in this regard. Its case law has consistently upheld bans on headscarves and veils giving States a wide margin of appreciation.[99] This wide margin comes at a cost to women though who are not able to express their religious beliefs in the way they want to or in the same way that men can. In its third party intervener's submission in the 2015 decision in *SAS v France*[100] before the Strasbourg Court, Amnesty International pointed out that the French law banning veils covering full face (*niqab*) risked Muslim women experiencing a distinct form of discrimination due to the intersection of sex with other factors such as religion, and such discrimination might express itself in the form of stereotyping of sub-groups of women.[101] It also noted that the assumption that women wore headscarves or veils only under coercion was an expression of gender-based and religion-based stereotyping and ending gender-based discrimination would require a far more nuanced approach.[102] Similarly, the British AG Eleanor Sharpston noted in her Opinion in *Bougnaoui*[103] that there was no consensus as to whether the headscarf was a symbol of oppression of women or a feminist statement, as it represented 'a woman's right to assert her choice and her religious freedom to be a Muslim who wishes to manifest her faith in that way'.[104] She further noted that either view would 'no doubt find support in individual cases and particular contexts'.[105] Considering gender alongside all other issues in therefore vital for a full understanding of the cases and any impact decisions might have.

In some EU Member States, where the population is ethnically more diverse there is a long tradition of recognising discrimination and enacting policies and legislation that is aimed at tackling multiple strands of discrimination, particularly sex and race discrimination, whereas other Member States, where immigration flows are more recent, such as Germany[106] and Spain have resisted implementing

99 See *Dakir v Belgium*, App No 4619/12 (ECtHR 11 July 2017); *Belcacemi and Oussar v Belgium*, App No 37798/13 (ECtHR 11 July 2017); *Sahin v Turkey*, App No 44774/98 (ECtHR 29 June 2004); *SAS v France*, 2014-III ECtHR 341.

100 *SAS v France* (n 99).

101 ibid para 90.

102 ibid para 91.

103 Case C-188/15 *Asma Bougnaoui and Other v Micropole SA* [2016] EU:C:2016:553, Opinion of AG Sharpston.

104 ibid para 75.

105 ibid.

106 Case C-329/04 *Commission v Germany* [2005] EU:C:2005:263 concerned Germany's failure to pass all necessary legislation to bring national law into line with the Racial Equality Directive 2000/43.

anti-discrimination legislation.[107] Additionally, in some Member States, such as France, the measurement of racial discrimination is also highly contested, and the country has developed a legal and institutional framework against racial discrimination due to the 'colour blind' republican model of French integration.[108] Rather naively the assumption in France up until the 1990s appears to have been that discrimination against non-French citizens disappears once individuals obtain French citizenship.[109] Even if it is still necessary to increase the efforts of fighting institutional discrimination in France, some changes in the attitudes have followed after the pressure from the EU and due to publication of research that French young people from migrant background faced discrimination, particularly in the field of employment and recruitment.[110] However, what is common among all Member States is that they experience more recent and diverse immigration flows with increasing numbers of labour migrants from eastern Europe as well as asylum seekers and refugees from the Middle East and Latin America.[111] Additionally, in many Member States, migrants and ethnic minorities, specifically the Roma population, are not treated as equal members of society and experience various forms of discrimination, even if they were citizens.[112]

Associative disability discrimination

The judgement in *Coleman*[113] introduced the principle of 'discrimination by association' into European non-discrimination law. It firmly attached liability to the act of discrimination and can thus be hailed as a landmark decision. The facts in the case were as follows. Ms Coleman worked as a legal secretary for a law firm, Attridge Law, at the time of the birth of her disabled son in 2002.[114] He suffered from apnoeic attacks and congenital laryngomalacia and bronchomalacia, requiring 'specialised and particular care' which was provided by Ms Coleman as his primary carer.[115] When the son was three years old Ms Coleman accepted voluntary redundancy and, consequently, ceased working for Attridge Law.[116] She then brought a claim against the former employer in the Employment Tribunal, alleging that she had been subject to unfair constructive dismissal and had been

107 Isabelle Carles, Erica Howard and Eleonore Kofman, 'Gendered experiences of racial discrimination: Comparative socio-legal research' in Dagmar Schiek and Anna Lawson (eds), *European Union Non-Discrimination Law and Intersectionality: Investigating the Triangle of Racial, Gender and Disability Discrimination* (Taylor and Francis 2011) 227 and 230.
108 ibid.
109 ibid 230.
110 ibid.
111 ibid.
112 ibid.
113 Case C-303/06 *S Coleman v Attridge Law and Steve Law* [2008] ECR I-5603; 3 CMLR 27.
114 ibid paras 19–20.
115 ibid para 20.
116 ibid para 21.

treated less favourably than other employees because she was the primary carer of a disabled child.[117] According to her, that treatment caused her to stop working for her former employer.[118] The tribunal stayed the proceedings and made a preliminary reference to the Court of Justice to determine whether the relevant national law, the Disability Discrimination Act 1995, accurately implemented the Framework Directive[119] in this area because section 3(A)(1) of the 1995 Act referred to 'the disabled person [being] treated less favourably by comparison to other employees who are not disabled and there is no justification for that treatment'.[120] This effectively precluded Coleman's claim based on discrimination by association. The national court's reference to the Court of Justice identified four questions, which in essence concerned a single issue of law: whether the Framework Directive only protected from direct discrimination and harassment employees who were themselves disabled or could the protection be extended to the non-disabled employee, who had been the victim of direct discrimination and harassment by the employer, because of her association with a disabled person.[121]

In *Coleman* it was held that the Directive 'has the objective of creating within the Community a level playing field as regards equality'.[122] Therefore, the Court concluded that the principle of equal treatment applied 'not to a particular category of person',[123] but to 'all forms of discrimination grounds of disability'.[124] Limiting the scope was 'liable to deprive that directive of an important element of its effectiveness and to reduce the protection which it is intended to guarantee'.[125] Therefore *Coleman* focused on the discriminatory act itself rather than on the practically difficult and theoretically problematic issue of determining comparators[126] or even the personal scope of the provisions. This approach moves

117 For a more detailed consideration of the facts, see Tim Connor, 'Case C-303/06, Coleman v. Attridge Law' (2010) 16(1) *Columbia Journal of European Law* 141; Tim Connor, 'Discrimination by Association: A Step in the Right Direction' (2010) 31(1) *Journal of Social Welfare and Family Law* 59.

118 *Coleman* (n 113) para 22.

119 Directive 2000/78/EC.

120 23 May 2006. London (South) Employment Tribunal. Case number 2303745/2005. An appeal by Attridge Law concerning the permissibility of a preliminary reference in the context of determining a preliminary issue was dismissed by the Employment Appeal Tribunal. *Attridge Law and Another v Coleman* (2007) 2 *Common Market Law Review* 24.

121 Case C-303/06 *S Coleman v Attridge Law and Steve Law* [2008] EU:C:2008:61, Opinion of AG Maduro, point 6.

122 *Coleman* (n 113) para 47.

123 ibid para 38.

124 ibid.

125 ibid para 51.

126 Many jurisdictions have begun to develop the equality principle beyond the limitations of the 'comparator model' or 'like treatment' approach. For instance, instead of requiring a pregnant woman to be compared to a similarly situated male comparator, the new approach takes the view that detrimental treatment on grounds of pregnancy itself constitutes discrimination on grounds of gender. This is the approach adopted by the Court of Justice in a series of equality cases where the Court has held that since only women have the capacity

us beyond a pure non-discrimination model in which discrimination against a person with certain characteristics is prohibited and begins to take a more holistic view. Since Ms Coleman was treated unfairly, and the treatment was the result of one of the prohibited grounds, her treatment by her employer should be unlawful. This appears common sense. It is also an approach which could move equality generally and gender equality specifically towards an approach which allows us to focus more on the behaviour of the person or institution discriminating rather than on technical issues as to who an appropriate comparator might be. This is potentially important as we will see in relation to intersectionality below.

However, the question whether the concept of discrimination by association applies in the context of other forms of discrimination is worth considering further. *Coleman* held that 'The principle of equal treatment enshrined in. . . [The Framework Directive] . . . applies not to a particular category of persons but by reference to the grounds mentioned in Article 1.'[127] In principle, therefore, it is arguable that liability for discrimination by association applies on the grounds 'religion or belief . . . age or sexual orientation as regards employment'.[128] The Court seemed to agree, noting that the equal treatment principle of the Framework Directive 'must not be interpreted strictly, that is, as prohibiting only direct discrimination on grounds of disability and relating exclusively to disabled people'.[129] Further support can be found in the Preamble to the Framework Directive, which notes that the Community Charter of the Fundamental Social Rights of Workers 'refers both to the general combating of every form of discrimination and to the need to take appropriate action for the social and economic integration of disabled people'.[130] It therefore looks promising that discrimination by association is a concept which is here to stay and which will establish itself in EU equality law not just in relation to disability. In fact, in 2015 the Court of Justice decided *CHEZ*,[131] confirming discrimination by association in the context of race discrimination.

The Court could, however, have gone further in *Coleman* had it chosen to take up the theme of 'human dignity' discussed at length by AG Poiares Maduro in the case. It must be questioned whether the Court's refusal to take up this theme is an opportunity missed. The adoption of the notion of 'human dignity'

---

to become pregnant, discrimination on grounds of pregnancy is necessarily discrimination on grounds of sex. See Sandra Fredman, 'Reversing Roles: Bringing Men into the Frame' (2014) 10(4) *International Journal of Law in Context* 442, 445–446 doi:10.1017/S1744552314000214.

127 ibid para 38.

128 Directive 2000/78, art 1.

129 *Coleman* (n 113) para 43.

130 ibid referring to Directive 2000/78, recital 6 (emphasis added).

131 Case C-83/14 *'CHEZ Razpredelenie Bulgaria' AD v Komisia za zashtita ot diskriminatsia* [2015] EU:C:2015:480. The case concerned access to services rather than employment but confirms that, where someone not themselves part of the Roma community suffers because of race discrimination against the Roma as they live in a predominantly Roma area, they can bring a claim.

as the basis underpinning the introduction of the concept of associative discrimination would have laid the foundations for future jurisprudential development and could have provided the basis for a holistic approach to equality. We turn to this next.

Intersectionality, human dignity and a holistic approach

The concept of 'human dignity' is not new to EU law.[132] AG Maduro attempted to establish a foundation to equality jurisprudence which would govern the interpretation of the Framework Directive and see 'human dignity' as fundamental to equality. Although the AG's approach was ultimately not taken up by the Court of Justice, it is an approach which would facilitate the consideration of gender alongside other factors and which might be more sensitive to gender implications and one which could be employed in a variety of policy areas. While AG Maduro's approach has been welcomed by some, it has been criticised by others.[133] The perceived danger appears to be that any attempt to establish what remains essentially an abstract and subjective notion of 'human dignity' as a legal test, will effectively hand interpretative control over the development of that concept to national courts. For instance, in *Omega Spielhallen*[134] the Court of Justice accepted by implication that the concept of 'human dignity' bore potential for significantly differing meanings from Member State to Member State.[135] It held that:

> It is not indispensable in that respect for the restrictive measure issued by the authorities of a Member State to correspond to a conception shared by all Member States as regards the precise way in which the fundamental right or legitimate interest in question is to be protected.[136]

In the light of the foregoing discussion, it might have been deliberate on the part of the Court of Justice that the judgement in *Coleman* failed to elevate the

132 In several jurisdictions, the judiciary have endorsed the incorporation of the use of dignity in domestic interpretations of European equality law. See, eg, Gay Moon and Robin Allen, 'Dignity Discourse in Discrimination Law: A Better Route to Equality?' (2006) 6 *European Human Rights Law Review* 610, 626. They refer to the 'exponential growth in dignity discourse in the courts of England and Wales'. See also Christopher McCrudden, 'Human Dignity and European Equality Law After Coleman' (2008) 2 *European Gender Equality Law Review* 18. A number of decisions where the concept of 'human dignity' has considered include, eg, Case 168/91 *Christos Konstantinidis v Stadt Altensteig-Standesamt and Landratsamt Calw – Ordnungsamt* [1993] ECR I-1191; Case C-36/02 *Omega Spielhallen- und Automatenaufstellungs-GmbH v Oberbürgermeisterin der Bundesstadt Bonn* [2004] ECR I-9609; *P v S* (n 35).

133 See, eg, Errol P Mendes, 'Taking Equality into the 21st Century: Establishing the Concept of Equal Human Dignity' (2000) 12(1) *National Journal of Constitutional Law* 3, 10–12.

134 *Omega* (n 132) paras 34–37.

135 The implication in *Omega* was that the German approach to dignity was not a conception of dignity that was common to other Member States. See also Case C-244/06 *Dynamic Medien Vertriebs GmbH v Avides Media AG* [2008] ECR I-505, para 44.

136 *Omega* (n 132) para 37.

concept of 'human dignity' to act as the foundation upon which future developments could be based – the Court has not traditionally been keen to allow definitional and interpretative issues to the Member States. Taking the approach it did leaves the Court, rather than the Member State, in control. It is, however, a missed opportunity to help the Court develop a coherent jurisprudence which could also deal with multiple or intersectional discrimination. A focus on human dignity would not require a strict legal categorisation of grounds but instead would allow the Court to focus on the experience of the claimant.

It has been widely argued that although multiple and intersectional discrimination has been increasingly discussed by scholars and the policy makers within the EU and hardly any court in the United States disagrees fundamentally with the major premise of intersectionality theory, there are various interpretations of the key concepts, most significant target groups and available evidence for discrimination and policy making in this field.[137] However, both legal advocacy organisations bringing discrimination case claims to courts and the judiciary have been unresponsive to efforts to bring claims for discrimination based on intersectional 'identity traits designated for protection' that are listed as prohibited grounds in anti-discrimination laws.[138] This has dampened the efforts to advance the theory of intersectionality in a legal context.[139] However, the approach to equality legislation where most national courts in Europe look at merely one single discrimination ground fails to address multiple discrimination based on for example race and gender.[140] Isabelle Carles and her colleagues argue that men and women experience different kind of discrimination and react in different ways to discrimination.[141] According to Suzanne Goldberg, due to the institutional legitimacy and capacity constraints the courts tend to simplify cases before them and resist more complex and holistic analysis demanded by intersectional identity theory.[142] She suggests that this could be so because identity is primarily a social construct and therefore secondary to a legal construct.[143] Hence, defining the boundaries of protected identity categories, such as gender, sexual orientation and disability,

137 Carles, Howard and Kofman (n 107) 227. Mieke Verloo, 'Multiple Inequalities, Intersectionality and the European Union' (2006) 13(3) *European Journal of Women's Studies* 211; Kimberlé Williams Crenshaw, 'Demarginalizing the Intersection of Race and Sex: A Black Feminist Critique of Antidiscrimination Doctrine, Feminist Theory and Antiracist Politics' (1989) 8 *University of Chicago Legal Forum* 139; Sandra Fredman, 'Double Trouble: Multiple Discrimination and EU Law' (2005) 2 *European Anti-Discrimination Law Review* 13; Maria Y Lee, 'Being Wary of Categories: Is It Possible to Move Away from Categorisations in Anti-Discrimination Law?' (2017) 1 *University of Vienna Law Review* <https://viennalawreview.com/index.php/vlr/article/view/1863> accessed 9 April 2018.

138 Suzanne B Goldberg, 'Identity-based discrimination and the barriers to complexity' in Schiek and Lawson (n 107) 177 and 180.

139 ibid 178.

140 Carles, Howard and Kofman (n 107) 227.

141 ibid.

142 Goldberg (n 138) 178.

143 ibid 189.

involves individual experience and sensibilities to a much larger degree than defining breach of contract doctrine or proximate cause in tort law.[144] It has been argued that the main obstacle to changing judicial approaches is teaching judges and litigators to see the multiple identities of claimants and the relationships of dominance and subordination that lie at the root of discrimination.[145] Changing this is likely to require a combination of training and legislation to clarify the legal basis for considering all grounds of discrimination in cases where only one ground has been alleged and to redefine discrimination so that it includes considerations of relationships of dominance and subordination based on the prohibited grounds of discrimination.[146]

In order to translate intersectional claims meaningfully in the adjudication process, the courts must move away from the demand that female litigants produce a comparator, or the closest substitute, to show that without the protected characteristic(s), they would have been treated fairly in the workplace or other environment.[147] The use of a comparator is fraught with institutional difficulties, whereas more holistic assessment would enable the court to consider a range of evidence that may indicate an employer's hostility or bias towards a subset of workers, such as women wearing headscarves, older people or people with disabilities. This would be particularly helpful in workplaces where comparator proof does not exist or would be subject to scepticism because of the relatively low number of 'comparable' employees who lack the same protected traits as the claimant.[148] Although the criticism of this approach may be that the courts appear undisciplined and try to stretch beyond their institutional capacity, this can hardly be a bad thing if it results in a fairer outcome for litigants who are being arbitrarily discriminated against. All grounds of discrimination that can be identified with the claimant, eg sex, religion, ethnic origin and race, must be considered in order to account for the relationship of dominance between the claimant and the defendant and the claimant and the court.[149] For instance, if the justification offered for certain dress code includes the aim of avoiding conflict between groups, the court must examine whether the groups are identifiable by race or ethnic origin, religion and sex.[150] If so, the presumption must that the dress code is intended to maintain the position of a group, which shares a dominant characteristic in a society, and the justification is unacceptable. If the defendant is unable to provide evidence on the issue, the rules on burden of proof in EU Directives require that any doubt is resolved in good faith and to the benefit of the claimant.[151] To decide otherwise,

144 ibid.

145 Lynn Roseberry, 'The Assimilationist Anti-Discrimination Paradigm and the Immigrant Muslim Woman: Suggestions on How to Re-Conceptualize Discrimination Claims' in Schiek and Lawson (n 107) 207.

146 ibid 207–208.

147 Goldberg (n 138) 189.

148 ibid.

149 Roseberry (n 145) 207.

150 ibid.

151 ibid.

the claimant's gender is isolated from her ethnic background or race, beliefs and culture, which results in her personal traits becoming irrelevant as additional grounds of discrimination.

Conclusion

We have attempted to discuss a much more inclusive approach to the wider equality case law of the Court of Justice which deals with alleged discrimination on grounds of a number of protected characteristics, including sexual orientation, race, religion and disability. We therefore argue that a more intersectional approach to equality law would put human dignity at the heart of the consideration. At the moment, most national courts and the Court of Justice look at merely one single discrimination ground, and so they fail to address the impact of multiple discrimination on women based, for instance, on gender and race, gender and sexual orientation, gender and religious beliefs, gender and class, or gender and disability. Especially, the early approach of the Court was merely to look at the discrimination on the grounds of nationality. Although the decision in *Konstantinidis*[152] hardly warrants the intersectional approach because it does not concern a female applicant who would face discrimination on the grounds of gender and another ground, we have seen throughout the chapter that the Advocates General of the Court often take more accommodating approach towards discrimination cases and have attempted to establish a foundation to equality jurisprudence which would govern the interpretation of the Framework Directive and which would see 'human dignity' as fundamental to equality. Although it is generally accepted that human dignity has been incorporated judicially as a general principle of EU law,[153] the Court has been less willing to accept its interpretation as suggested by the Advocates-General over the years.[154] For instance, in *Konstantinidis*[155] AG Jacobs suggested that the applicant did not show proof of actual damage of a tangible nature,

> in order to bring into operation the prohibition of discrimination. Community law does not regard the migrant worker (or the self employed migrant)

152 *Konstantinidis* (n 132).

153 AG Jacobs stated in 1993 that 'the constitutional traditions of the Member States in general allow for the conclusion that there exists a principle according to which the State must respect not only the individual's physical well-being, but also his dignity, moral integrity and sense of personal identity'. See Case C-168/91 *Christos Konstantinidis v Stadt Altensteig-Standesamt and Landratsamt Calw-Ordnungsamt* [1993] ECR I-1191, Opinion of AG Jacobs, para 39.

154 In Omega, the Court held that 'the Community legal order undeniably strives to ensure respect for human dignity as a general principle of law'. *Omega* (n 132) para 34. See also Case C-377/98 *Netherlands v Parliament and Council* [2001] ECR I-7079.

155 *Konstantinidis*, Opinion of AG Jacobs (n 153), points 2 and 25. The case concerned a Greek national who worked in Germany as a self-employed masseur and assistant hydrotherapist. He requested German authorities to transcribe his name in Roman characters as 'Christos Konstantinidis' on the ground that such a spelling indicated the correct

> purely as an economic agent and a factor of production entitled to the same salary and working conditions as nationals of the host State; it regards him as a human being who is entitled to live in that State 'in freedom and dignity' . . . and to be spared any difference in treatment that would render his life less comfortable, physically or psychologically, than the lives of the native population.[156]

Similarly, AG Mengozzi's Opinion in *Léger* could be seen to caution against making prejudiced assumptions about an entire group of individuals based on sexual orientation. Unfortunately, the Court itself was not very progressive in its reasoning. This is similar to judicial interpretation of equality and dignity in courts outside Europe, including Canada and South Africa. Christopher McCrudden has noted that dignity plays an 'increasingly important foundational role in the judicial interpretation of the meaning of constitutional anti-discrimination prohibition'.[157] For instance, the Supreme Court of Canada has interpreted the purpose of the 'right to equality' to mean the prevention of:

> the violation of essential human dignity and freedom through the imposition of disadvantage, stereotyping, or political or social prejudice, and to promote a society in which all persons enjoy equal recognition at law as human beings or as members of. . . [the] society, equally capable and deserving of concern, respect and consideration.[158]

Until the Court accepts a more inclusive approach towards equality cases, we have 'a level playing field as regards equality', which discriminates against groups of women based on the very characteristics which the equality law purports to protect.

Bibliography

Ahmed T, 'The Opposition of the CJEU to the ECHR as a Mechanism of International Human Rights' (2017) 4(2) *Journal of International and Comparative Law* 1

Antokolskaia M, *Harmonisation of Family Law in Europe: A Historical Perspective* (Intersentia 2006)

Arnull A, *The European Union and Its Court of Justice* (2nd edn, Oxford University Press 2006)

pronunciation of his name. The Court merely noted that the freedom of establishment in the Treaty meant that Mr Konstandinitis could not be discriminated against because his nationality, but mentioned nothing about dignity.

156 ibid point 24.

157 Christopher McCrudden, 'Human Dignity and judicial Interpretation of Human Rights' (2008) 19(4) *European Journal of International Law* 655, 690 doi:10.1093/ejil/chn043.

158 *Law v Canada (Minister of Employment and Immigration)* (1999) 1 SCR 497, para 51.

Arnull A, Eeckhout P and Tridimas T, *Continuity and Change in EU Law: Essays in Honour of Sir Francis Jacobs* (Oxford University Press 2008)
Auchmuty R, 'Feminist Approaches to Sexuality and Law Scholarship' (2015) 15(1) *Legal Information Management* 4
Barnard C, *EU Employment Law* (4th edn, Oxford University Press 2012)
Bell M, 'Gender Identity and Sexual Orientation: Alternative Pathways in EU Equality Law' (2012) 60 *AJCL* 127
Bernitz U, Weatherill S and De Vries S (eds), *The Protection of Fundamental Rights in the EU After Lisbon* (Hart 2013)
Besson S, 'Gender Discrimination Under EU and ECHR Law: Never Shall the Twain Meet?' (2008) 8(4) *Human Rights Law Review* 647 doi:10.1093/hrlr/ngn023
Carles I, Howard E and Kofman E, 'Gendered Experiences of Racial Discrimination: Comparative Socio-Legal Research' in Schiek D and Lawson A (eds), *European Union Non-Discrimination Law and Intersectionality: Investigating the Triangle of Racial, Gender and Disability Discrimination* (Taylor and Francis 2011)
Connor T, 'Case C-303/06, Coleman v. Attridge Law' (2010) 16(1) *Columbia Journal of European Law* 141
———, 'Discrimination by Association: A Step in the Right Direction' (2010) 31(1) *Journal of Social Welfare and Family Law* 59.
Council Directive 2000/43/EC of 29 June 2000 Implementing the Principle of Equal Treatment Between Persons Irrespective of Racial or Ethnic Origin [2000] OJ L180/22
Council Directive 2000/78/EC of 27 November 2000 Establishing a General Framework for Equal Treatment in Employment and Occupation [2000] OJ L303/16
Council Regulation (EC, Euratom) No 723/2004 of 22 March 2004 Amending the Staff Regulations of Officials of the European Communities and the Conditions of Employment of Other Servants of the European Communities [2004] OJ L124/1
Curry-Sumner I, 'Same-sex Relationships in a European Perspective' in Scherpe JM (ed), *European Family Law Vol. III: Family Law in a European Perspective* (Edward Elgar 2016)
David M and Guerrina R, 'Gender and European External Relations: Dominant Discourses and Unintended Consequences of Gender Mainstreaming' (2013) 39 *Women's Studies International Forum* 53 doi:10.1016/j.wsif.2012.06.005
De Baere G and Gutman K, 'The Impact of the European Union and the European Court of Justice on European Family Law' (2015) 1 *European Family Law* 5
de Búrca G, 'After the EU Charter of Fundamental Rights: The Court of Justice as a Human Rights Adjudicator?' (2013) 13 *Maastricht Journal of European and Comparative Law* 168
Fitzpatrick B, 'The "Mainstreaming" of Sexual Orientation into European Equality Law' in Meenan H (ed), *Equality Law in an Enlarged European Union* (Cambridge University Press 2007) 316
Fredman S, 'Double Trouble: Multiple Discrimination and EU Law' (2005) 2 *European Anti-Discrimination Law Review* 13
———, 'Reversing Roles: Bringing Men into the Frame' (2014) 10(4) *International Journal of Law in Context* 442, 445–446 doi:10.1017/S1744552314000214
Goldber SB, 'Identity-based Discrimination and the Barriers to Complexity' in Schiek D and Lawson A (eds), *European Union Non-Discrimination Law and*

Intersectionality: Investigating the Triangle of Racial, Gender and Disability Discrimination (Taylor and Francis 2011)

Gragl P, *The Accession of the European Union to the European Convention on Human Rights* (Hart 2013)

Guillemard A-M, 'The Advent of a Flexible Life-course and the Reconfiguration of Welfare' in Andersen JG, Guillemard A-M, Jensen PH and Pfau-Effinger B (eds), *The Changing Face of Welfare: Consequences and Outcomes from a Citizenship Perspective* (Policy Press 2005)

Guth J, 'When Is a Partner Not a Partner? Conceptualisations of "Family" in EU Free Movement Law' (2011) 33(2) *Journal of Social Welfare and Family Law* 193 doi:10.1080/09649069.2011.617078

Helfer LR and Voeten E, 'International Courts as Agents of Legal Change: Evidence from LGBT Rights in Europe' (2014) 68 *International Organization* 77

Kochenov D (ed), *EU Citizenship and Federalism: The Role of Rights* (Cambridge University Press 2016)

Lee MY, 'Being Wary of Categories: Is It Possible to Move Away from Categorisations in Anti-Discrimination Law?' (2017) 1 *University of Vienna Law Review* <https://viennalawreview.com/index.php/vlr/article/view/1863> accessed 9 April 2018

Lenaerts K and Gutman K, 'The Comparative Law Method and the European Court of Justice: Echoes Across the Atlantic' (2016) 64(4) *The American Journal of Comparative Law* 841 doi:10.1093/ajcl/avw017

Lock T, 'EU Accession to the ECHR: Implications for the Judicial Review in Strasbourg' (2011) 35(6) *European Law Review* 777

———, 'Walking on a Tightrope: The Draft ECHR Accession Agreement and the Autonomy of the EU Legal Order' (2011) 48(4) *Common Market Law Review* 1025

McCrudden C, 'Human Dignity and European Equality Law After Coleman' (2008) 2 *European Gender Equality Law Review* 18

———, 'Human Dignity and Judicial Interpretation of Human Rights' (2008) 19(4) *European Journal of International Law* 655 doi:10.1093/ejil/chn043

McGlynn C, 'Challenging the European Harmonisation of Family Law: Perspectives on "the Family"' in Boelki-Woelki K (ed), *Perspectives for the Unification and Harmonisation of Family Law in Europe* (Intersentia 2003)

Mendes EP, 'Taking Equality into the 21st Century: Establishing the Concept of Equal Human Dignity' (2000) 12(1) *National Journal of Constitutional Law* 3, 10–12.

Miles J, 'Unmarried Cohabitation in a European Perspective' in Scherpe JM (ed), *European Family Law Vol. III: Family Law in a European Perspective* (Edward Elgar 2016)

Moon G and Allen R, 'Dignity Discourse in Discrimination Law: A Better Route to Equality?' (2006) 6 *European Human Rights Law Review* 610

Mulder J, 'Some More Equal Than Others? Matrimonial Benefits and the CJEU's Case Law on Discrimination on the Grounds of Sexual Orientation' (2012) 19 *Maastricht Journal of European and Comparative Law* 505

Pattison P and Guth J, 'The Road Less Travelled: Gender Identity Discrimination in the US and UK' (2015) 17 *Atlantic Law Journal* 85

Regulation (EU, Euratom) No 1023/2013 of the European Parliament and of the Council of 22 October 2013 [2013] OJ L287/15

Regulation No 30/65/EEC, 4/65/Euratom of the Councils of 16 March 1965 amending the Staff Regulations of Officials and the Conditions of Employment of Other Servants of the European Economic Community and the European Atomic Energy Community [1965] OJ 47/701

Roseberry L, 'The Assimilationist Anti-Discrimination Paradigm and the Immigrant Muslim Woman: Suggestions on How to Re-Conceptualize Discrimination Claims' in Schiek D and Lawson A (eds), *European Union Non-Discrimination Law and Intersectionality: Investigating the Triangle of Racial, Gender and Disability Discrimination* (Taylor and Francis 2011)

Schiek D, 'Age Discrimination Before the ECJ: Conceptual and Theoretical Issues' (2011) 48(3) *Common Market Law Review* 777

Storgaard LH, 'EU Law Autonomy Versus European Fundamental Rights Protection: On Opinion 2/13 on EU Accession to the ECHR' (2015) 15(3) *Human Rights Law Review* 485

Treaty Establishing the European Community [2002] OJ C325/33

Treaty Establishing the European Economic Community (Rome 25 March 1957)

Treaty of the Functioning of the European Union [2012] OJ C 326/47

Treaty on European Union [2012] OJ C326/13

Tryfonidou A, 'Discrimination on the Grounds of Sexual Orientation and Gender Identity' in Vogenauer S and Weatherill S (eds), *General Principles of Law: European and Comparative Perspectives* (Hart 2017)

Verloo M, 'Multiple Inequalities, Intersectionality and the European Union' (2006) 13(3) *European Journal of Women's Studies* 211

Williams Crenshaw K, 'Demarginalizing the Intersection of Race and Sex: A Black Feminist Critique of Antidiscrimination Doctrine, Feminist Theory and Antiracist Politics' (1989) 8 *University of Chicago Legal Forum* 139

7 European Union citizenship – free movement for all?

With Sophie Mayat[1]

> So we have blazed a trail of destruction – leaving the other countries to survey the wreckage of what was once EU citizenship.[2]

Much has been written about European Union (EU) citizenship[3] and it lends itself well to a gendered analysis.[4] On the face of it, EU citizenship decisions appear mostly gender neutral. As has been argued earlier in this book, there are some areas of EU law where a gendered reading of the law is relatively easy and obvious and where measures have clearly been implemented in order to enhance equality. In other areas, however, this is more difficult. EU citizenship is such an area, but a gendered reading can result in a more holistic and full understanding of the issues and possible solutions. Although many decisions discussed in this

1 Sophie Mayat graduated from the University of Bradford in 2016 with a first class LLB Law degree. She presented a gendered analysis of the decision in *McCarthy* (see below) in her final year dissertation and many of the ideas presented in this chapter were developed in conversation with her. She currently works as a legal advisor at Wakefield Metropolitan District Council. We would like to thank her for her input, ideas, support and for keeping our hope of a new generation of feminist lawyers alive.

2 Charlotte O'Brien, 'The ECJ Sacrifices EU Citizenship in Vain: *Commission v United Kingdom*' (2017) 54(1) *Common Market Law Review* 209, 241.

3 See eg Michael Dougan, 'The bubble that burst: Exploring the legitimacy of the case law on the free movement of union citizens' in Maurice Adams, Henri de Waele, Johan Meeusen and Gert Straetmans (eds), *Judging Europe's Judges: The Legitimacy of the Case Law of the European Court of Justice* (Hart 2013); Michael Dougan, Niamh Nic Shuibhne and Eleanor Spaventa (eds), *Empowerment and Disempowerment of the European Citizen* (Hart 2012); Charlotte O'Brien, *Unity in Adversity: EU Citizenship, Social Justice and the Cautionary Tale of the UK* (Hart, 2017); Dimitry Kochenov (ed), *EU Citizenship and Federalism: The Role of Rights* (Cambridge University Press 2017); Willem Maas, *Creating European Citizens* (Rowman and Littlefield 2007); Willem Maas, 'Free Movement and the Difference that Citizenship Makes' (2017) 23(1) *Journal of European Integration History* 85; Oxana Golynker, *Ubiquitous Citizens of Europe: The Paradigm of Partial Migration* (Intersentia 2006).

4 See Jessica Guth, 'Law as the object and agent of integration: Gendering the Court of Justice of the European Union, its decisions and their impact' in Gabriele Abels and Heather MacRae (eds), *Gendering European Integration Theory: Engaging New Dialogues* (Barbara Budrich 2016) where some of these ideas have previously been discussed.

chapter could be argued to have significance for the gender dynamics of citizenship law because they have offered the Court of Justice of the European Union[5] an opportunity to consider the impacts of, for instance, pregnancy, childbirth and care responsibilities on the status of EU migrant women under EU law, the Court has not often addressed the broader issues about the extent to which EU citizenship law can genuinely claim to embody a commitment to gender equality.[6]

EU citizenship was arguably a construct designed to bring the people of Europe closer to the Union and make it meaningful to them in more than just an economic sense.[7] Although it might also be true that EU citizenship was intended primarily as a symbolic concept, it is clear that the citizenship provisions offer concrete rights to EU citizens and that it has become the fundamental status[8] of at least some nationals of EU Member States. Whether it is a useful fundamental status for all, and for women in particular, is part of the focus of this chapter. The free movement of people and citizenship case law provides a plethora of examples highlighting how gendered analysis could have more fully informed decisions. Jo Shaw, for example, has suggested that the decisions of the Court – and EU policy generally – privilege certain EU citizens over others and construct gender roles in certain ways.[9] The EU model of citizenship appears to be built on full labour market participation by all. In a heterosexual family set up, this usually includes women as workers *and* primary carers and men as the main earners.[10] This chapter explores the implications of this and how a gendered reading of the

5 While the Court of Justice of the European Union consists of the Court of Justice, the General Court and specialised courts, we refer exclusively to the Court of Justice in this Chapter. See Treaty on European Union [2012] OJ C326/13 (TEU), art 19(1).

6 See eg Samantha Currie, 'Pregnancy-related Employment Breaks, the Gender Dynamics of Free Movement Law and Curtailed Citizenship: Jessy Saint Prix' (2016) 53 *Common Market Law Review* 543.

7 Samantha Currie, 'The transformation of union citizenship' in Michael Dougan and Samantha Currie (eds), *50 Years of the European Treaties: Looking Back and Thinking Forward* (Hart 2009).

8 Case C-184/99 *Rudy Grzelczyk v Centre public d'aide sociale d'Ottignies-Louvain-la-Neuve* [2001] ECR I-06193.

9 Jo Shaw, 'Importing gender: The challenge of feminism and the analysis of the EU legal order' (2000) 7(3) Journal of European Public Policy 406 doi:10.1080/135017600050086107; Jo Shaw, 'Mainstreaming Equality and Diversity in the European Union' (2005) 58 *Current Legal Problems* 255.

10 See also Emanuela Lombardo and Mieke Verloo, 'Institutionalizing Intersectionality in the European Union?' (2009) 11(4) *International Feminist Journal of Politics* 478 doi:10.1080/14616740903237442; Emanuela Lombardo and Petra Meier, 'Framing Gender Equality in the European Union Political Discourse' (2008) 15(1) *Social Politics: International Studies in Gender, State and Society* 101 doi:10.1093/sp/jxn001; Jessica Guth, 'When Is a Partner Not a Partner? Conceptualisations of 'Family' in EU Free Movement Law' (2011) 33(2) *Journal of Social Welfare and Family Law* 193; Charlotte O'Brien, 'Social Blind Spots and Monocular Policy Making: The ECJ's Migrant Worker Model' (2009) 46(4) *Common Market Law Review* 1107; Charlotte O'Brien, 'I Trade, Therefore I Am: Legal Personhood in the European Union' (2013) 50 *Common Market Law Review* 1643.

legal framework and case law could lead us to a more nuanced understanding of the lives of EU citizens.

The chapter is structured as follows. We examine early case law which established some key principles in the area of citizenship and free movement and argue that, while these cases benefitted women, the advancement of women's rights or a particular awareness of gender issues was not what drove the Court to make those decisions. Rather they were part of the Court establishing its own position as well as an attempt to move along European integration. We then examine a series of cases concerning non-economically active EU citizens and those construed as welfare tourists to ask whether a gendered understanding of these cases could lead to better outcomes for EU citizens and a more nuanced application of EU Law. Finally, we turn to a number of cases concerning residence and associated rights of carers to highlight how the Court initially continued its rights expansion before more recently deconstructing the established citizenship law to the detriment of EU citizenship generally and women and children particularly. In order to set the discussions that follow in context, we first briefly set out the legal framework governing EU citizenship.

The legal framework on EU citizenship

Article 20 of the Treaty on the Functioning of the European Union[11] (TFEU) establishes EU citizenship and Article 21 TFEU makes it clear that EU citizens have the right to move and reside freely within the EU. However, according to the latter provision, the right to free movement and the right of residence are subject to the conditions and limitations set out in any secondary legislation giving the Treaty provisions effect. Most of these conditions and limitations can be found in the Citizens' Rights Directive (CRD).[12] Whereas under Article 6 CRD all EU citizens benefit from the right of residence in the host Member State for a period of three months, the right of residence for periods in excess of that is subject to fulfilment of the criteria outlined in Article 7. Article 7 stipulates, *inter alia*, that residence in another Member State is lawful where there is economic activity or self-sufficiency and where there is no burden on the social assistance systems of the host State. While this does not mean that EU migrants have to be workers, provide services or run a business, it accentuates the economic rationale behind the free movement provisions. It also puts into question the notion that all nationals of Member States are truly EU citizens in the fullest sense. Economic activity or economic self-sufficiency is the key to unlocking residence rights,

11 Treaty on the Functioning of the European Union [2012] OJ C 326/47.

12 Directive 2004/38/EC of the European Parliament and of the Council of 29 April 2004 on the right of citizens of the Union and their family members to move and reside freely within the territory of the Member States amending Regulation (EEC) No 1612/68 and repealing Directives 64/221/EEC, 68/360/EEC, 72/194/EEC, 73/148/EEC, 75/34/EEC, 75/35/EEC, 90/364/EEC, 90/365/EEC and 93/96/EEC [2004] OJ L158/77 (CRD).

which in turn is the key to unlocking other rights and, as we shall see throughout this chapter, these are keys that can easily be taken away or lost.

The CRD also affords rights to family members of EU nationals regardless of their nationality. The rationale for these rights, which were first developed through case law,[13] is primarily economic in nature and bound up with free movement rights of the EU national, who would be discouraged from moving between Member States if their spouses or partners or children were not able to accompany or join them.[14] Article 7(2) CRD ensures that non-EU national family members are afforded residence and associated rights, provided that their EU national family member who they rely on fulfils the requirements of economic activity or self-sufficiency. Article 12 CRD makes provisions for the retention of rights by the third-country national in the case of the EU national's death or departure from the host State and Article 13 in cases of divorce or annulment of the marriage or registered partnership.

Although the provisions in the secondary legislation might not appear gendered, they are. It is more likely that women will find themselves in those roles, which do not carry rights *per se*, but which derive rights from someone else. The majority of caring roles, for example, are undertaken by women, who may not be able to fulfil the conditions set out in the legislative framework, and will therefore fall on the wrong side of the limitations laid down in the CRD. They are also more likely to accompany or join their male spouses or partners who appear to be mobile and thus more likely to move to another Member State.[15] The Treaty provisions are maybe aspirational. Perhaps it is unrealistic to expect such transnational solidarity that would make equal treatment of EU nationals with nationals of a host State a reality in all circumstances. However, the conditions arguably render the provisions meaningless for those who need the protection of the law the most. Damien Chalmers and his colleagues summarise this issue well: '[y]et the practical effect of these conditions is that "expensive" members of

13 eg Case 32/75 *Anita Cristini v Société nationale des chemins de fer français* [1975] ECR 1085; Case C-85/96 *Maria Martínez Sala v Freistaat Bayern* [1998] ECR I-02691; Case C-237/94 *John O'Flynn v Adjudication Officer* [1996] ECR I-2617; Case 75-63 *Hoekstra (née Unger) v Bestuur der Bedrijfsvereniging voor Detailhandel en Ambachten* [1964] ECR 00177; Case C-122/84 *Kenneth Scrivner and Carol Cole v Centre public d'aide sociale de Chastre* [1985] ECR 1027; Case 235/87 *Annunziata Matteucci v Communauté française of Belgium and Other* [1988] ECR 5589; Case C-413/99 *Baumbast and R v Secretary of State for the Home Department* [2002] ECR I-07091.

14 The Court has also made the argument in the context of short stays in host Member States, holding that there is no deprivation of the EU law rights of an EU citizen, who has no intention to reside in the host State for longer than three months, because this indicates that they do not intend to move permanently to the host State. Therefore, short stays do not discourage EU citizens from moving to another Member State. See Joint Cases C-456/12 *O v Minister voor Immigratie, Integratie en Asiel, and Minister voor Immigratie, Integratie en Asiel v B* [2014] EU:C:2014:135.

15 See eg Louise Ackers, *Shifting Spaces: Women, Citizenship and Migration in the European Union* (Policy Press 1999); Louise Ackers and Bryony Gill, *Moving People and Knowledge: Scientific Mobility in an Enlarging Europe* (Edward Elgar 2008).

society do not enjoy free movement rights. [. . .] Union Citizenship is a citizenship for all Europeans who are not poor or sick'[16] – we would also add, Europeans who are not caring for the sick, young, elderly or supporting spouses to not be poor. While the Court initially seemed to opt for a liberal and generous interpretation of the legal framework in order to give rights to as many EU citizens as possible, case law since 2014 suggests this carefully crafted citizenship safety net is being dismantled and that this is likely to have a significant impact on those most vulnerable EU citizens and their families.[17]

An expansionist agenda? The early case law

In its 2001 decision in *Grzelczyk*[18] the Court famously proclaimed that EU citizenship would become the fundamental status of all EU citizens.[19] EU citizenship was formally introduced into EU law by Treaty amendments as a way of bringing Europe closer to its people and enhancing the legitimacy of the EU.[20] EU citizenship was seen as encouraging a European identity and a way of making the EU meaningful in more than just an economic sense.[21] However, elements of citizenship were already apparent in the founding Treaty[22] and have been developed throughout the history of the EU. Economic free movement rights bear the hallmarks of citizenship, albeit for a selected few. The granting of social rights to the economic elite and the extension of some of those rights to families and economically inactive individuals can all be couched in citizenship terms. The constitutionalisation of citizenship rights through inclusion in the Treaty on European Union[23] can thus be seen as signifying a new chapter in the development of the status of the individual in the EU.[24] As Samantha Currie notes:

16 Damian Chalmers, Gareth Davies and Giorgio Monti, *European Union Law: Text and Materials* (Cambridge University Press 2014) 478.
17 See O'Brien, 'The ECJ Sacrifices EU Citizenship in Vain' (n 2).
18 *Grzelczyk* (n 8).
19 An aspirational statement which is now codified in recital 3 preamble of the CRD.
20 Treaty of Amsterdam amending the Treaty on European Union, the Treaties establishing the European Communities and certain related acts, as signed in Amsterdam on 2 October 1997, art 1(4): 'In Article A the second paragraph shall be replaced by the following: 'This Treaty marks a new stage in the process of creating an ever closer union among the peoples of Europe, in which decisions are taken as openly as possible and as closely as possible to the citizen.' See also Chalmers, Davies and Monti (n 16); Louise Ackers and Peter Dwyer, *Senior Citizenship? Retirement, Migration and Welfare in the European Union* (Polity Press 2002); Samantha Currie, *Migration, Work and Citizenship in the Enlarged European Union* (Ashgate 2008) chapter 1.
21 Currie, 'The transformation of union citizenship' (n 7).
22 Treaty establishing the European Economic Community (Rome, 25 March 1957) (Treaty of Rome).
23 Treaty on European Union [2012] OJ C326/13.
24 Jo Shaw, 'The Many Pasts and Futures of Citizenship in the European Union' (1997) 22 *European Law Review* 554. For developments of these arguments and analysis of early EU citizenship more generally see, eg Maas, *Creating European Citizens* (n 3); Siofra O'Leary, *The Evolving Concept of Community Citizenship: From the Free Movement of Persons to Union*

> Citizenship, therefore, stretches further than the articulation in Articles 17–22 EC[25] [now Articles 20–25 TFEU] per se, so as to incorporate the traditional economic free movement provisions, read alongside the extensive interpretation provided by the ECJ of the social rights of economic migrants. It also finds expression via the equal treatment principle in Article 12 EC [now Article 18 TFEU] and various pieces of secondary legislation.[26]

Whichever way citizenship is considered in the EU context there is no escaping the fact that the citizenship provisions are inextricably linked to free movement. In order for any of the citizenship provisions to become active, some kind of cross-border element is necessary. It is, of course, possible to argue that at least this was the principle until the controversial *Zambrano*[27] judgement, which we consider below.[28] While this close link with migration has been seen by some as limiting the scope and effectiveness of EU citizenship,[29] its impact on free movement rights is nonetheless worth noting and celebrating. In its 1998 judgement in *Martínez Sala*[30] the Court agreed that there did not always have to be a link between an EU migrant carrying out some kind of economic activity in the form of employment or self-employment and their right to receive social advantages. Since Maria Martínez Sala was lawfully residing in Germany, the Court held that she should be entitled to equal treatment with nationals of the host State. Although Mrs Martínez Sala had been previously employed in Germany,[31] the Court appeared to suggest that her economic activity, or rather the lack of it at the point of application, should be irrelevant to the consideration as to her entitlements. The important factor was her lawful residence under national law,

---

Citizenship (Kluwer 1996); Samantha Besson and André Utzinger, 'Introduction: Future Challenges of European Citizenship: Facing a Wide-Open Pandora's Box' (2007) 13 *European Law Journal* 573; Gareth Davies, '"Any Place I Hang My Hat?" or: Residence Is the New Nationality' (2005) 11 *European Law Journal* 43; Gareth Davis, 'Citizenship of the Union . . . rights for all?' (2002) 27 *European Law Review* 121; Dora Kostakopoulou, 'European Union Citizenship: Writing the Future' (2007) 13 *European Law Journal* 623; Eleanor Spaventa, 'Seeing the Wood Despite the Trees? On the Scope of Union Citizenship and its Constitutional Effects' (2008) 45 *Common Market Law Review* 13.

25 Treaty establishing the European Community [2002] OJ C325/33 (EC Treaty).

26 Currie, *Migration, Work and Citizenship* (n 20) 149.

27 Case C-34/09 *Gerardo Ruiz Zambrano v Office National de l'Emploi (ONEm)* [2011] ECR I-01177.

28 Currie, 'The transformation of union citizenship' (n 7).

29 ibid. See also Anonymous, 'Two-speed European Citizenship? Can the Lisbon Treaty Help Close the Gap?' (2008) 45 *Common Market Law Review* 1.

30 *Martínez Sala* (n 13).

31 Although the Court was unable to determine whether Maria Martínez Sala was 'a worker within the meaning of Article 48 of [EEC] treaty and [Article 7(2) of] Regulation No 1612/68' or an employed person within the meaning of Article 2 in conjunction with Article 1 of Regulation (EEC) No 1408/71 due to insufficient information by the national court, it nevertheless noted that she was a jobseeker and that she had a patchy work history, with various short periods of employment. Even though she was not working at the time of the decision, she received social assistance under the German Federal Social Welfare Law. See ibid para 34.

and that residence entitled her to equal treatment. This decision had far-reaching consequences, and it is a decision to be welcomed from a gender perspective because it allowed those who could demonstrate lawful residence to claim equal treatment even where they did not meet the definition of an EU migrant worker or self-employed person.

The approach taken by the Court in *Martínez Sala* is taken further in *Baumbast*[32] where the Court granted residence rights to the Baumbast family despite the fact that Mr Baumbast was no longer working in the host State, the United Kingdom (UK), but was employed by a German company outside Europe. Hence, the family did not meet the sufficient resources and health insurance requirements set out in the legal provisions. The Court held: 'The Treaty of the European Union does not require that citizens of the Union pursue a professional or trade activity, . . . in order to enjoy the rights provided in Part Two of the EC Treaty, on citizenship of the Union'.[33] However, most of the citizenship cases actually involve the application of some limitations to that basic premise. In *Grzelczyk*, for example, the sufficient resources requirement placed on students was not overruled. In *Trojani*[34] the Court noted that lawful residence could be withdrawn in cases where the requirements of lawful residence, ie sufficient resources, were no longer met. Similarly, in *Bidar*[35] and *Förster*,[36] a period of residence could be required to establish a 'genuine link' with the society of the host State before financial assistance such as subsidised student loans or student maintenance grant would be granted.[37] In fact, most of these citizenship decisions can be understood in terms of the requirement that there is a 'real and effective degree of connection between the claimant and the Member State'.[38] Starting with Maria Martinez Sala, it is evident that she had spent considerable time in the host State, and had previously contributed to the German economy through her economic activity. Similarly, Rudy Grzlyczyk had spent some time in the host State and had gone to considerable effort to support himself for the first three years of study. He had therefore established a degree of connection with the host State. It is also easy to see this link in *Baumbast* where the family had spent a considerable time in the

32 *Baumbast* (n 13).

33 ibid

34 Case C-456/02 *Michel Trojani v Centre public d'aide sociale de Bruxelles* (CPAS) [2004] EU:C:2004:488.

35 Case C-209/03 *R on the application of Dany Bidar v London Borough of Ealing and Secretary of State for Education and Skills* [2005] ECR I-02119.

36 Case C-158/07 *Jacqueline Förster v Hoofddirectie van de Informatie Beheer Groep* [2008] ECR I-08507.

37 See eg *Bidar* (n 35) para 55. O'Brien calls this a 'real link'. See O'Brien, *Unity in Adversity* (n 3) 35.

38 Case C-359/13 *B Martens v Minister van Onderwijs, Cultuur en Wetenschap* [2015] EU:C:2015:118, para 37: 'the proof required to demonstrate the genuine link must not be too exclusive in nature or unduly favour one element which is not necessarily representative of the real and effective degree of connection between the claimant and the Member State, to the exclusion of all other representative elements'.

UK and were also clearly committed to staying there. While the requirement for a genuine link with the society of the host State has meant that EU citizenship stops short of granting rights to non-economically active migrants purely on the basis of their citizenship status, the principle of proportionality has been used to soften the blow of such a requirement and to grant rights and benefits to which there is, on a strict application of the legal provisions, no entitlement.

Baumbast provides a valuable example of how economic self-sufficiency will help EU citizens establish or, more accurately, retain, their residence rights in cases where they do not in reality meet the requirements set out in EU law. Although the family had no medical insurance in the UK within the meaning of Article 7 CRD, the family was not considered a burden on the host State because they had medical insurance in Germany, where they travelled to receive any treatment. Therefore, the family was not reliant on the social assistance system during their period of residence. Additionally, it was clear that Mr Baumbast had previously engaged in economic activity, thus contributing to the economy in the UK. Although the Court confirmed that the right of residence was subject to the limitations and conditions set out in the Treaty and secondary legislation, it went on to say: 'those limitations are applied in compliance with general principles of EU law and, in particular, the principle of proportionality'.[39] Taking all those matters into consideration, the Court felt that denying the family their right of residence was not proportionate.

Michael Dougan and Eleanor Spaventa provide a useful summary:

> Baumbast . . . illustrates the application of proportionality to the 'health insurance' requirement imposed . . . The earlier case of Grzelczyk illustrates (though more in hindsight than in the explicit reasoning of the judgment itself) the application of the principle of proportionality to the requirement of 'sufficient resources' set out in the Residency Directives.[40]

Recognising the role of the principle of proportionality in citizenship case law has allowed greater flexibility to deal with cases taking personal circumstances of citizens into account as suggested by Currie:

> the Court's use of proportionality has injected a greater degree of flexibility into the black-letter provisions and allowed it to extend residence (and equal treatment) rights to some individuals who fall outside of the formal legislative regime.[41]

39 *Baumbast* (n 13) para 94.

40 Michael Dougan and Eleanor Spaventa, 'Educating Rudy and the Non-English Patient: A Double Bill on Residency Rights Under Art 18 EC' (2003) 28 *European Law Review* 699, 703.

41 Currie, *Migration, Work and Citizenship* (n 20) 168.

However, this flexibility only appears to apply in situations where citizens are already self-sufficient and the Court has been less willing to expand this flexibility to other situations preferring to apply different tests to establish eligibility in those situations.[42] As Jessica Guth notes '[t]his makes no sense at is seems to be offering help to those least likely to need it and denying it to those most likely to require assistance'.[43] A gendered reading of the case law and its application allows us to highlight that this does not impact on all citizens equally. Women are more likely to fall into a category of citizens who are not deemed to be economically active. Economic activity has traditionally been narrowly construed to include employment and self-employed activity but has excluded other activities such as volunteering and care.[44] We return to the question of care below after considering the position of those who are not claiming economic activity but instead are basing their claims to social assistance on other citizenship provisions.

Martínez Sala together with early cases on EU migrant workers suggests that the Court was keen to extend rights to as many EU nationals as possible.[45] As a result, many EU migrant women gained access to rights they would otherwise not have been able to claim. For instance, cases on part-time work allowed women to claim worker status and the associated rights.[46] The status of a worker was found to give economically active EU citizens a wide range of rights both prior to and following the existence of the employment relationship.[47] Further case law highlighted that worker status was not linked to whether or not the work paid enough to live on,[48] thus allowing a claim to rights where otherwise women in particular would have been left vulnerable and without access to assistance.[49]

42 For the case law on students requiring a real or genuine link test, see eg *Bidar* (n 35); *Förster* (n 36).

43 Guth, 'Law as the object' (n 4).

44 See O'Brien, 'Social Blind Spots' (n 10); Charlotte O'Brien, 'Drudges, Dupes and Do-gooders? Competing Notions of 'Value' in the Union's Approach to Volunteers' (2011) 1(1) *European Journal of Social Law* 49.

45 The objective of arts 48–51 of the EEC Treaty was to establish 'as complete a freedom of movement for workers as possible'. See *Hoekstra* (n 13).

46 eg Case C-53/81 *DM Levin v Staatssecretaris van Justitie* [1982] ECR 01035; Case C-413/01 *Franca Ninni-Orasche v Bundesminister für Wissenschaft, Verkehr und Kunst* [2003] EU:C:2003:600.

47 See eg Case C-48/75 *Jean Noël Royer* [1976] EU:C:1976:57; Case C-292/89 *R v Immigration Appeal Tribunal, ex parte Gustaff Desiderius Antonissen* [1991] EU:C:1991:80; *Ninni-Orasche* (n 46).

48 *RH Kempf v Staatssecretaris van Justitie* [1986] ECR-01741, EU:C:1986:223.

49 There is significant evidence that those in precarious and low-paid part-time work are more likely to be women. See eg Charlotte O'Brien, 'Civis Capitalist Sum: Class as the New Guiding Principle of EU Free Movement Rights' (2016) 53(4) *Common Market Law Review* 937, 938; Colette Fagan and Jill Rubery, 'Advancing Gender Equality Through European Employment Policy: The Impact of the UK's EU Membership and the Risks of Brexit' (2017) *Social Policy and Society* 1 doi:10.1017/S1474746417000458; Jo McBride, Andrew Smith, and Marcell Mbala, '"You end up with Nothing": The Experience of Being a Statistic

However, these cases also reveal the Court's desire to claim jurisdiction for itself and to ensure that it, and not the Member States, took control of defining and developing key concepts of EU law.[50] The focus of the Court appears to be the expansion of rights to EU citizens and EU integration rather than necessarily improving the position for women. Although the Court may have had some awareness of gender when deciding these cases, there is little evidence of this in the judgements. There is more evidence of its instrumentalism and protecting and expanding its own position and reach. Judgements following *Martínez Sala* prove an ever-increasing scope of citizenship, with links between economic activity and citizenship rights seemingly weakening with every decision.[51] However, a hierarchy of citizens has remained, and it is this hierarchy that was eventually also codified in Article 7[52] CRD which puts economic activity and economic self-sufficiency at the top of that hierarchy.

The rights of (EU citizen) children and their primary carers

Although early cases reiterate the economic underpinnings of EU law and the reluctance to impose financial burdens on Member States, there is some indication that other categories of EU citizens might also be seen as worth affording rights to. There is a body of case law after 2000 which is concerned with the rights of carers and particularly the rights they may derive from EU national children they care for. This can be seen as a positive step towards greater equality, and it may also be evidence that the Court is willing to take into consideration and accept gendered considerations when considering citizenship status. However, a careful reading of case law reveals an economic undertone in citizen judgements where the Court suggests that despite the rights of EU citizen children to attend school in the host State are considered 'independent'[53] under Article 10 of Regulation

---

of "in-work Poverty" in the UK' (2017) 1 *Work, Employment and Society* 1–2 doi:10.1177/0950017017728614; Office for National Statistics, 'People in Employment on a Zero-hours Contract: Mar 2017' 2 <www.ons.gov.uk/employmentandlabourmarket/peopleinwork/earningsandworkinghours/articles/contractsthatdonotguaranteeaminimumnumberofhours/mar2017> accessed 26 November 2017.

50 The objective of the provisions of the Treaty concerning workers would be deprived of all effect and frustrated if the meaning of the concept of 'workers' could be unilaterally fixed and modified by Member States. See *Hoekstra* (n 13).

51 eg *Martínez Sala* (n 13); *Baumbast* (n 13).

52 Directive 2004/38/EC, art 7(1)(b): 'All Union citizens shall have the right of residence on the territory of another Member State for a period of longer than three months . . . if they have sufficient resources for themselves and their family members not to become a burden on the social assistance system of the host Member State during their period of residence and have comprehensive sickness insurance cover in the host Member State.'

53 *Baumbast* (n 13) para 21: 'As regards the children, the Adjudicator decided that they enjoyed an independent right of residence under Article 12 of Regulation No 1612/68.'

492/2011,[54] such rights exist in the first place because of an EU citizen worker parent.[55] Hence, although in *Zhu and Chen*[56] the Court appears to recognise the right of a minor EU citizen child to reside in the host State as a self-standing right, many of the cases deliberating the residence rights of EU national children emphasise the link between economic activity of the children's fathers even though the Court does not seem to require that the primary carer-mother meets the requirements of EU migrant worker or self-sufficiency. Therefore, a careful reading of the citizenship cases appears to emphasise a link between the rights of the EU citizen children and the fathers, or another male member of the same household, who either currently works, or has previously worked in the host State. Hence, more recent case law discussed later in this chapter demonstrates the fact that the children are EU citizens themselves and attend school in the host State does not guarantee the children or the primary carer mothers any rights in themselves in cases where no EU citizen worker is present. Hence, it appears that the carers' rights are subordinate to and dependent on their children and ultimately their economically active (ex-)husbands or (ex-)partners.

Even though the carer-parents in the Court's 2004 decision in *Zhu and Chen*[57] were not EU nationals, the link between the Chinese national parents' economic self-sufficiency and the rights of their Irish national child, who at the time of the decision was four years old, are very visible, in that her parents are considered to have sufficient resources to support themselves. At the same time this decision can been seen as rather significant as it visibly expands the citizenship case law. In this case the Court was prepared to recognise the rights of third-country national parent-carers of their EU national child. There was no question of the carers becoming a burden on a host State since the parents were self-sufficient and had enough money to look after themselves and their daughter without needing recourse to social assistance.[58] In this decision the Court also rejected the suggestion that a child could not take advantage of the rights of free movement and residence simply because she had never moved from one Member State to another Member State.[59] According to the Court, the capacity of a

54 Regulation 1612/68 was repealed by Regulation (EU) No 492/2011 of the European Parliament and of the Council of 5 April 2011 on freedom of movement for workers within the Union [2011] OJ L141/1. Regulation No 492/2011, art 10 reproduced the wording of Regulation 1612/68, art 12.

55 *Baumbast* (n 13) para 55: 'to permit children of a citizen of the Union . . . to continue their education in the host Member State only where they cannot do so in their Member State of origin would offend not only the letter of Article 12 of Regulation No 1612/68. . . but also its spirit'.

56 eg, Case C-200/02 *Kunqian Catherine Zhu and Man Lavette Chen v Secretary of State for the Home Department* [2004] ECR I-9925 (*Zhu and Chen*).

57 ibid.

58 Mr Chen was a director and the majority shareholder of a company established in China for which he and his wife worked. He travelled frequently to the UK for the purposes of his work and his wife joined him on one of such trips in 2000. ibid paras 7–8.

59 ibid para 18.

national of a Member State to be the holder of rights guaranteed by the Treaty and by secondary law on the free movement of persons could not be made conditional upon the attainment of a minimum age prescribed for the acquisition of legal capacity to exercise those rights personally.[60] In later case law, the Court has also indicated that children should not be penalised for the fact that they have moved to another Member State with their parents while being unable to independently exercise their rights.[61]

However, case law following the enactment of the CRD suggests that carers do not have to meet the requirements of EU migrant worker or self-sufficiency in Article 7, but can, in fact, derive rights even where they are, for all intents and purposes, a burden on the host State. The 2010 cases of *Ibrahim*[62] and *Teixera*[63] are useful illustrations. In both cases women who had been spouses of EU nationals prior to separation or divorce and who were primary carers for their children applied for housing benefit in the UK. The housing benefit was denied on the basis that neither Ms Ibrahim nor Ms Teixera had the right to reside in the UK under EU law. However, the Court held that their children had a children of EU migrant workers and that with that right came a right of residence for both the children themselves and their primary carer, regardless of their nationality. In essence, the Court decided that this type of right of residence was not subject to the self-sufficiency conditions in the Directive. The Court also noted, however, that the right to reside would end when the child reached the age of majority, unless it could be shown that the child required the presence of the parent-carer in order to complete their education. *Teixera* nevertheless appears to demonstrate the understanding that obligations relating to childcare may necessitate women to take a break from employment because women are more likely to be primarily responsible for providing care than men.[64]

There are similar decisions concerning the assumption that children forming part of an EU citizen worker's household retain the right to education even in

60 ibid para 20.

61 In *Martens* (n 38) the Court held that rules which made the access to the finance subject to minimum number of years residence rule for its own citizens, who had been resident outside the Netherlands prior to their studies, were discriminatory. This was because Ms Martens had moved to Belgium with her father when she were a minor and could not fulfil the requirement to have resided in the Netherlands for a continuous period of three years in the six years prior to the commencement of her university studies.

62 Case C-310/08 *London Borough of Harrow v Nimco Hassan Ibrahim and Other* [2010] ECR I-01065. Ms Ibrahim was a sole parent of Somali nationality who had separated from her Danish citizen husband who had worked in the UK. All her four children (aged from one to nine) were Danish.

63 Case C-480/08 *Maria Teixeira v London Borough of Lambeth and Other* [2010] ECR I-01107. Ms Teixeira was a lone parent of Portuguese nationality who had divorced from her Portuguese husband who worked in the UK. Although she was not working when her Portuguese daughter started school in the UK, she herself had worked intermittently in the UK since 1989 and she also worked for various periods during her daughter's education. ibid paras 20–21.

64 See eg O'Brien, 'I trade, therefore I am' (n 10).

the event of a divorce. In *Alarape*[65] the Court confirmed that a Nigerian ex-spouse of an EU citizen could continue to have a derived right of residence in the UK on the basis of Articles 12 and 13(1) CRD,[66] provided that her 22-year-old Nigerian national son remained 'in need of the presence and care of that parent in order to be able to continue and to complete his education'.[67] Ms Alarape relied on her derived right of residence of a family member of an EU citizen, who had exercised their rights in the UK stemming from the EC Treaty between 2004 and 2010. However, the national authorities considered that the EU citizen had been a worker only for two years in that period.[68] The mother and son argued that they shared a common household in London. However, in practice, Mr Tijani lived away from home in Edinburgh and resided with his mother in London only during holidays and occasional weekends because he had enrolled on doctoral studies at the University of Edinburgh.[69] In *NA*[70] a Pakistani national wife of a German national husband could not rely on the retention of her right of residence in the UK on the basis of Article 13 CRD where the commencement of divorce proceedings post-dated the departure of her husband from the UK.[71] This was so even if she had been the victim of domestic violence during the marriage.[72] Instead, the Court merely noted that Article 13(2) CRD required that her EU citizen husband must reside in the host Member State, in accordance with Article 7(1) CRD, until the date of the commencement of divorce proceedings. Because NA's husband had left the UK she was not entitled to rely on Article 13(2)(c), which stipulated it was necessary to ensure that the third-country national spouse would not lose their right to residence in the host State

65 Case C-529/11 *Olaitan Ajoke Alarape and Olukayode Azeez Tijani v Secretary of State for the Home Department* [2013] EU:C:2013:290 (*Alarape*).

66 Directive 2004/38, arts 12 and 13(1) protect non-national parents who are at risk of losing their rights of residence in a host State as a result of a marriage breakdown. Such parents may have a derived right of residence which enables them to stay in the host Member State during the period of their children's education in situations where the latter enjoy the right to continue their education in the host State under Directive 2004/38.

67 *Alarape* (n 65) para 49.

68 ibid para 18.

69 During her period of residence in the UK from July 2004 to 2009 Ms Alarape had worked on a part-time self-employed basis, with a monthly income of around £1,600, on which she paid taxes and national insurance contributions. The Court also noted that Mr Tijani had been in full-time education since arriving in the UK in 2004, first at school and subsequently at university. Between 2006 and 2008 he also worked part-time. *Alarape* (n 65) paras 15–17.

70 Case C-115/15 *Secretary of State for the Home Department v NA* [2016] All ER (D) 93 (Jul), EU:C:2016:487.

71 Case C-115/15 *Secretary of State for the Home Department v NA* [2016] EU:C:2016:259, Opinion of AG Wathelet, para 11. See also *NA* (n 70) para 36. In *Singh and Others*, the Court had held that in accordance with art 7(1) CRD, the EU citizen, who was the spouse of a third-country national, had to reside in the host Member State up to the commencement of divorce proceedings in order for that spouse to claim the retention of his or her right of residence in the host Member State on the basis of art 13(2) CRD. Case C-218/14 *Kuldip Singh and Others v Minister for Justice and Equality* [2015] EU:C:2015:476, para 66.

72 *NA*, Opinion of AG Wathelet (n 71) para 13.

in 'particularly difficult circumstances, such as having been a victim of domestic violence while the marriage or registered partnership was subsisting'.[73] The outcome is absurd in that the Court suggested that had her abusive husband stayed in the UK until she was divorced, she would have been able to rely on Article 13(2)(c). However, because he had decided to settle in Pakistan, she was only able to reside in the UK due to having acquired the custody of the couple's two German national daughters, who were both born in the UK and attended school there.[74]

Although the Court noted that that the Commission's proposal for the CRD stated that the purpose of Article 13(2) 'was to offer certain legal safeguards to third-country nationals whose right of residence was dependent on a family relationship by marriage and who could therefore be open to blackmail accompanied by threats of divorce',[75] accordingly such safeguards were necessary only in the event of final divorce since the right of residence of a third-country national spouse was not affected in the event of *de facto* separation.[76] Therefore, had NA not been the primary carer of her children, who were German nationals, she would have had to leave the UK.

Two key issues arise from a gendered reading of this case law. First, the Court chose a restrictive interpretation when it did not have to. It could have approached the question differently and offered a more expansive and gender-aware interpretation of the law. Second, the Court missed the dangers of making the rights of primary carers (usually women) dependent on the rights of their children. We consider these issues next.

The judgement in *NA* ignores the reality of NA's life and position. It fails to engage with the domestic violence she suffered and the options open to her. Arguably it also achieves the exact opposite of what section 13(2)(c) was intended to achieve.[77] Helen Oosterum-Staples argues convincingly that even a strict reading of the legislation does not automatically lead to the conclusion the Court reached. She notes:

> The crucial difference between the two sub-sections [13(2)a and 13(2)c] is that the word 'divorce' is not used in sub-section (c). [. . .] Even if we acknowledge that a literal reading of Article 13(2)(a) of the Citizens Directive merits the conclusion that the EU-citizen's departure from the host-Member State entails the loss of the right of residence derived from Article

73 *NA* (n 70) para 50.

74 *NA*, Opinion of AG Wathelet (n 71) paras 14–15.

75 *NA* (n 70) para 47.

76 ibid. For case law concerning the right of residence for third-country national spouses after separation, see Case 267/83 *Aissatou Diatta* [1985] EU:C:1985:67; *Ibrahim* (n 62); Case C-244/13 *Ewaen Fred Ogieriakhi v Minister for Justice and Equality and Others* [2014] EU:C:2014:2068.

77 Helen Oosterum-Staples, 'Residence Rights for Caring Parents Who Are Also Victims of Domestic Violence' 19 (2017) *European Journal of Migration and Law* 396.

> 7(2) of the Citizens Directive that cannot be repaired by Article 13(2)(a) of that Directive, the omission of any reference to the initiation of divorce proceedings in sub-section (c) challenges the Court of Justice's conclusion that the same holds true for victims of domestic violence.[78]

The second issue is that the residence rights were afforded to the female primary carer in *Ibrahim*, *Teixera*, *Alarape* and *NA* on the basis of the children's dependence on their primary carer mothers, who in turn derived their right to education from the EU citizen worker. This was so even in *Alarape* where the son had already reached the age of majority. The primary carer mothers' rights are subordinate to and dependent on their children and ultimately their husbands or partners. The rights do not attach to personhood and the carers are not valued in their own right. While these cases provide a temporary solution to a residency gap which arises when third-country nationals are left behind by the EU national spouses or partners, the solution is only ever temporary and any rights would be lost when the children reach majority and/or leave the host State. The two issues raised taken together present a worrying picture in situations where women find themselves in vulnerable situations or are the victims of domestic violence. The spouse could, for example, threaten to or actually remove the children, exerting an enormous amount of power over the victim and potentially leaving her without any rights at all, thus forcing her to leave the host country which may have been her home for a considerable amount of time.

These cases show some awareness that these issues are gendered and that men and women are likely to experience these situations differently or, rather, are likely to be in different roles. Women are more likely to be the primary carer and find themselves in the sort of situations the women in the above cases found themselves in. Certainly, in many of these cases it seems that male migrants are highly mobile, perhaps due to the flexible nature of their work as self-employed persons or as employees in companies which may have offices in more than one Member State or even outside the EU or simply because it is easier for them to extract themselves from caring responsibilities and other local ties. Therefore, because of their mobility, men appear to be more likely to be able to establish rights through economic activity and have the ability to relocate to another Member State, or even outside the EU.

There are also some rather worrying economic undertones in these cases. It appears that women are unlikely to be able to relocate due to the more inflexible nature of their jobs or perhaps lack of work, children's education, or inability to afford relocation. Allowing primary carers of EU migrant worker's children to reside in the territory of the host State while their children are in education, but not after their children complete their education, suggests that the Court considers the residence as a way of supporting the preparation for the next generation of workers. The main purpose of residence is to help children complete education and prepare for work or other economic activity. What happens after that is also

78 ibid 412.

very important though. If residence rights are lost at that point when children no longer attend school or university, women who have devoted their time in the host State to caring for their children could be forced to leave. The contribution they have made to their children, the community and the host State is ignored. They are deemed expensive (because they rely on social assistance) and, once the children can be self-sufficient, they are no longer useful. This situation is exacerbated in the very situations where they need the protection of EU law most – for example in situations of domestic violence. Although the drafting history of Article 13(2)(c) CRD suggests that the legislators intended to offer protection to victims of domestic violence or other difficult circumstances, the decision in *NA* has achieved the opposite and actually privileges the perpetrators.[79]

While the cases concerning primary carer-parents have resulted in citizenship case law which enables women to retain their rights of residence in the host State, more recent case law demonstrates that the Court is returning to what commentators call 'market citizenship',[80] with the requirements that the carers must have sufficient resources for themselves to not to become a burden on the social assistance system of the host States.

Highlighting the genderedness of citizenship case law: *Zambrano* and *McCarthy*

Although in recent case law concerning the right to social assistance for non-workers the Court has taken an increasingly restrictive approach towards citizenship rights, maintaining that the rights are linked to economic activity, it is worth examining two citizenship cases concerning the right of residence for third country national family members, *Zambrano*[81] and *McCarthy*,[82] decided in quick succession in 2011. These cases help highlight how a gendered reading of the citizenship case law allows us to ask questions and take into consideration issues of which we might otherwise not take account. Although the cases might not seem that similar, the legal issues raised by the national courts are essentially almost identical because they concern the right of residence for family members of 'static' EU citizens. In *Zambrano*, a residence permit was granted to Columbian parents on the basis of their children's EU citizenship status. In *McCarthy*, a residence permit was refused to a Jamaican spouse of a dual British–Irish citizen. Guth has argued that '[i]n both cases the legal issue . . . is whether a right to reside in the EU can be derived by a third-country national from an EU national who has always resided in their home State. In *Zambrano* the answer was yes, in *McCarthy* the

79 Oosterum-Staples (n 77).

80 See eg, Jo Shaw, 'Importing Gender: The Challenge of Feminism and the Analysis of the EU Legal Order' (2000) 7(3) *Journal of European Public Policy* 406 doi:10.1080/13501760050086107.

81 *Zambrano* (n 27).

82 Case C-434/09 *Shirley McCarthy v Secretary of State for the Home Department* [2011] EU:C:2011:277.

answer was no'.[83] The basis for the difference in outcome is that if the children, who had never exercised their EU law rights, would have been forced to leave the territory of the EU, they would have been deprived of the 'substance' of their EU law rights. In contrast, Mrs McCarthy would not be deprived of her rights if she did not fulfil the substantive requirements which EU law imposed on EU citizens wishing to reside in the host Member State for more than three months.[84]

While it is worth acknowledging the limit of EU law rights in a sense that the Treaties contain only a limited set of rights to free movement and residence under Articles 20 and 21 TFEU, which are only activated upon moving from one's State of origin to another Member State, the British Advocate General (AG), Eleonor Sharpston, has noted that not all cases concerning Article 21 TFEU have required cross-border movement in order to protect fundamental rights. According to her, 'the Court has opted for a generous interpretation of Article 21 TFEU in order to protect fundamental rights' and to create legal certainty in a delicate area of both EU law and domestic law.[85] She specifically noted that in *Zhu and Chen*, the 'movement' took place from England to Northern Ireland. Catherine Zhu's mother nevertheless became entitled to a derived right of residence as a result of this movement and the acquisition of Irish nationality by her daughter 'through application of the extraterritorial rule that then formed part of that Member State's nationality law'.[86] Although Sharpston appears to suggest that EU law can only operate within the confines of national law, we have argued in Chapter 3 that the Court sometimes uses its political power, especially in relation to EU citizenship and fundamental rights. Therefore, these two cases are the main focus of this section in order to examine the extent to which gendered assumptions may have influenced the outcomes.

Despite his unsuccessful application for asylum in 1999, Gerardo Ruiz Zambrano, a Colombian national, continued to live in Belgium and obtained work although he should have been unable to pursue any employment while the authorities determined his application for legalising his situation.[87] After the birth of their two children in Belgium, he and his Columbian wife unsuccessfully applied for residence permits.[88] The Court, who heard the case in 2011, held that under Article 20 TFEU, the Zambrano family could not be refused the right of residence because their minor children, who had acquired Belgian nationality at birth, were dependent upon their parents.[89] Similarly, Belgium could not

83 Guth, 'Law as the Object' (n 4).

84 Case C-434/09 *Shirley McCarthy v Secretary of State for the Home Department* [2010] EU:C:2010:718, Opinion of AG Kokott, point 44.

85 Case C-34/09 *Gerardo Ruiz Zambrano v Office national de l'emploi (ONEM)* [2010] EU:C:2010:560, Opinion of AG Sharpston, point 141.

86 ibid point 137.

87 *Zambrano* (n 27) paras 14–18.

88 ibid para 23. For further details, see Jessica Guth and Edward Mowlam, 'The evolution of European Union citizenship; Where does Zambrano take us?' (2012) 46(1) *The Law Teacher* 75 doi: 10.1080/03069400.2012.644972.

89 *Zambrano* (n 27) para 45.

refuse to grant Mr Zambrano a work permit, if this deprived the children of the 'genuine enjoyment of the substance of the rights attaching to the status of EU citizen'.[90] The decision is controversial not only because the case highlights the incompetence of Belgian authorities to determine the family's application for legalising their situation,[91] but also due to its departure from other cases determining the right of residence for third-country national family members.[92]

In contrast, although Shirley McCarthy held dual Irish–UK nationality, she had never exercised her EU free movement rights. She applied for a right of residence for her Jamaican husband but was refused, as she was not a 'qualified person' under the EU law.[93] Consequently, her husband, George McCarthy, could not claim attached spousal rights.[94] The Court noted:

> However, no element of the situation of Mrs McCarthy, as described by the national court, indicates that the national measure at issue in the main proceedings has the effect of depriving her of the genuine enjoyment of the substance of the rights associated with her status as a Union citizen, or of impeding the exercise of her right to move and reside freely within the territory of the Member States, in accordance with Article 21 TFEU.[95]

The Court further noted that the dual citizenship acquired by Mrs McCarthy had no implications for her ability to rely on EU law:

> Indeed, the failure by the authorities of the United Kingdom to take into account the Irish nationality of Mrs McCarthy for the purposes of granting her a right of residence in the United Kingdom in no way affects her in her right to move and reside freely within the territory of the Member States, or any other right conferred on her by virtue of her status as a Union citizen.[96]

In applying citizenship provisions to *McCarthy*, the Court took a restrictive approach, choosing to consult Article 21 TFEU and applying limitations to free movement on the basis that Mrs McCarthy was a 'static' citizen who had never left

90 ibid.
91 ibid para 26.
92 See eg Case C-256/11 *Murat Dereci and Others v Bundesministerium für Inneres* [2011] ECR I-11315, para 74 where the Court held that provisions on EU citizenship did not preclude Member States from refusing a right of residence to a third-country national on its territory in cases where their EU citizen family member whom they relied on for a derived right of residence had never exercised their right to freedom of movement, provided that the refusal did not lead to the 'denial of the genuine enjoyment of the substance of the rights conferred by virtue of their status' as an EU citizen.
93 Directive 2004/38/EC, part 1(6).
94 *McCarthy* (n 82) para 20.
95 ibid para 49.
96 ibid.

England.[97] A gendered approach to the situation as well as the legal analysis in *McCarthy* allows us to see this case differently and to argue that, the same way as Zambrano's children would have been deprived of the genuine enjoyment of their EU law rights, Mrs McCarthy is also deprived of that enjoyment. Anastasia Iliopoulou Penot has noted that '[t]he Court attaches no significance to a literal reading of the Directive. Its reasoning is inspired by the will to guarantee the effectiveness of the right of residence of Union citizens through the protection of their family life'.[98] Questions arise why the Court did not extend this reasoning to Shirley McCarthy's family and why the Court was unwilling to keep her family together.[99] A gendered look can reveal how traditional factual and legal analysis can miss things which we might consider important. The German AG, Juliane Kokott, noted Mrs McCarthy's dependence on the State and in turn the potential burden placed upon the social welfare system. However, the judgement fails to address the reality that, much like the Somalian mother of four in *Ibrahim*,[100] Mrs McCarthy was a homemaker, caring for three children of whom one was severely disabled.

These facts are important in a gendered reading of the case. They allow us to pose 'what if' scenarios to better understand how EU law works. For instance, had Shirley McCarthy been in a different financial situation and able to pay for her disabled child's care while working herself, the Court may have chosen to employ the same reasoning as in *Zambrano*. Alternatively, she may not have needed that reasoning in the first place as she may have been in a position to move to another Member State to trigger her EU law rights. In fact, she may not have needed the help of EU law at all because she may have met the UK immigration rules, which stipulate an income threshold for her husband to join her. More importantly, however, a gendered reading allows us to question whether the law was applied in a way that seems meaningful. The legal questions relate to the scope and limitations of the citizenship provisions in the TFEU and, more specifically perhaps, the distinction between 'static' and 'mobile' EU citizen and the way the definition of economic activity is to be conceptualised and applied in any given situation. *Zambrano* indicated that mobility was not a requirement. Similarly, other cases concerning EU national children[101] confirm that this is not necessarily a novel approach. Yet, this appears to be the stumbling block for the

97 *McCarthy*, Opinion of AG Kokott (n 84) point 43: 'a "static" Union citizen such as Mrs McCarthy is not discriminated against at all compared with "mobile" Union citizens'.

98 Anastasia Iliopoulou Penot, 'The transnational character of union citizenship' in Michael Dougan, Niamh Nic Shuibhne, and Eleanor Spaventa (eds), *Media of Empowerment and Disempowerment of the European Citizen* (Hart 2012) 15 and 27.

99 CMA McCauliff, 'EU Citizenship: Why Can't the Advocated General Keep Sheila McCarthy's Family Together?' (2013) 36(5) *Fordham International Law Journal* 1372.

100 Indeed, Ms Ibrahim was a housewife with four children of whom the youngest was one and she depended entirely on social assistance to cover her family's living expenses and housing costs. *Ibrahim* (n 62) paras 19–20.

101 See eg those discussed in section concerning EU citizen children and their carer-parents.

Court in *McCarthy* although the Court does not offer any clear explanation as to why this is the case.

Therefore, EU law appears to afford protection only to highly mobile citizens who may at some point in their lives be in a position to move from one Member State to another. The possibility of triggering EU law free movement rights at a later stage of one's life is thus protected in *Zambrano*. However, EU law fails to provide any consideration for individuals like Shirley McCarthy, who may experience circumstances that prevent cross-border mobility even where the granting of EU law rights might actually increase the potential for engagement with EU law provisions. Hence, the nature of free movement provisions and their application may also serve as indirect discrimination on the basis of disability or poverty.[102]

The second hurdle in gendered reading appears to be the lack of economic activity. It is clear that Mrs McCarthy has never worked and is dependent on her country of nationality for assistance. Therefore, she appears to be the kind of EU citizen to whom very few EU rights apply because she is not economically active and has neither intention nor the means to leave her home State. However, not granting Mr McCarthy the right of residence makes no sense economically because it is not clear whether he would be able to work and support the family. Therefore, the Court appears to suggest that Mr Zambrano is perhaps a more 'worthy' recipient of rights derived from EU law. The Court specifically noted the contribution Mr Zambrano made to the economy of the host State:

> at the time of his second child's birth, Mr Ruiz Zambrano had sufficient resources from his working activities to provide for his family. His work was paid according to the various applicable scales, with statutory deductions made for social security and the payment of employer contributions.[103]

Therefore, Mr Zambrano's self-sufficiency is one of the reasons for the Court's decision to regularise the family's situation.

To claim that women such as Shirley McCarthy are not prevented from enjoying their EU law rights seems absurd, considering that care responsibilities still predominantly fall on women who often either do not work, or work limited hours, and therefore rely on State benefits or other assistance. Carer-parents with young children, who attend full-time education, often earn very little and need to resort to the State to supplement their income. Therefore, women with care responsibilities are simply not in a position to uproot themselves and their families and move to another Member State – only to exercise the right to bring their third-country national spouse with them. Their situation is exactly the same as in *Zambrano* where the young children were not in a position to move to another

102 It is worth highlighting that the Court does not take into account the level of disability of Mrs McCarthy's child.

103 *Zambrano* (n 27) para 20.

EU Member State in order to avoid having to have to leave the EU altogether since their parents enjoyed no right of residence in Belgium.

However, the *McCarthy* judgement does not demonstrate awareness of the fact that sole parents with young children are unlikely to be mobile. Hence, the question arises that if the Court was prepared to grant residence rights in *Zambrano* where there was no cross-border element, why did it not allow the same rights in *McCarthy* which did not concern any less 'the very enjoyment of the substance of rights conferred by the status of EU citizenship'. If the EU citizenship rights concerned merely free movement linked to economic activity, the answer would perhaps be affirmative. However, *Zambrano* does not concern free movement linked to economic activity. Although the Court does not make explicit reference to the analogy between family reunification cases of the European Court of Human Rights and the deprivation of the children of their EU citizenship if their father is unable to obtain a residence permit and a work permit in Belgium,[104] there are family reunification cases before the latter court where the host State is unable to require the families to leave its territory due to the degree of integration of the family in that State.[105]

However, we argue that there is only a lack of economic activity if this is defined in a traditional and narrow sense. Louise Ackers argues that assumption that care work fails to qualify as 'work' for EU citizenship purposes[106] enforces a hierarchy in the enjoyment of citizenship provisions.[107] Although the Court has recognised the value of unpaid domestic work in its case law,[108] it has only done so where care work enables the male member of the household to pursue economic activity which allows the family to be self-sufficient. However, the Court is less willing to accept care work as genuine economic activity in its own right. Isabella Moebius and Erika Szyszczak have criticised the Court's distinction between employment and care work as it allows for the work of women to remain invisible for the purpose of EU law.[109] The unpaid and invisible nature of what is usually seen as a female caring role leads to economic and legal disadvantages.[110] The principle of unpaid work goes against the EU ideals of an economically active citizen; the lack of clarification and recognition of unpaid work allows for the facilitation of

104 *Zambrano* (n 27) para 44.

105 See, eg, *Sen v The Netherlands*, no 31465/96, § 31, 21 December 2001.

106 *Martínez Sala* (n 13).

107 Louise Ackers, 'Women, Citizenship and European Community Law: The Gender Implications of the Free Movement Provisions' (1994) 16(4) *Journal of Social Welfare and Family Law* 391.

108 See eg *Baumbast* (n 13); *Zhu and Chen* (n 56); Case C-60/00 *Mary Carpenter v Secretary of State for the Home Department* [2002] ECR I-6279.

109 Isabella Moebius and Erika Szyszczak, 'Of Raising Pigs and Children' (1998) 18(1) *Yearbook of European Law* 125.

110 Clare McGlynn, 'European Union Family Values: Ideologies of "Family" and "Motherhood" in European Union Law' (2001) 8 *Social Politics* 325. See also Clare McGlynn, 'Ideologies of Motherhood in European Community Sex Equality Law' (2000) 6 *European Law Journal* 29.

'market citizenship'.[111] This explanation of citizenship is formed on the principle of granting free movement rights in return for economic activity in the host State.[112]

However, a gendered approach recognises care work as a necessary duty of life and notes that, without two adult members of the household to share the burden of maintaining or caring for the family, the family is unable to attain self-sufficiency or make substantial use of their EU citizenship rights. Although there is no mention of the role of Mr Zambrano's wife in caring for their children, the Court indirectly recognised these issues and addressed them by granting residency and working rights to allow the family to remain self-sufficient and within EU territory. The current structure of EU citizenship provisions promotes the underlying principles of dependency with families; whilst *Zambrano* shows that the Court, or EU law, protects the interests of children in some cases, it leaves carers and particularly lone parents in a vulnerable position.[113] Since the care of children still falls disproportionately to women, lone parents are more likely to be women.[114] Hence, legislation and decisions, which have adverse impacts on lone parents, also indirectly have an adverse impact on women. Charlotte O'Brien has argued that, compared to two-parent families, single-parent families are nearly seven times as likely to have a total family income in the lowest income quintile.[115] Single-parent families are also less likely to have a full-time worker in the family, and it is likely that they may not be in work at all if they have young children.[116] Additionally, lone parents find it more difficult to find work and, thus, take longer to find work, and they are likely to have an immediate need for benefits, partly due to childcare that is inflexible and incompatible with low-income, low-status jobs.[117] As a result, single parents' inability to access the means to provide basic subsistence for their children is also a significant barrier to accessing a job market.[118] Therefore, women, who are also lone parents and who exercise their free movement rights, may see the welfare of their children compromised. This can be seen in many of the cases discussed above, including *Ibrahim*, *Teixera*, *Alarape*, *NA* and *McCarthy*, but also those we are yet to discuss, including *Dano*[119] and *Alimanovic*.[120] In fact, hardly any case law exists where the single parent is male,

111 Shaw, 'Importing Gender' (n 80).
112 Michelle Everson, 'The legacy of the market citizen' in Jo Shaw and Gillian More (eds), *New Legal Dynamics of European Union* (Clarendon 1995) 73–89.
113 Ackers (n 107).
114 See Charlotte O'Brien, 'THE pillory, the Precipice and the Slippery Slope: The Profound Effects of the UK's Legal Reform Programme Targeting EU Migrants' (2015) 37(1) *Journal of Social Welfare and Family Law* 111, 129.
115 ibid 114.
116 ibid.
117 ibid.
118 ibid.
119 Case C-333/13 *Elizabeta Dano v Jobcenter Leipzig* [2014] EU:C:2014:2358.
120 Case C-67/14 *Jobcenter Berlin Neukölln v Nazifa Alimanovic and Others* [2015] EU:C:2015:597.

but carers are predominantly women, regardless whether they were caring for their own children, the children of their spouses from previous relationships,[121] or their grandchildren.[122]

The EU ideals of citizenship provisions fundamentally allow for the 'cherry-picking' of economic citizenship criteria. In doing so, it is able to mask the gender inequality this approach perhaps inadvertently produces.[123] A better approach might be to focus on gender equity with the idea of men and women being treated using different approaches to achieve the same outcome.[124] This reflects their different roles. The gender equity approach implies fairness as the life experiences and expectations of men and women are taken in to consideration in a bid to compensate for the historical and social disadvantages women face.[125] This approach would make allowances for the fact that Mrs McCarthy worked although she did not get paid. She would not be considered a burden upon the State and instead made contributions by working as a full-time carer to her disabled child as well as looking after her other children. A gender equity approach would consider that society often requires mothers to take on the role of primary carer for children and so restricts them in applying for rights under Article 7 CRD.[126] In similar vein, O'Brien argued in favour of an integrated interpretation approach that:

> the reach of free movement rights should be defined according to a duty of both formal and substantive equal treatment. The scope of migrant work should be subject to the same principles as the content of Community law. In this way some asymmetry could be redressed; not by attempting to Europeanise the social, but by socializing the (already European) economic.[127]

In contrast with *Zambrano*, the Court's analysis in *McCarthy* is extremely limited because it failed to recognise as a deprivation of EU citizenship rights any other situation than expulsion from EU territory. According to it, the decision had no adverse impact on Mrs McCarthy's free movement rights or enjoyment of the substance of EU rights.[128] An alternative argument suggests that EU citizenship provides freedoms and, in fact, the literal application of the law to Mrs McCarthy's circumstances places restrictions upon her EU citizenship as it renders her incapable of achieving family reunification in her home State. The Court failed to

121 *Carpenter* (n 107).

122 Case C-457/12 *S and G v Minister voor Immigratie, Integratie en Asiel* [2014] EU:C:2014:136 (*S and G*).

123 Francesca Strumia, 'Remedying the Inequalities of Economic Citizenship in Europe: Cohesion Policy and the Negative Right to Move' (2011) 17(6) *European Law Journal* 725.

124 Sylvia Walby, 'The European Union and Gender Equality: Emergent Varieties of Gender Regime' (2004) 11(1) *Social Politics* 4.

125 ibid.

126 Directive 2004/38/EC, art 7.

127 O'Brien, 'Social Blind Spots' (n 10) 1107.

128 *McCarthy* (n 82) para 49.

consider the practical ramifications Mrs McCarthy faced due to her inability to move to another Member State due to her dependent child. Requiring her to move to another Member State could force her to use the social welfare systems of the host State for the provision of care, thus becoming a greater burden upon the host State and causing detriment to her child. In contrast, in *Zambrano*, the required permits were granted to facilitate the care of the children and prevent forced migration.[129] The pertinent difference in these cases is gendered because of the degree of self-sufficiency and definition of economic activity recognised by the Court.

Considering these two cases together gives us an insight into assumptions made and issues taken for granted or constructed in a particular way and these have gendered implications. In addition, the two cases suggest that there needs to be a particular type of relationship in order for derived residence rights to apply: that of carer, ideally parent and child. Other cases[130] have hinted at this as explored above – where there is a carer of an EU national child, residence and associated rights are granted more often than not. However, this is not always the case. The Court's 2012 decision in *S and G*[131] suggests that its reasoning is occasionally rather hostile towards women. In this case the Court stated that the mere fact that it might appear desirable that sponsor S's son was cared for by his third-country national mother-in-law, who was also the son's biological grandmother was insufficient in itself to constitute such a dissuasive effect.[132] Such a conclusion seems absurd because, in *Carpenter*, Mr Carpenter's Philippine wife, Mary Carpenter, was not related to her husband's children in any way, but her presence and care of Mr Carpenter's children were considered more important than the care of sponsor S's mother-in-law who was directly related to the couple's son.

The Court is rather less willing to allow partners and spouses to derive such rights from each other:

> Thus, whereas in *Zambrano* the company (and indeed authorisation to work) of a carer-parent was considered essential for the continued residence of the citizen on the territory of the Union, in *McCarthy* the same logic did not apply to the company of a spouse.[133]

As argued above, the acknowledgement of carers' rights is an important development in EU law and one which potentially benefits women as carers across the EU. However, Guth notes that:

> the cases seem to require women to do it all: They need to be able to work and ideally work in a Member State other than their own in order to benefit

129 *Zambrano* (n 27) para 43
130 See eg *Zhu and Chen* (n 56); *Ibrahim* (n 62); *Teixera* (n 63).
131 *S and G* (n 122).
132 ibid para 43.
133 Stephen Coutts, 'Case C- 434–09: Shirley McCarthy v. Secretary of State for the Home Department' (10 May 2011) <http://globalcit.eu/case-c-434-09-shirley-mccarthy-v-secretary-of-state-for-the-home-department/> accessed 9 April 2018.

> from the right to have their third country family member join them and if there is a relationship of caring present, chances of rights being granted seem to increase dramatically.[134]

Additionally, the recent decisions that grandparents are not automatically considered as an ideal carer for their grandchildren seem rather absurd. The EU ideal of full labour market participation and a lack of recognition of caring responsibilities as economic activity taken together mean that the realities of women's lives is not accurately reflected in the stories heard in the Court and thus also not accurately translated into legal solutions which are gender aware. This leads Guth to ask a series of questions in relation to these two cases:

> What then if, in the *Zambrano* case, Mr Zambrano had not featured? What if it was Mrs Zambrano who had claimed the right of residence? What if she had not worked because she had been looking after the (EU national) children? Would the reasoning have been the same? What if Mr Zambrano had still been in Colombia and had asked to join his family in Belgium? Would he have been granted residence in the way that McCarthy's Jamaican husband was not?[135]

She rightly notes that 'from a gender perspective all these questions matter' and that many questions that could have been asked in *McCarthy* were not because they were either deemed irrelevant or it did not occur to anyone that they might be pertinent. Applying a gender lens to the cases allows those questions to be asked and allows us to question whether *Zambrano* and *McCarthy* should have been treated differently.

Dismantling EU citizenship: economic (in)activity and access to benefits

Considerable ambiguity existed over the exact scope of free movement rights under Article 21 TFEU after its inclusion in the Treaty in 2009, specifically in terms of whether an economically inactive EU citizen whose period of residence in the host State is longer than three months, but shorter than five years, should be entitled to benefits available to the nationals of the host State. While in the 2013 decision in *Brey*[136] the blanket refusal to grant social assistance to any EU citizen not meeting the self-sufficiency requirements was held to be inconsistent with Articles 7(1)(b), 8(4), 24(1) and 24(2) CRD, the case also narrowed the scope of social assistance.[137] This was achieved by widening the scope of the

134 Guth, 'Law as the object' (n 4).
135 ibid.
136 Case C-140/12 *Pensionsversicherungsanstalt v Peter Brey* [2013] EU:C:2013:565.
137 ibid para 80. The Court was prepared to acknowledge that automatically excluding an economically inactive EU citizen from obtaining a complementary supplement 'whatever

benefits that can lawfully be withheld from EU migrants. The Court's reluctance to expand citizenship rights further become even more pronounced in its post-2013 case law.[138] The narrowing appears to coincide with the aftermath of the 2008 global financial crisis and the lifting of the restrictions for free movement for citizens of two new Member States, Bulgaria and Romania, in 2012.[139] While the cases discussed in relation to EU citizen children and their parent-carers suggest an expansionist agenda in which the Court's aim was to increase the reach of citizenship rights and require the Member States to show a degree of solidarity to their European neighbours, post-2013 judgements emphasise the limitations and conditions on the exercise of free movement.[140] Adam Weiss has argued that the recent citizenship case law demonstrates that EU citizens are expected to start their lives in another Member State as 'economically active', 'economically self-sufficient', or the family member of someone in either two categories.[141] If the EU citizen fails to meet those criteria, Article 14 CRD implies that they can be sent back to their country of origin. Indeed, Article 14(4)(b) specifically stipulates that jobseekers and their family members 'may not be expelled for as long as the Union citizens can provide evidence that they are continuing to seek employment and that they have a genuine chance of being engaged'. Additionally, Article 24 CRD explicitly states that EU citizens can be denied social security payments aimed at providing a minimum subsistence income in the host State under Regulation 883/2004.[142] In recent cases concerning access for EU citizens the Court maintained its case law on benefits for jobseekers[143] and showed its commitment to gender equality by finding that EU citizens maintain their 'worker' status as residents even during maternity periods.[144]

However, 2014 and 2015 saw a number of cases involving sole-parent women who had moved from one Member State to another and claimed the possibility to use Article 21 TFEU to support residence rights and access social assistance available to nationals of the host State by relying on the principle of equal treatment.

---

the circumstances' because he had no right to reside in the host State under art 7 CRD was contrary to the Directive because he had been issued with residence certificate.

138 eg *Dano* (n 119); *Alimanovic* (n 120).

139 Blauberger and Schmidt note that the interior ministers of Austria, Germany, the Netherlands and the UK alleged in 2013 that the free movement provisions in the Treaty enabled systematic abuse EU law in order to gain access to welfare systems of host States. Michael Blauberger and Susanne K Schmidt, 'Welfare Migration? Free Movement of EU Citizens and Access to Social Benefits' (2014) *Research and Politics* 1, 1 doi:10.1177/2053168014563879.

140 Currie, 'Pregnancy-related Employment Breaks' (n 6) 558.

141 Adam Weiss, 'Free Movement and Roma Emancipation: How Immigration Lawyers Can Combat Antigypyism' (2016) *Immigration, Asylum and Nationality Law* 253, 259.

142 Regulation (EC) No 883/2004 of the European Parliament and of the Council of 29 April 2004 on the coordination of social security systems [2004] OJ L 166/1, art 70(2)(a).

143 Cases C-22/07 and C-23/08 *Athanasios Vatsouras and Josif Koupatantze v Arbeitsgemeinschaft (ARGE) Nürnberg 900* [2009] ECR I-04585. However, see *Alimanovic* (n 120).

144 Case C-507/12 *Jessy Saint Prix v Secretary of State for Work and Pensions* [2014] EU:C:2014:2007.

In many of these cases the Court considered that the applicants were economically inactive and, thus, had no right of residence under EU law – even though the applicants enjoyed the right of residence under national law. In a number of cases, Germany had issued residency permits to the applicants and their children. However, unlike in *Brey*, the issuance of residency permits under national law appeared to be of no relevance since, according to the Court, the applicants were considered as a burden on the social assistance system of the host State. For instance, in the 2014 judgement in *Dano*[145] a Romanian national could not benefit from the right of residence under EU law in the host State because she was not in paid employment. Similarly, in the 2015 judgement in *Alimanovic*[146] a Swedish national mother and daughter, who had reached the age of majority, were unable to rely on EU law because they were no longer considered as workers in the host State. Both women had held temporary jobs in Germany for less than a year and stopped working. Since Ms Alimanovic had been in work, but only for 11 months, and not within the previous year, the Court was quick to apply Article 7(3) CRD in a literal sense, stressing that Ms Alimanovic had been unemployed for longer than the six months.

This is important from the gendered point of view because in citizenship judgements delivered in 2010 the Court put very little emphasis on the provisions in the CRD according to which a worker retains a status of a worker under Article 45 TFEU despite no longer being in the labour market. For instance, in *Ibrahim*, the Court disregarded the requirements for both Ms Ibrahim and her husband from whom she was separated to fulfil the conditions of Article 7 CRD. The Court appeared to suggest that the right of residence for neither Mr Yusuf, as the former worker, nor Ms Ibrahim, as the primary carer-parent, was dependent on the fulfilment of the conditions of Article 7 CRD, even though it noted that under this provision, the former worker should have both a comprehensive sickness insurance cover and sufficient resources for himself and his family. It did this by contrasting the CRD and Article 10 of Regulation No 1612/68, under which there is a right of the spouse and descendants of an EU citizen worker 'to install themselves with him in the latter State',[147] and explaining that Article 10 had been replaced with Article 7(1)(b) and (d) and (2) CRD, which stipulated that the family members of an EU citizen, who resided in a host State 'without being a worker or self-employed person there have the right to accompany or join that citizen, provided that he has sufficient resources for himself and the family members and has comprehensive sickness insurance cover in the host Member State'.[148] It nevertheless did not question the fact that Mr Yusuf appeared to no longer be a worker.

In the cases concerning retention of worker status by female applicants who had previously worked in the host State, albeit for a brief period of time, specifically

145 *Dano* (n 119).
146 *Alimanovic* (n 120).
147 *Ibrahim* (n 62) para 27.
148 ibid.

Alimanovic and *Saint Prix*,[149] the Court has appeared to cement its retreat from the expansive conceptualisation of citizenship. The Court has also made it very clear that host States were under no obligation under EU law to provide access to social assistance available to EU citizens who did not fulfil the conditions of Article 7 CRD. Since this is quite a departure from many of the cases discussed in this chapter, the decisions have gendered implications when the applicants are women. Although in *Brey* the Court interpreted the CRD as requiring a host Member State to take account of the individual situation of an economically inactive EU citizen before adopting an expulsion measure or finding that their residence was placing an unreasonable burden on its social assistance system,[150] no case-by-case assessment of personal circumstances was considered necessary in *Alimanovic*.[151] Significantly, this judgement removed the proportionality requirement in cases concerning jobseekers.[152] *Brey* is significant from the gendered perspective because it raises a question why should German pensioner Peter Brey's situation be substantially different from that of Romanian Elizabeta Dano and Swedish Nazifa Alimanovic, considering that they were all economically inactive – in the Court's opinion. Is this because Mr Brey is his wife's carer and suffers from ill health or has a disability?[153] Additionally, the Swedish AG, Nils Wahl, notes that Mr Brey claims to have been a 'victim of discrimination' in Germany on grounds his Russian origin and therefore moved to Austria.[154] Therefore, the judgement appears to indicate that the authorities should investigate whether he qualified for social assistance which under Regulation 883/2004 can be used to guarantee either 'a minimum subsistence income' or protection to a disabled EU citizen, who has a close link to the 'social environment' of the host State.[155] It is not certain how much Wahl's opinion influenced the judgement. But he seemingly had difficulties 'to grasp how a single individual can become an unreasonable burden on the finances of a Member State', finally concluding that there would hardly be an 'unreasonable burden' in the case of a one-off payment of a few hundred Euros, but recurring payments which were likely to continue for the foreseeable future would be unreasonable.[156] Although Wahl pointed out that

149 *Saint Prix* (n 144) [2014] EU:C:2014:2007.
150 *Brey* (n 136) paras 64, 69 and 78.
151 *Alimanovic* (n 120) para 59.
152 This had been confirmed previously in *Dano* where the Court had removed the requirement of a case-by-case assessment in situations where the claimant seemingly moved to the host State solely for the purpose of claiming social assistance, but had no intention of finding work. For another case concerning jobseekers, see Case C-299/14 *Vestische Arbeit Jobcenter Kreis Recklinghausen v Jovanna García-Nieto and Others* [2016] EU:C:2016:114.
153 The case facts note that Mr Brey was a recipient of German invalidity pension and care allowance. *Brey* (n 136) para 16.
154 Case C-140/12 *Peter Brey v Pensionsversicherungsanstalt* [2013] EU:C:2013:337, Opinion of AG Wahl, point 86.
155 Regulation 883/2004, art 70(2)(a).
156 *Brey*, Opinion of AG Wahl (n 154) point 88.

Mr Brey was 'unable to demonstrate any prior links to Austrian society that would justify those payments' and that his situation would have been different had he, for instance, 'worked, resided and paid taxes there on a previous occasion',[157] the Court considered that Mr Brey's situation warranted the investigation of his individual circumstances. Hence, *Brey* can be argued to demonstrate apparent gender bias because, in contrast in *Dano*, the Court ruled out the possibility of economically inactive EU citizens to be treated the same way as any national of the host State on the grounds that the equal treatment rule in Article 24(1) CRD[158] applied only where a person had a right to reside in the host State.[159]

In *Dano* the Court dedicated a considerable portion of the judgement to explaining that Article 7(1)(b) CRD sought to prevent economically inactive, non-resident EU citizens from claiming entitlement to social benefits under the same conditions as those applicable to nationals of the host State. Thus, pursuant to Article 7, Member States had the possibility of refusing to grant social benefits to economically inactive EU citizens who exercised their right to freedom of movement solely in order to obtain social assistance in another Member State.[160] According to it, denying the host States such possibility would result in the arrival in their territory of persons who would not have sufficient resources to provide for themselves and who would automatically be entitled to social security payments intended to cover a minimum subsistence income.[161] Hence, allowing such 'abuses' would have run counter to an objective of the CRD, namely preventing EU citizens from becoming an unreasonable burden on the social assistance system of the host State.[162]

In this case, the Court further took the opportunity to clarify the status of jobseekers under Article 24(2) CRD, which concerns the right to social assistance of the host State during the first three months of residence.[163] According to this provision, the host States were not 'obliged to confer entitlement to social assistance during the first three months of residence or, where appropriate, the longer period provided for in Article 14(4)(b)'. In effect, the host States may restrict jobseekers and their families from accessing social assistance during the first three months of their residence without this being inconsistent with EU law. Despite the equal treatment rule in Article 24(1) CRD, Ms Dano could not claim equal treatment with German nationals in terms of access to social benefits because her residence in Germany did not comply with the conditions of the CRD.[164] Hence,

157 ibid.
158 Directive 2004/38, art 24(1) provides that all EU citizens 'residing in the territory of another EU Member State on the basis of that Directive enjoyed equal treatment with the nationals of that State within the scope of the Treaty'.
159 *Dano* (n 119) para 68.
160 ibid para 78.
161 ibid para 79.
162 ibid para 74 referring to Directive 2004/38, preamble, recital 10.
163 or where appropriate, the period of seeking employment extending beyond the first three months.
164 *Dano* (n 119) para 69.

she should have been employed or have had sufficient financial resources and a comprehensive sickness insurance cover for herself and for her son. Without either, she had not the right to equal treatment, effectively making her a second-class EU citizen.

Unlike in previous case law concerning EU citizen children and their carer parents, the Court did not address in any way the right of Ms Dano's child, Florian, to education in Germany under EU law. Even though Ms Dano argued that she took care of her sister's children, the Court did not address this in more detail or consider whether her sister was a worker whose household she could have formed part of as 'other family member' under Article 3 CRD. Nor did the Court address Ms Dano's origin as a Roma or that the 10 million Roma, who became EU citizens in 2004 and 2007, are the most marginalised ethnic minorities in Europe.[165] Although Roma can challenge discrimination based on race or ethnicity in the labour market and a wide range of other areas of life, including education, housing and social support under the Race Equality Directive,[166] the Employment Equality Directive[167] and the protection of the European Convention on Human Rights,[168] they are, *inter alia*, excluded from the labour markets of many central and eastern European Member States where their share of the population is highest.[169] Additionally, the European Union Fundamental Rights Agency has noted that the Roma are economically deprived as a consequence of discrimination.[170] Although the Roma would be most in need of social support, if they moved to another EU Member State, the recent citizenship case law means that the Roma are significantly disadvantaged.[171] None of this is addressed in the *Dano* judgement, whereas AG Wahl noted that Peter Brey had moved to Austria due to alleged discrimination he faced in Germany due to his Russian heritage.[172] Hence, the judgements suggest that it is appropriate for the Court to adopt an empathetic approach towards a German pensioner who cares for his wife. However, it does not feel empathy for the Roma woman, who has only attended school for three years in Romania and who is barely literate.[173] There is no indication

165 Egle Dagilyte and Margaret Greenfields, 'United Kingdom Welfare Benefit Reforms in 2013–2014: Roma Between the Pillory, The Precipice and the Slippery Slope' (2015) 37(4) *Journal of Social Welfare and Family Law* 476 doi:10.1080/09649069.2015.1121954.

166 Council Directive 2000/43/EC of 29 June 2000 implementing the principle of equal treatment between persons irrespective of racial or ethnic origin [2000] OJ L180/22, art 3.

167 Council Directive 2000/78/EC of 27 November 2000 establishing a general framework for equal treatment in employment and occupation [2000] OJ L303/16.

168 Convention for the Protection of Human Rights and Fundamental Freedoms (European Convention on Human Rights, as amended) (ECHR).

169 eg, Romania, Bulgaria Slovakia, and Hungary. See Weiss (n 141).

170 EU Fundamental Rights Agency, *Poverty and Employment: The Situation of Roma in 11 EU Member States* (Fundamental Rights Agency 2014) doi:10.2811/50875.

171 Weiss (n 141) 261–262.

172 *Brey*, Opinion of AG Wahl (n 154) point 86.

173 *Dano* (n 119) para 39.

that the fact that Elizabeta Dano has left school after a mere three years of primary education is an inherently debilitating factor.

Weiss has argued that, despite the fact that the first legal instrument at EU level focusing on integration and recognising States' obligations towards Roma was introduced in 2013,[174] EU law places obstacles in the way of Roma to prove that they can use their EU citizenship to move to another EU Member State and shed the consequences of their unequal status in the State of their origin because EU law does not allow an EU citizen who has moved to another Member State to acquire the host State's citizenship.[175]

Additionally, the provisions of the CRD demonstrate that there are no obligations for the host States to provide funding for students other than workers, self-employed persons, persons who retain such status, and members of their families, before they have legally resided in the host State for a continuous period of five years. Therefore, this provision merely codifies existing case law, such as *Grzelczyk*,[176] *Lair*[177] and *Brown*.[178] However, the host States' attempts to prevent EU migrants from claiming in-work benefits and accessing social housing, for instance, as the UK Government proposed to do during the first four years of EU migrants' residence in the UK before it decided to exit the EU, are seemingly inconsistent with the Court's case law and the provisions of both the Treaty and the Citizens' Rights Directive.[179]

Commission v UK[180] appears to complete the project of dismantling EU citizenship. While seemingly gender neutral, the decision concerns EU citizens' access to child benefit and tax credits in the UK. Tax credits are primarily intended to support low-income workers with children and combine poverty alleviation with incentives to work.[181] Although these in-work benefits do not target female labour force participation specifically, evidence suggests that higher rates of women are eligible and use tax credits than men.[182] Additionally, in-work benefits have a positive impact on female employment, particularly single mothers.[183] Hence,

174 ibid referring to Council Recommendation on effective Roma integration measures in the Member States [2013] OJ C378.

175 ibid 259.

176 *Grzelczyk* (n 8).

177 Case 39/86 *Sylvie Lair v Universität Hannover* [1988] ECR 03161 (equal access to university education and training grants).

178 Case 197/86 *Steven Malcolm Brown v Secretary of State for Scotland* [1988] ECR 03205.

179 Steve Peers, 'The Nine Labours of Cameron: Analysis of the Plans to Change EU Free Movement Law' *EU Law Analysis* (28 November 2014) <http://eulawanalysis.blogspot.co.uk/2014/11/the-nine-labours-of-cameron-analysis-of.html> accessed 28 November 2014.

180 Case C-308/14 *Commission v UK* [2016] EU:C:2016:436.

181 Claudia Olivetti and Barbara Petrongolo, 'The Economic Consequences of Family Policies: Lessons from a Century of Legislation in High-Income Countries' (2017) 31(1) *Journal of Economic Perspectives* 205.

182 ibid 225–226.

183 ibid.

Commission v UK is not only disturbing from a gendered point of view but it also appears to 'destroy . . . any possibility of a claim based on proportionality, or asserting a . . . right to a case-by-case assessment of personal circumstances'.[184] According to O'Brien, the judgement confirms the Member States' 'prerogative to discriminate on the grounds of nationality', and it thus, extinguishes EU citizenship, albeit doing this 'furtively', since the term citizenship or Article 18 TFEU are not mentioned once in the judgement. Hence, the Court's 'failure to engage with primary law, while dismissing and eviscerating it, is striking'.[185] The judgement rests on the conclusion that, while the test for lawful residence is in itself indirectly discriminatory, the process of checking residence documents in order to access child benefit and tax credits, which are considered social security benefits under Regulation 883/2004,[186] is justified and proportionate. According to the Court, EU citizens were 'required to prove that they in fact enjoy a right to reside lawfully in United Kingdom territory [only in specific cases]' and that verification was not systematic but carried out 'only in the event of doubt'.[187] Hence, the verification was proportionate, appropriate 'for securing the attainment of the objective of protecting public finances' and did not exceed what was 'necessary to attain that objective'.[188] However, EU migrants, who seek to rely on child benefits and tax credits, are most likely to be parents who need these the most.[189] Hence, the decision is likely to have an adverse impact on EU migrants with children, and specifically single parents.

Rethinking the EU citizen and her rights

EU citizenship law has developed from purely economic beginnings to the recognition that EU migrants are more than simply human resources. The case law of the Court shows this recognition and subsequent development quite clearly. It shows that the Court has on occasion appeared gender aware but also that it has missed opportunities which could have led to a more nuanced and holistic understanding of how EU citizenship plays out in the real lives of real women in the EU. Part of the problem is that the EU has, it seems, an ideal EU citizen in mind. It legislates and decides cases on the basis of an able-bodied person who is fully integrated into the labour market of a host State. That is the yard stick by which all shall be measured. Where caring responsibilities or other activities are recognised, they are recognised as an add on – as something that needs to be done in addition to the economic activity rather than being seen as a different form of useful activity which makes a contribution to the host State. This can

184 O'Brien, 'The ECJ sacrifices EU Citizenship in Vain' (n 2) 242.
185 ibid.
186 Regulation (EC) 883/2004 of 29 April 2004 on the coordination of social security systems [2004] OJ L166/1.
187 *Commission v UK* (n 180) paras 83–84.
188 ibid para 85.
189 See O'Brien, 'The Pillory' (n 113) 129.

leave women in the position where they have to do it all: Work, care and provide for their families. O'Brien suggests a different way of thinking:

> An alternative approach to economic rationality is here advocated, in which the choice is not between economic utilitarianism and individualistic human rights, but a choice between definitions of 'utility', a choice that should take account of the long-term interests of society.[190]

A gendered analysis of the law in this area allows us to rethink utility. It helps us to reconceptualise who an EU citizen is, and should be, and to value the diversity of EU citizens. It means we can more easily see how women like Maria Martínez Sala and Shirley McCarthy and even Elizabeta Dano should be valued, and valued not in spite of their lack of economic activity, but because of who they are and everything else they do.

O'Brien notes the importance of evaluating the law in an area as a whole rather than each step in isolation. She says:

> EU citizenship is the subject of incremental and painstaking construction. In allowing ourselves to get caught up with dissecting each separate instalment that comes with each new case, we risk accepting without scrutiny what should be a controversial ideological framework – that of an economic/market citizenship. Within this framework, rights do not attach to personhood; rather rights are triggered, interpreted, delineated and weighed according to a miscellany of conditions. As a result, claimants can face 'social welfare cliff edges' – tipping them over the edge of the cliff, from full protection to none – on the basis of apparently arbitrary tricks of circumstance.[191]

So, while looking at each case in turn we can say something about the extent to which the Court has or has not been gender aware and whether or not gendered considerations were taken into account in its decisions. We can consider whether different questions could have and should have been asked and whether that would have altered the outcome. And, when we do this, we see some promising decisions: we see part-time work being recognised, we see carers' rights being recognised in some cases and we see an overall expansion of citizens' rights. However, what we do not see is rights attaching to personhood and we still see conditions which make presumption about who are EU citizens that are based on an ideal which many women in particular cannot meet. This leaves a far greater proportion of women than men facing the 'social welfare cliff edges' with no safety net or support. That is where the challenge for EU citizenship really lies.

190 Charlotte O'Brien, 'Equality's False Summits: New Varieties of Disability Discrimination, "Excessive" Equal Treatment and Economically Constricted Horizons' (2011) 36(1) *European Law Review* 26–50, 27.

191 O'Brien, 'I trade, therefore I am' (n 10) 1643.

Bibliography

Ackers L, *Shifting Spaces: Women, Citizenship and Migration in the European Union* (Policy Press 1999)

———, 'Women, Citizenship and European Community Law: The Gender Implications of the Free Movement Provisions' (1994) 16(4) *Journal of Social Welfare and Family Law* 391

Ackers L and Gill B, *Moving People and Knowledge: Scientific Mobility in an Enlarging Europe* (Edward Elgar 2008).

Blauberger M and Schmidt SK, 'Welfare Migration? Free Movement of EU Citizens and Access to Social Benefits' (2014) *Research and Politics* 1 doi:10.1177/2053168014563879

Chalmers, D, Davies G and Monti G, *European Union Law: Text and Materials* (Cambridge University Press 2014)

Council Directive 2000/43/EC of 29 June 2000 Implementing the Principle of Equal Treatment Between Persons Irrespective of Racial or Ethnic Origin [2000] OJ L180/22

Council Directive 2000/78/EC of 27 November 2000 Establishing a General Framework for Equal Treatment in Employment and Occupation [2000] OJ L303/16

Council Directive 92/85/EEC of 19 October 1992 on the Introduction of Measures to Encourage Improvements in the Safety and Health at Work of Pregnant Workers and Workers Who Have Recently Given Birth or Are Breastfeeding [1992] OJ L 348/1

Council Recommendation on Effective Roma Integration Measures in the Member States [2013] OJ C378

Coutts S, 'Case C- 434–09: Shirley McCarthy v. Secretary of State for the Home Department' (10 May 2011) <http://globalcit.eu/case-c-434-09-shirley-mccarthy-v-secretary-of-state-for-the-home-department/> accessed 9 April 2018

Currie S, 'Pregnancy-related Employment Breaks, the Gender Dynamics of Free Movement Law and Curtailed Citizenship: Jessy Saint Prix' (2016) 53 *Common Market Law Review* 543

———, 'Two-speed European Citizenship? Can the Lisbon Treaty Help Close the Gap? (2008) 45 *Common Market Law Review* 1

———, 'The Transformation of Union Citizenship' in Dougan M and Currie S (eds), *50 Years of the European Treaties: Looking Back and Thinking Forward* (Hart 2009)

Dagilyte E and Greenfields M, 'United Kingdom Welfare Benefit Reforms in 2013–2014: Roma Between the Pillory, the Precipice and the Slippery Slope' (2015) 37(4) *Journal of Social Welfare and Family Law* 476 doi:10.1080/09649069.2015.1121954

Directive 2004/38/EC of the European Parliament and of the Council of 29 April 2004 on the Right of Citizens of the Union and Their Family Members to Move and Reside Freely Within the Territory of the Member States Amending Regulation (EEC) No 1612/68 and Repealing Directives 64/221/EEC, 68/360/EEC, 72/194/EEC, 73/148/EEC, 75/34/EEC, 75/35/EEC, 90/364/EEC, 90/365/EEC and 93/96/EEC [2004] OJ L158/77

Dougan M, 'The Bubble That Burst: Exploring the Legitimacy of the Case Law on the Free Movement of Union Citizens' in Adams M, de Waele H, Meeusen J and Straetmans G (eds), *Judging Europe's Judges: The Legitimacy of the Case Law of the European Court of Justice* (Hart 2013)

Everson M, 'The Legacy of the Market Citizen' in Shaw J and More G (eds), *New Legal Dynamics of European Union* (Clarendon 1995)

Golynker O, *Ubiquitous Citizens of Europe: The Paradigm of Partial Migration* (Intersentia 2006)

Guth J, 'Law as the Object and Agent of Integration: Gendering the Court of Justice of the European Union, Its Decisions and Their Impact' in Abels G and Macrae H (eds), *Gendering European Integration Theory Engaging New Dialogues* (Barbara Budrich 2016)

———, 'When Is a Partner Not a Partner? Conceptualisations of "Family" in EU Free Movement Law (2011) 33(2) *Journal of Social Welfare and Family Law* 193

Guth J and Mowlam E, 'The evolution of European Union citizenship: where does Zambrano take us?' (2012) 46(1) *The Law Teacher* 75 doi:10.1080/03069400.2012.644972

Iliopoulou Penot A, 'The Transnational Character of Union Citizenship' in Dougan M, Shuibhne NN and Spaventa E (eds), *Media of Empowerment and Disempowerment of the European Citizen* (Hart 2012)

Income Support (General) Regulations (1987) SI 1987/1967

Kochenov D (ed), *EU Citizenship and Federalism: The Role of Rights* (Cambridge University Press 2017)

Lombardo E and Meier P, 'Framing Gender Equality in the European Union Political Discourse' (2008) 15(1) *Social Politics: International Studies in Gender, State and Society* 101 doi:10.1093/sp/jxn001

Lombardo E and Verloo M, 'Institutionalizing Intersectionality in the European Union?' (2009) 11(4) *International Feminist Journal of Politics* 478 doi:10.1080/14616740903237442

Maas W, *Creating European Citizens* (Rowman and Littlefield 2007)

———, 'Free Movement and the Difference That Citizenship Makes' (2017) 23(1) *Journal of European Integration History* 85

McCauliff CMA, 'EU Citizenship: Why Can't the Advocated General Keep Sheila McCarthy's Family Together?' (2013) 36(5) *Fordham International Law Journal* 1372

McGlynn C, 'European Union Family Values: Ideologies of "Family" and "Motherhood" in European Union Law' (2001) 8 *Social Politics* 325

———, 'Ideologies of Motherhood in European Community Sex Equality Law' (2000) 6 *European Law Journal* 29

Moebius I and Szyszczak E, 'Of Raising Pigs and Children' (1998) 18(1) *Yearbook of European Law* 125

O'Brien C, 'Drudges, Dupes and Do-gooders? Competing Notions of "Value" in the Union's Approach to Volunteers' (2011) 1(1) *European Journal of Social Law* 49

———, 'Equality's False Summits: New Varieties of Disability Discrimination, "Excessive" Equal Treatment and Economically Constricted Horizons' (2011) 36(1) *European Law Review* 26

———, 'I Trade, Therefore I Am: Legal Personhood in the European Union' (2013) 50 *Common Market Law Review* 1643

———, 'Social Blind Spots and Monocular Policy Making: The ECJ's Migrant Worker Model' (2009) 46(4) *Common Market Law Review* 1107

———, 'The Pillory, the Precipice and the Slippery Slope: The Profound Effects of the UK's Legal Reform Programme Targeting EU Migrants' (2015) 37(1) *Journal of Social Welfare and Family Law* 111

———, *Unity in Adversity: EU Citizenship, Social Justice and the Cautionary Tale of the UK* (Hart 2017)

Olivetti C and Petrongolo B, 'The Economic Consequences of Family Policies: Lessons from a Century of Legislation in High-Income Countries' (2017) 31(1) *Journal of Economic Perspectives* 205

Peers S, 'The Nine Labours of Cameron: Analysis of the Plans to Change EU Free Movement Law' *EU Law Analysis* (28 November 2014) <http://eulawanalysis.blogspot.co.uk/2014/11/the-nine-labours-of-cameron-analysis-of.html> accessed 28 November 2014

Regulation (EC) No 883/2004 of the European Parliament and of the Council of 29 April 2004 on the Coordination of Social Security Systems [2004] OJ L 166/1

Schiek D, 'Intersectionality and the Notion of Disability in EU Discrimination Law' (2016) 53(1) *Common Market Law Review* 35

Shaw J, 'Importing Gender: The Challenge of Feminism and the Analysis of the EU Legal Order' (2000) 7(3) *Journal of European Public Policy* 406 doi:10.1080/13501760050086107

———, 'Mainstreaming Equality and Diversity in the European Union' (2005) 58 *Current Legal Problems* 255

Shuibhne NN and Spaventa E (eds), *Empowerment and Disempowerment of the European Citizen* (Hart 2012)

Strumia F, 'Remedying the Inequalities of Economic Citizenship in Europe: Cohesion Policy and the Negative Right to Move' (2011) 17(6) *European Law Journal* 725

Treaty on the Functioning of the European Union [2012] OJ C 326/47

Walby, S, 'The European Union and Gender Equality: Emergent Varieties of Gender Regime' (2004) 11(1) *Social Politics* 4

Weiss A, 'Free Movement and Roma Emancipation: How Immigration Lawyers Can Combat Antigypyism' (2016) *Immigration, Asylum and Nationality Law* 253

8 Concluding thoughts

> We need more feminist judges: judges who understand women's experiences and take seriously harm to women and girls, who ask the gender question, 'How might this law, statute, or holding affect men and women differently?'; who interpret equal protection and discrimination law in light of those provisions' broad social change purposes; who value women's lives and women's work; who do not believe women to be liars, whores, or deserving of violence by nature; who question their own stereotypes and predilections and listen to evidence; and who, simply put, believe in equal justice for all.[1]

Throughout this book we have tried to highlight the importance of stopping and pausing to consider what other questions can be asked of policy, fact patterns and case law in order to consider gender as a factor and to look at things differently. We have argued that, although the Court of Justice of the European Union (CJEU) is clearly a key driver for some of the most significant developments in (gender) equality law, it has also missed many an opportunity to advance women's rights. The Court has not always been the gender-aware court it is sometimes heralded to be and, in fact, unless gender is specifically and obviously at issue, the Court is not actually very good at recognising gender as a factor. Our analysis has shown that the Court is often blind to gender and to possible unintended consequences of EU law and policy and its own decisions. In these short concluding remarks, we suggest that perhaps the only way to achieve genuine awareness of how gender impacts on the various experiences of women in various circumstances highlighted in this book is to go back to where we started – the composition of the Court. However, even this may not be sufficient given the reliance of the Court on preliminary references which are in turn reliant on national legal systems. We suspect therefore that the answers may not lie in law and legal systems at all, but in the continued activism of women and men across the world who believe that promoting greater equality is better for everyone, regardless of their gender, class, race or disability, and who understand the importance of legal decisions in reacting to social attitudes as well as shaping them.

1 Sally J Kenney, *Gender and Justice: Why Women in the Judiciary Really Matter* (Routledge 2013) 15–16.

Gendering the court and the outcomes of its work

> In order to determine what equality requires in any given case it is useful to recall the values underlying equality. These are *human dignity* and personal autonomy.[2]

It may be worth reminding the Court of this. While the cases we have analysed have shown that the Court does have a history of making decisions which have advanced gender equality, these cases are the ones where gender is obvious and where there has also been something in it for the Court. In cases where gender is not the key issue, the Court is far less aware of the gendered nature of its decision. In Chapters 6 and 7 we can see how gender can make a difference to our understanding of the cases and can give us a much better understanding of the lives of the individual claimants, the issues faced by them and how the decision of the Court might ultimately impact on them. It is in relation to these cases that the Court must do better. Further, the Court appears to make thing unnecessarily complex and complicated by maintaining the strict distinction between its own jurisdiction and that of the European Court of Human Rights. While the latter is far from perfect, the two courts working together to develop holistic equality and fundamental rights principles could be a force to be reckoned with and could also help the CJEU to shift its focus from a market-driven rationale to embracing fundamental rights throughout its jurisprudence.

Our analysis suggests that, whether or not gender is considered important depends on the actors involved in the cases. We have noted several examples where the Advocates-General of the Court have offered gender-aware opinions which have not been followed by the Court. It may be that having a greater number of women on the Court so that women can more easily work together, share concerns and make their voices heard would make a significant difference to Europe's women. Much of the empirical work cited in Chapters 3 and 4 suggests this may be the case. However, we also acknowledge that untangling gender from all the other characteristics of judges is difficult. Some may simply be making better decisions because they are better judges; others might be making poor decisions in relation to gender not because they do not care about equality and women's rights but because they are blind to the issues. We need judges who are willing to have their eyes opened. As Kenney suggests[3] we perhaps need feminist judges in order to take the next steps and continue forwards, ideally without taking any backward steps along the way.

What's next for gender and the CJEU?

The Court must, we suggest, move away from its focus on market citizenship and economically underpinned rationales. It has been argued that participation

2 Case C-303/06 *S Coleman v Attridge Law and Steve Law* EU:C:2008:61, AG Maduro, para 8.
3 Kenney (n 1).

in the formal labour market has a potential to increase women's income.[4] However, in this context in countries which provide no social protection or access to health care, after having become employed women are then expected to be able to 'buy education and better health care'.[5] Although, as Bussman notes in relation to the impact open trade can have on women's lives, some women may receive health insurance coverage through their employment in the formal labour market, the argument of the economics is nevertheless rather simplistically that women's welfare has potential to improve when they assume a more active role in economic life through their participation in the formal labour market because the higher income enables women to pay for medical[6] and educational services for themselves and for their children.[7] Additionally, according to this line of thinking, new jobs for women in the industrial sector can delay marriage and child-bearing which in turn is thought to improve women's health and enable girls and women to continue with higher education.[8] According to Bussmann, the higher female labour force participation is – regardless of the specific sector – the higher the women's personal income will be.[9] The problems with these lines of arguments are that they offer a rather simplistic view that participation in the labour market is the answer to everything and that all jobs are able to provide women with sufficient salary to pay for all their (health care and educational) needs. This line of argument is particularly problematic in the context of the EU's relationship with the rest of the world and one which needs much further exploration.

However, even within the EU this line of argument is problematic as we have seen in Chapter 7 in particular. Although employment is usually viewed as the best route out of poverty, there is also evidence that there are crucial issues over low pay, limited working hours and constrained employment opportunities, which result in underemployment and severe financial challenges.[10] For example since 2002, the UK has seen increasing non-traditional patterns of work, when job growth in full-time employment has been replaced by job growth in unpredictable, temporary, part-time, zero-hours,[11] 'gig economy' type employment. While this is perhaps extreme in the UK, it does reflect an emerging trend across the EU. Commentators have noted the (gendered) impact that this has on EU

4 Margit Bussmann, 'The Effect of Trade Openness on Women's Welfare and Work Life' (2009) 37(6) *World Development* 1027, 1028 doi:10.1016/j.worlddev.2008.10.007
5 ibid 1028.
6 ibid.
7 ibid.
8 ibid.
9 Eg, a flourishing export industry will create new jobs for both men and women, who are thought to benefit from more employment opportunities in the export sector. See Bussmann (n 4) 1028.
10 See Jo McBride, Andrew Smith, and Marcell Mbala, '"You end up with Nothing": The Experience of Being a Statistic of "in-work Poverty" in the UK' (2017) 1 *Work, Employment and Society* 1, 2 doi:10.1177/0950017017728614.
11 This refers to contracts where employees are not guaranteed any hours in a given week.

citizens.[12] Women are required to do it all because they are valued only as market citizens and the care work, unpaid domestic labour and other contributions to society made by women remain invisible.

According to Anna Elomäki, EU gender policies have from the very beginning of their formulation been incorporated under the logic of the market.[13] The adoption of neoliberal policies has led to the dismantling of State protection that was previously provided to employees and eroded by the aspirations to create 'flexible' labour markets to attract capital and to enable States to compete. Where the cuts in State welfare provision have not been accompanied by an equivalent expansion in affordable market provision, the shortfall has been compensated by the unpaid labour of women, particularly among low-income groups. Elomäki argues that the prevalence of economic gender equality discourses in the EU and at national levels has been facilitated by the aspirations towards evidence-based policy making and new governance technologies, which require translating activities into a financial calculation as part of 'good and efficient government'.[14] How this plays out in all areas of EU law and policy making needs careful investigation.

We have focused exclusively on equality law and citizenship in this book and can thus only tell part of the story. The areas covered are areas where gender is either obvious or easily identifiable as relevant. Elsewhere we consider more difficult areas predominantly linked to the external relations of the EU. However, there are more policy areas and legal developments that can and should be fully scrutinised from a gender perspective as the very brief comments above clearly indicate. Only having a complete picture of how the Court engages with issues in different policy settings will allow us to evaluate the Court fully. It may be that in some areas it is very gender aware and in others not at all. Where this is the case, feminist scholars interested in the EU and its institutions can make a difference by highlighting the unconscious biases and missed opportunities and hope that our voices will be heard.

Overall, though, we need more research. We need work which considers some of the questions we have raised from perspectives other than gender and which

12 See for example Johanna Kantola and Emanuela Lombardo (eds), *Gender and the Economic Crisis in Europe: Politics, Institutions and Intersectionality* (Springer 2017); Roberta Guerrina, 'Gendering European economic narratives: Assessing the costs of the crisis to gender equality' in Johanna Kantola and Emanuela Lombardo (eds), *Gender and the Economic Crisis in Europe: Politics, Institutions and Intersectionality* (Palgrave MacMillan 2017); Mary Daly, 'What Adult Worker Model? A Critical Look at Recent Social Policy Reform in Europe from a Gender and Family Perspective' (2011) 18(1) *Social Politics: International Studies in Gender, State and Society* 1; Anna van der Vleuten, *The Price of Gender Equality: Member States and Governance in the European Union* (Routledge 2007).

13 Anna Elomäki, 'The Economic Case for Gender Equality in the European Union: Selling Gender Equality to Decision-makers and Neoliberalism to Women's Organizations' (2015) 22(3) *European Journal of Women's Studies* 288, 290–291. See also Johanna Kantola, *Gender and the European Union* (Palgrave Macmillan 2010).

14 Elomäki (n 13) 290; Johanna Kantola and Judith A Squires, 'From State Feminism to Market Feminism?' (2012) 33(4) *International Political Science Review* 382.

brings new theoretical frameworks, new questions and new approaches to analysing and understanding the Court. Our work has been desked-based and, while it has been informative, interesting and has provided us with very rich material for analysis, it can only take us so far. In order to really understand the Court, we need detailed empirical work which can pick up on the themes of this book. We need to understand how gender plays out but also how other characteristics shape the work of the Court. What difference does the background, legal tradition, race or ethnicity, sexual orientation or religion make? How do judges negotiate their day-to-day work in a highly political and increasingly politisised environment and how do they see their roles? This work might sound like it is simply academic fancy, something to sustain an academic career, but we suggest that it is important on a practical level too. Understanding the Court is the first step to changing it for the better, to force it to become more gender aware, more aware of inequalities and unintended consequences of its decisions and actions as both a political and legal institution. Understanding it better also means that we can utilise it more effectively. If we fully understand how the Court works, how it thinks and what makes it tick, litigation strategies can be tailored to be more effective to both win cases and to guide the Court in a particular direction in its jurisprudence. This could make a significant difference to everyone living in the EU and possibly beyond.

Bibliography

Bussmann M, 'The Effect of Trade Openness on Women's Welfare and Work Life' (2009) 37(6) *World Development* 1027 doi:10.1016/j.worlddev.2008.10.007

Daly M, 'What Adult Worker Model? A Critical Look at Recent Social Policy Reform in Europe from a Gender and Family Perspective' (2011) 18(1) *Social Politics: International Studies in Gender, State and Society* 1

Elomäki A, 'The Economic Case for Gender Equality in the European Union: Selling Gender Equality to Decision-makers and Neoliberalism to Women's Organizations' (2015) 22(3) *European Journal of Women's Studies* 288

Guerrina R, 'Gendering European Economic Narratives: Assessing the Costs of the Crisis to Gender Equality' in Kantola J, and Lombardo E (eds), *Gender and the Economic Crisis in Europe: Politics, Institutions and Intersectionality* (Palgrave MacMillan 2017)

Kantola J, *Gender and the European Union* (Palgrave MacMillan 2010)

Kantola J and Lombardo E (eds), *Gender and the Economic Crisis in Europe: Politics, Institutions and Intersectionality* (Springer 2017)

Kantola J and Squires JA, 'From State Feminism to Market Feminism?' (2012) 33(4) *International Political Science Review* 382

Kenney SJ, *Gender and Justice: Why Women in the Judiciary Really Matter* (Routledge 2013)

McBride J, Smith A and Mbala M, '"You end up with Nothing": The Experience of Being a Statistic of "in-work Poverty" in the UK' (2017) 1 *Work, Employment and Society* 1 doi:10.1177/0950017017728614

van der Vleuten A, *The Price of Gender Equality: Member States and Governance in the European Union* (Routledge 2007)

Index

For Product Safety Concerns and Information please contact our EU representative GPSR@taylorandfrancis.com
Taylor & Francis Verlag GmbH, Kaufingerstraße 24, 80331 München, Germany

www.ingramcontent.com/pod-product-compliance
Ingram Content Group UK Ltd.
Pitfield, Milton Keynes, MK11 3LW, UK
UKHW022127190926
475702UK00013B/1686

9780367588120

Operations Management and Data Analytics Modelling